STATUTORY AND ADMINISTRATIVE LAW SUPPLEMENT

To Accompany

CONTRACTS

Exchange Transactions and Relations

THIRD EDITION

By

IAN R. MACNEIL

and

PAUL J. GUDEL

NEW YORK, NEW YORK

FOUNDATION PRESS

2002

COPYRIGHT © 1978 FOUNDATION PRESS

COPYRIGHT © 2002 By FOUNDATION PRESS

      395 Hudson Street

      New York, NY 10014

      Phone Toll Free 1–877–888–1330

      Fax (212) 367–6799

      fdpress.com

ISBN 1–58778–463–7

 TEXT IS PRINTED ON 10% POST CONSUMER RECYCLED PAPER

ACKNOWLEDGMENTS

We wish to express our appreciation for permission to reprint portions of the following materials:

Model Rules of Professional Conduct, American Bar Association @ 1998.

Comments to: Uniform Consumer Code, 1968 @ 1969, Uniform Consumer Credit Code, 1974 @ 1977, Uniform Consumer Sales Practices Act @ 1971, Uniform Deceptive Trade Practices Act @ 1966, Uniform Land Transactions Act @ 1975, 1977, National Conference of Commissioners on Uniform State Laws. (The National Conference is the author of the uniform laws in the supplement.)

The following annotations and comments to Uniform Commercial Code 2-708, published by West Publishing Co., Inc. (and in the case of the Illinois Code Comments, Burdette Smith Co.):

California Code Comments, John A. Bohn and Charles J. Williams, West's Annotated California Codes @ 1964.

Illinois Code Comment, William B. Davenport, Smith-Hurd Illinois Annotated Statutes @ 1963.

Wisconsin Annotations, West's Wisconsin Statutes Annotated @ 1964.

Notes of Decision, Uniform Laws Annotated-Uniform Commercial Code (Master Edition) @ 1976, 1977, 1978.

P.J.G.
I.R.M.

*

TABLE OF CONTENTS

PART IV: FOREIGN

*

STATUTORY AND ADMINISTRATIVE LAW SUPPLEMENT

To Accompany

CONTRACTS

Exchange Transactions and Relations

*

INTRODUCTION

All statutes and administrative regulations bearing most significantly on matters treated in the principal book appear in this supplement, *except the Uniform Commercial Code*. (The supplement includes annotations to UCC 2–708, to be used in connection with the problem on p. 97 of the principal book.) The statutes and administrative regulations are set out separately in a supplement, not because they are less important than the cases and materials in the main book, but solely to facilitate reference.

These statutes and administrative regulations are in the following sequence: (1) Federal, including constitution; (2) National, non-federal, such as Uniform and Model acts and the Model Rules of Professional Conduct; (3) State legislation; (4) Foreign legislation. Within categories items are listed alphabetically.

Omissions are denoted by * * *, except where the numbering or lettering of paragraphs themselves clearly shows the omission.

Note: *This supplement is intended only for use in connection with law school courses and has been edited accordingly. It would be unwise to use it as a source book for other purposes.*

PART I: FEDERAL

UNITED STATES CONSTITUTION

Art. 1, § 10. No State Shall enter into any Treaty, Alliance, or Confederation; grant Letters of Marque and Reprisal; coin Money; emit Bills of Credit; make any Thing but gold and silver Coin a Tender in Payment of Debts; pass any Bill of Attainder, ex post facto Law, or Law impairing the Obligation of Contracts, or grant any Title of Nobility.

Amend. 13, § 1. Neither slavery nor involuntary servitude, except as a punishment for crime whereof the party shall have been duly convicted, shall exist within the United States, or any place subject to their jurisdiction.

§ 2. Congress shall have power to enforce this article by appropriate legislation.

Amend. 14, § 1. All persons born or naturalized in the United States, and subject to the jurisdiction thereof, are citizens of the United States and the State wherein they reside. No State shall make or enforce any law which shall abridge the privileges or immunities of. citizens of the United States; nor shall any State deprive any person of life, liberty, or property, without due process of law; nor deny to any person within its jurisdiction the equal protection of the laws. * * *

§ 5. The Congress shall have power to enforce, by appropriate legislation, the provisions of this article.

UNITED STATES ARBITRATION ACT

9 U.S.C.

§ 1. "Maritime Transactions" and "Commerce" Defined; Exceptions to Operation of Title

"Maritime transactions", as herein defined, means charter parties, bills of lading of water carriers, agreements relating to wharfage, supplies furnished vessels or repairs to vessels, collisions, or any other matters in foreign commerce which, if the subject of controversy, would be embraced within admiralty jurisdiction; "commerce", as herein defined, means commerce among the several States or with foreign nations, or in any Territory of the United States or in the District of Columbia, or between any such Territory and another, or between any such Territory and any State or foreign nation, or between the District of Columbia and any State or Territory or foreign nation, but nothing herein contained shall apply to contracts of employment of seamen, railroad employees, or any other class of workers engaged in foreign or interstate commerce.

§ 2. Validity, Irrevocability, and Enforcement of Agreements to Arbitrate

A written provision in any maritime transaction or a contract evidencing a transaction involving commerce to settle by arbitration a controversy thereafter arising out of such contract or transaction, or the refusal to perform the whole or any part thereof, or an agreement in writing to submit to arbitration an existing controversy arising out of such a contract, transaction, or refusal, shall be valid, irrevocable, and enforceable, save upon such grounds as exist at law or in equity. for the revocation of any contract.

§ 3. Stay of Proceedings Where Issue Therein Referable to Arbitration

If any suit or proceeding be brought in any of the courts of the United States upon any issue referable to arbitration under an agreement in writing for such arbitration, the court in which such suit is pending, upon being satisfied that the issue involved in such suit or proceeding is referable to arbitration under such an agreement, shall on application of one of the parties stay the trial of the action until such arbitration has been had in accordance with the terms of the agreement, providing the applicant for the stay is not in default in proceeding with such arbitration.

§ 4. Failure to Arbitrate Under Agreement; Petition to United States Court Having Jurisdiction for Order to Compel Arbitration; Notice and Service Thereof; Hearing and Determination

A party aggrieved by the alleged failure, neglect, or refusal of another to arbitrate under a written agreement for arbitration may petition any United States district court which, save for such agreement, would have jurisdiction under Title 28, in a civil action or in admiralty of the subject matter of a suit arising out of the controversy between the parties, for an order directing that such arbitration proceed in the manner provided for in such agreement. Five days' notice in writing of such application shall be served upon the party in default. Service thereof shall be made in the manner provided by the Federal Rules of Civil Procedure. The court shall hear the parties, and upon being satisfied that the making of the agreement for arbitration or the failure to comply therewith is not in issue, the court shall make an order directing the parties to proceed to arbitration in accordance with the terms of the agreement. The hearing and proceedings, under such agreement, shall be within the district in which the petition for an order directing such arbitration is filed. If the making of the arbitration agreement or the failure, neglect, or refusal to perform the same be in issue, the court shall proceed summarily to the trial thereof. If no jury trial be demanded by the party alleged to be in default, or if the matter in dispute is within admiralty jurisdiction, the court shall hear and determine such issue. Where such an issue is raised, the party alleged to be in default may, except in cases of admiralty, on or before the return day of the notice of application, demand a jury trial of such issue, and upon such demand the

3

court shall make an order referring the issue or issues to a jury in the manner provided by the Federal Rules of Civil Procedure, or may specially call a jury for that purpose. If the jury find that no agreement in writing for arbitration was made or that there is no default in proceeding thereunder, the proceeding shall be dismissed. If the jury find that an agreement for arbitration was made in writing and that there is a default in proceeding thereunder, the court shall make an order summarily directing the parties to proceed with the arbitration in accordance with the terms thereof.

§ 5. Appointment of Arbitrators or Umpire

If in the agreement provision be made for a method of naming or appointing an arbitrator or arbitrators or an umpire, such method shall be followed; but if no method be provided therein, or if a method be provided and any party thereto shall fail to avail himself of such method, or if for any other reason there shall be a lapse in the naming of an arbitrator or arbitrators or umpire, or in filling a vacancy, then upon the application of either party to the controversy the court shall designate and appoint an arbitrator or arbitrators or umpire, as the case may require, who shall act under the said agreement with the same force and effect as if he or they had been specifically named therein; and unless otherwise provided in the agreement the arbitration shall be by a single arbitrator.

§ 6. Application Heard as Motion

Any application to the court hereunder shall be made and heard in the manner provided by law for the making and hearing of motions, except as otherwise herein expressly provided.

§ 7. Witnesses Before Arbitrators; Fees; Compelling Attendance

The arbitrators selected either as prescribed in this title or otherwise, or a majority of them, may summon in writing any person to attend before them or any of them as a witness and in a proper case to bring with him or them any book, record, document, or paper which may be deemed material as evidence in the case. The fees for such attendance shall be the same as the fees of witnesses before masters of the United States courts. Said summons shall issue in the name of the arbitrator or arbitrators, or a majority of them, and shall be signed by the arbitrators, or a majority of them, and shall be directed to the said person and shall be served in the same manner as subpoenas to appear and testify before the court; if any person or persons so summoned to testify shall refuse or neglect to obey said summons, upon petition the United States district court for the district in which such arbitrators, or a majority of them, are sitting may compel the attendance of such person or persons before said arbitrator or arbitrators, or punish said person or persons for contempt in the same manner provided by law for securing the attendance of witnesses or their punishment for neglect or refusal to attend in the courts of the United States.

§ 8. Proceedings Began by Libel in Admiralty and Seizure of Vessel or Property

If the basis of jurisdiction be a cause of action otherwise justiciable in admiralty, then, notwithstanding anything herein to the contrary, the party claiming to be aggrieved may begin his proceeding hereunder by libel and seizure of the vessel or other property of the other party according to the usual course of admiralty proceedings, and the court shall then have jurisdiction to direct the parties to proceed with the arbitration and shall retain jurisdiction to enter its decree upon the award.

§ 9. Award of Arbitrators; Confirmation; Jurisdiction; Procedure

If the parties in their agreement have agreed that a judgment of the court shall be entered upon the award made pursuant to the arbitration, and shall specify the court, then at any time within one year after the award is made any party to the arbitration may apply to the court so specified for an order confirming the award, and thereupon the court must grant such an order unless the award is vacated, modified, or corrected as prescribed in sections 10 and 11 of this title. If no court is specified in the agreement of the parties, then such application may be made to the United States court in and for the district within which such award was made. Notice of the application shall be served upon the adverse party, and thereupon the court shall have jurisdiction of such party as though he had appeared generally in the proceeding. If the adverse party is a resident of the district within which the award was made, such service shall be made upon the adverse party or his attorney as prescribed by law for service of notice of motion in an action in the same court. If the adverse party shall be a nonresident, then the notice of the application shall be served by the marshal of any district within which the adverse party may be found in like manner as other process of the court.

§ 10. Same; Vacation; Grounds; Rehearing

In either of the following cases the United States court in and for the district wherein the award was made may make an order vacating the award upon the application of any party to the arbitration—

(a) Where the award was procured by corruption, fraud, or undue means.

(b) Where there was evident partiality or corruption in the arbitrators, or either of them.

(c) Where the arbitrators were guilty of misconduct in refusing to postpone the hearing, upon sufficient cause shown, or in refusing to hear evidence pertinent and material to the controversy; or of any other misbehavior by which the rights of any party have been prejudiced.

(d) Where the arbitrators exceeded their powers, or so imperfectly executed them that a mutual, final, and definite award upon the subject matter submitted was not made.

5

(e) Where an award is vacated and the time within which the agreement required the award to be made has not expired the court may, in its discretion, direct a rehearing by the arbitrators.

§ 11. Same; Modification or Correction; Grounds; Order

In either of the following cases the United States court in and for the district wherein the award was made may make an order modifying or correcting the award upon the application of any party to the arbitration—

(a) Where there was an evident material miscalculation of figures or an evident material mistake in the description of any person, thing, or property referred to in the award.

(b) Where the arbitrators have awarded upon a matter not submitted to them, unless it is a matter not affecting the merits of the decision upon the matter submitted.

(c) Where the award is imperfect in matter of form not affecting the merits of the controversy.

The order may modify and correct the award, so as to effect the intent thereof and promote justice between the parties.

§ 12. Notice of Motions to Vacate or Modify; Service; Stay of Proceedings

Notice of a motion to vacate, modify, or correct an award must be served upon the adverse party or his attorney within three months after the award is filed or delivered. If the adverse party is a resident of the district within which the award was made, such service shall be made upon the adverse party or his attorney as prescribed by law for service of notice of motion in an action in the same court. If the adverse party shall be a nonresident then the notice of the application shall be served by the marshal of any district within which the adverse party may be found in like manner as other process of the court. For the purposes of the motion any judge who might make an order to stay the proceedings in an action brought in the same court may make an order, to be served with the notice of motion, staying the proceedings of the adverse party to enforce the award.

§ 13. Papers Filed with Order on Motions; Judgment; Docketing; Force and Effect; Enforcement

The party moving for an order confirming, modifying, or correcting an award shall, at the time such order is filed with the clerk for the entry of judgment thereon, also file the following papers with the clerk:

(a) The agreement; the selection or appointment, if any, of an additional arbitrator or umpire; and each written extension of the time, if any, within which to make the award.

(b) The award.

(c) Each notice, affidavit, or other paper used upon an application to confirm, modify, or correct the award, and a copy of each order of the court upon such an application.

The judgment shall be docketed as if it was rendered in an action.

The judgment so entered shall have the same force and effect, in all respects, as, and be subject to all the provisions of law relating to, a judgment in an action; and it may be enforced as if it had been rendered in an action in the court in which it is entered. * * *

AUTOMOBILE DEALERS' DAY IN COURT ACT

15 U.S.C.

§ 1221. Definitions

As used in this chapter—

(a) The term "automobile manufacturer" shall mean any person, partnership, corporation, association, or other form of business enterprise engaged in the manufacturing or assembling of passenger cars, trucks, or station wagons, including any person, partnership, or corporation which acts for and is under the control of such manufacturer or assembler in connection with the distribution of said automotive vehicles.

(b) The term "franchise" shall mean the written agreement or contract between any automobile manufacturer engaged in commerce and any automobile dealer which purports to fix the legal rights and liabilities of the parties to such agreement or contract.

(c) The term "automobile dealer" shall mean any person, partnership, corporation, association, or other form of business enterprise resident in the United States or in any Territory thereof or in the District of Columbia operating under the terms of a franchise and engaged in the sale or distribution of passenger cars, trucks, or station wagons.

(d) The term "commerce" shall mean commerce among the several States of the United States or with foreign nations, or in any Territory of the United States or in the District of Columbia, or among the Territories or between any Territory and any State or foreign nation, or between the District of Columbia and any State or Territory or foreign nation.

(e) The term "good faith" shall mean the duty of each party to any franchise, and all officers, employees, or agents thereof to act in a fair and equitable manner toward each other so as to guarantee the one party freedom from coercion, intimidation, or threats of coercion or intimidation from the other party: *Provided*, That recommendation, endorsement, exposition, persuasion, urging or argument shall not be deemed to constitute a lack of good faith.

§ 1222.   Authorization of Suits Against Manufacturers; Amount of Recovery; Defenses

An automobile dealer may bring suit against any automobile manufacturer engaged in commerce, in any district court of the United States in the district in which said manufacturer resides, or is found, or has an agent, without respect to the amount in controversy, and shall recover the damages by him sustained and the cost of suit by reason of the failure of said automobile manufacturer from and after August 8, 1956, to act in good faith in performing or complying with any of the terms or provisions of the franchise, or in terminating, canceling, or not renewing the franchise with said dealer: *Provided*, That in any such suit the manufacturer shall not be barred from asserting in defense of any such action the failure of the dealer to act in good faith.

§ 1223.   Limitations

Any action brought pursuant to this chapter shall be forever barred unless commenced within three years after the cause of action shall have accrued.

§ 1224.   Antitrust Laws as Affected

No provision of this chapter shall repeal, modify, or supersede, directly or indirectly, any provision of the antitrust laws of the United States.

§ 1225.   State Laws as Affected

This chapter shall not invalidate any provision of the laws of any State except insofar as there is a direct conflict between an express provision of this chapter and an express provision of State law which can not be reconciled.

CIVIL RIGHTS ACT OF 1866

42 U.S.C.

§ 1981.   Equal Rights Under the Law

All persons within the jurisdiction of the United States shall have the same right in every State and Territory to make and enforce contracts, to sue, be parties, give evidence, and to the full and equal benefit of all laws and proceedings for the security of persons and property as is enjoyed by white citizens, and shall be subject to like punishment, pains, penalties, taxes, licenses, and exactions of every kind, and to no other.

§ 1982.   Property Rights of Citizens

All citizens of the United States shall have the same right, in every State and Territory, as is enjoyed by white citizens thereof to inherit, purchase, lease, sell, hold, and convey real and personal property.

§ 1983. Civil Action for Deprivation of Rights

Every person who, under color of any statute, ordinance, regulation, custom, or usage, of any State or Territory, subjects, or causes to be subjected, any citizen of the United States or other person within the jurisdiction thereof to the deprivation of any rights, privileges, or immunities secured by the Constitution and laws, shall be liable to the party injured in an action at law, suit in equity, or other proper proceeding for redress.

CIVIL RIGHTS ACT of 1964[1]

42 U.S.C.

§ 2000e. (§ 701) Definitions

For the purposes of this subchapter—

(a) The term "person" includes one or more individuals, governments, governmental agencies, political subdivisions, labor unions, partnerships, associations, corporations, legal representatives, mutual companies, joint-stock companies, trusts, unincorporated organizations, trustees, trustees in cases under Title II, or receivers.

(b) The term "employer" means a person engaged in an industry affecting commerce who has fifteen or more employees for each working day in each of twenty or more calendar weeks in the current or preceding calendar year, and any agent of such a person, but such term does not include (1) the United States, a corporation wholly owned by the Government of the United States, an Indian tribe, or any department or agency of the District of Columbia subject by statute to procedures of the competitive service (as defined in section 2102 of Title 5), or (2) a bona fide private membership club (other than a labor organization) which is exempt from taxation under section 501(c) of Title 26, except that during the first year after March 24, 1972, persons having fewer than twenty-five employees (and their agents) shall not be considered employers.

(c) The term "employment agency" means any person regularly undertaking with or without compensation to procure employees for an employer or to procure for employees opportunities to work for an employer and includes an agent of such a person.

(d) The term "labor organization" means a labor organization engaged in an industry affecting commerce, and any agent of such an organization, and includes any organization of any kind, any agency, or employee representation committee, group, association, or plan so engaged in which employees participate and which exists for the purpose, in whole or in part,

---

1. Often referred to as Title VII. The number in parenthesis after each U.S.C. sec- tion number is the number of Act section.

of dealing with. employers concerning grievances, labor disputes, wages, rates of pay, hours, or other terms or conditions of employment, and any conference, general committee, joint or system board, or joint council so engaged which is subordinate to a national or international labor organization.

(f) The term "employee" means an individual employed by an employer, except that the term "employee" shall not include any person elected to public office in any State or political subdivision of any State by the qualified voters thereof, or any person chosen by such officer to be on such officer's personal staff, or an appointee on the policy making level or an immediate adviser with respect to the exercise of the constitutional or legal powers of the office. The exemption set forth in the preceding sentence shall not include employees subject to the civil service laws of a State government, governmental agency or political subdivision.

(j) The term "religion" includes all aspects of religious observance and practice, as well as belief, unless an employer demonstrates that he is unable to reasonably accommodate to an employee's or prospective employee's religious observance or practice without undue hardship on the conduct of the employer's business.

(k) The terms "because of sex" or "on the basis of sex" include, but are not limited to, because of or on the basis of pregnancy, childbirth, or related medical conditions; and women affected, childbirth or related medical conditions shall be treated the same for all employment-related purposes, including receipt of benefits under fringe benefit programs, as other persons not so affected but similar in their ability or inability to work, and nothing in section 2000e–2(h) of this title shall be interpreted to permit otherwise. The subsection shall not require an employer to pay for health insurance benefits for abortion, except where the life of the mother would be endangered if the fetus were carried to term, or expect where medical complications have arisen from an abortion: *Provided*, That nothing herein shall preclude an employer from providing abortion benefits or otherwise affect bargaining agreements in regard to abortion.

(m) The term "demonstrates" means meets the burdens of production and persuasion.

§ 2000e–1.   (§ 702) Subchapter Not Applicable to Employment of Aliens Outside State and Individuals for Performance of Activities of Religious Corporations, Associations, Educational Institutions, or Societies

(a) This subchapter shall not apply to an employer with respect to the employment of aliens outside any State, or to a religious corporation, association, educational institution, or society with respect to the employment of individuals of a particular religion to perform work connected with the carrying on by such corporation, association, educational institution, or society of its activities.

* * *

§ 2000e–2. (§ 703) Unlawful Employment Practices—Employer Practices

(a) Employer Practices

It shall be an unlawful employment practice for an employer—

(1) to fail or refuse to hire or to discharge any individual, or otherwise to discriminate against any individual with respect to his compensation, terms, conditions, or privileges of employment, because of such individual's race, color, religion, sex, or national origin; or

(2) to limit, segregate, or classify his employees or applicants for employment in any way which would deprive or tend to deprive any individual of employment opportunities or otherwise adversely affect his status as an employee, because of such individual's race, color, religion, sex, or national origin.

(b) Employment agency practices

It shall be an unlawful employment practice for an employment agency to fail or refuse to refer for employment, or otherwise to discriminate against, any individual because of his race, color, religion, sex, or national origin, or to classify or refer for employment any individual on the basis of his race, color, religion, sex, or national origin.

(c) Labor organization practices

It shall be an unlawful employment practice for a lab organization—

(1) to exclude or to expel from its membership, or otherwise to discriminate against, any individual because of his race, color, religion, sex, or national origin;

(2) to limit, segregate, or classify its membership or applicants for membership, or to classify or fail or refuse to refer for employment any individual, in any way which would deprive or tend to deprive any individual of employment opportunities, or would limit such employment opportunities or otherwise adversely affect his status as an employee or as an applicant for employment, because of such individual's race, color, religion, sex, or national origin; or

(3) to cause or attempt to cause an employer to discriminate against an individual in violation of this section.

(d) Training programs

It shall be an unlawful employment practice for any employer, labor organization, or joint labor-management committee controlling apprenticeship or other training or retraining, including on-the-job training programs to discriminate against any individual because of his race, color, religion, sex, or national origin in admission to, or employment in, any program established to provide apprenticeship or other training.

(e) Businesses or enterprises with personnel qualified on basis of religion, sex, or national origin; educational institutions with personnel of particular religion

Notwithstanding any other provision of this subchapter, (1) it shall not be an unlawful employment practice for an employer to hire and employ employees, for an employment agency to classify, or refer for employment any individual, for a labor organization to classify its membership or to classify or refer for employment any individual, or for an employer, labor organization, or joint labor-management committee controlling apprenticeship or other training or retraining programs to admit or employ any individual in any such program, on the basis of his religion, sex, or national origin in those certain instances where religion, sex, or national origin is a bona fide occupational qualification reasonably necessary to the normal operation of that particular business or enterprise, and (2) it shall not be an unlawful employment practice for a school, college, university, or other educational institution or institution of learning to hire and employ employees of a particular religion if such school, college, university, or other educational institution or institution of learning is, in whole or insubstantial part, owned, supported, controlled, or managed by a particular religion or by a particular religious corporation, association, or society, or if the curriculum of such school, college, university, or other educational institution or institution of learning is directed toward the propagation of a particular religion.

(h) Seniority or merit system; quantity or quality of production; ability tests; compensation based on sex and authorized by minimum wage provisions

Notwithstanding, any other provision of this subchapter, it shall not be an unlawful employment practice for an employer to apply different standards of compensation, or different terms, conditions, or privileges of employment pursuant to a bona fide seniority or merit system, or a system which measures earnings by quantity or quality of production or to employees who work in different locations, provided that such differences are not the result of an intention to discriminate because of race, color, religion, sex, or national origin, nor shall it be an unlawful employment practice for an employer to give and to act upon the results of any professionally developed ability test provided that such test, its administration or action upon the results is not designed, intended or used to discriminate because of race, color, religion, sex or national origin. It shall not be an unlawful employment practice under this subchapter for any employer to differentiate upon the basis of sex in determining the amount of the wages or compensation paid or to be paid to employees of such employer if such differentiation is authorized by the provisions of section 206(d) of Title 29.

(j) Preferential treatment not to be granted on account of existing number or percentage imbalance

Nothing contained in this subchapter shall be interpreted to require any employer, employment agency, labor organization, or joint labor-management committee subject to this subchapter to grant preferential treatment to any individual or to any group because of the race, color, religion, sex, or national origin of such individual or group on account of an imbalance which may exist with respect to the total number or percentage of persons of any race, color, religion, sex, or national origin employed by any employer, referred or classified for employment by any employment agency or labor organization, admitted to membership or classified by any labor organization, or admitted to, or employed in, any apprenticeship or other training program, in comparison with the total number or percentage of persons of such race, color, religion, sex, or national origin in any community, State, section, or other area, or in the available work force in any community, State, section, or other area.

(k)(1)(A) An unlawful employment practice based on disparate impact is established under this title only if—

(i) a complaining party demonstrates that a respondent uses a particular employment practice that causes a disparate impact on the basis of race, color, religion, sex or national origin and the respondent fails to demonstrate that the challenged practice is job related for the position in question and consistent with business necessity; or

(ii) the complaining party makes the demonstration described in subparagraph (C) with respect to an alternative employment practice and the respondent refuses to adopt such alternative employment practice.

(B)(i) With respect to demonstrating that a particular employment practice causes a disparate impact as describe in subparagraph (A)(i), the complaining party shall demonstrate that each particular challenged employment practice causes a disparate impact, except that if the complaining party can demonstrate to the court that the elements of a respondent's decisionmaking process are not capable of separation for analysis, the decisionmaking process may be analyzed as one employment practice.

(ii) If the respondent demonstrates that a specific employment practice does not cause the disparate impact, the respondent shall not be required to demonstrate that such practice is required by business necessity.

(C) The demonstration referred to by subparagraph (A)(ii) shall be in accordance with the law as it existed on June 4, 1989, with respect to the concept of "alternative employment practice".

(2) A demonstration that an employment practice is required by business necessity may not be used as a defense against a claim of intentional discrimination under this title.

(3) Notwithstanding any other provision of this title, a rule barring the employment of an individual who currently and knowingly uses or possesses a controlled substance, as defined in schedule I and II of section 102(6) of the Controlled Substances Act (21 U.S.C. 802(6)), other than the use or possession of a drug taken under the supervision of a licensed health care professional, or any other use or possession authorized by the Controlled Substances Act or any other provision of Federal law, shall be considered an unlawful employment practice under this title only if such rule is adopted or applied with an intent to discriminate because or race, color, religion, sex, or national origin. * * *

(*l*) It shall be an unlawful employment practice for a respondent, in connection with the selection or referral of applicants or candidates for employment or promotion, to adjust the scores of, use different cutoff scores for, or otherwise alter the results of, employment related tests on the basis of race, color, religion, sex or national origin.

(m) Except as otherwise provided in this title, an unlawful employment practice is established when the complaining party demonstrates that race, color, religion, sex or national origin was a motivating factor for any employment practice, even though other factors also motivated the practice.

§ 2000e–3.   (§ 704) Other Unlawful Employment Practices

(a) Discrimination for Making Charges, Testifying, Assisting, or Participating in Enforcement Proceedings

It shall be an unlawful employment practice for an employer to discriminate against any of his employees or applicants for employment, for an employment agency, or joint labor management committee controlling apprenticeship or other training or retraining, including on-the-job training programs, to discriminate against any individual, or for a labor organization to discriminate against any member thereof or applicant for membership, because he has opposed any practice made an unlawful employment practice by this subchapter, or because he has made a charge, testified, assisted, or participated in any manner in an investigation, proceeding, or hearing under this subchapter.

(b) Printing or publication of notices or advertisements indicating prohibited preference, limitation, specification, or discrimination; occupational qualification exception

It shall be an unlawful employment practice for an employer, labor organization, employment agency, or joint labor management committee controlling apprenticeship or other training or retraining, including on-the-job training programs, to print or publish or cause to be printed or published any notice or advertisement relating to employment by such an employer or membership in or any classification or referral for employment by such a labor organization, or relating to any classification or referral for employment by such an employment agency, or relating to admission to, or employment in, any program established to provide apprenticeship or other training by such a joint labor-management committee, indicating any preference, limitation, specification, or discrimination, based on race, color, religion, sex, or national origin, except that such a notice or advertisement may indicate a preference, limitation, specification, or discrimination based on religion, sex, or national origin when religion, sex, or national origin is a bona fide occupational qualification for employment.

§ 2000e–4.   (§ 705) Equal Employment Opportunity Commission

(a) Creation; Composition; Political Representation; Appointment; Term; Vacancies; Chairman and Vice Chairman; Duties of Chairman; Appointment of Personnel; Compensation of Personnel

There is hereby created a Commission to be known as the Equal Employment Opportunity Commission, which shall be composed of five members' not more than three of whom shall be members of the same political party. Members of the Commission shall be appointed by the President by and with the advice and consent of the Senate for a term of five years. * * *

§ 2000e–5. (§ 706) Enforcement Provisions—Power of Commission to Prevent Unlawful Employment Practices

(a) The Commission is empowered, as hereinafter provided, to prevent any person from engaging in any unlawful employment practice as set forth in section 2000e–2 or 2000e–3 of this title.

(b) Charges by persons aggrieved or member of Commission of unlawful employment practices by employers, etc.; filing; allegations; notice to respondent; contents of notice; investigation by Commission; contents of charges; prohibition on disclosure of charges; determination of reasonable. cause; conference, conciliation, and persuasion for elimination of unlawful practices; prohibition on disclosure of informal endeavors to end unlawful practices; use of evidence in subsequent proceedings; penalties for disclosure of information; time for determination of reasonable cause

Whenever a charge is filed by or on behalf of a person claiming to be aggrieved, or by a member of the Commission, alleging that an employer, employment agency, labor organization, or joint labor-management committee controlling apprenticeship or other training or retraining, including on-the-job training programs, has engaged in an unlawful employment practice, the Commission shall serve a notice of the charge (including the date, place and circumstances of the alleged unlawful employment practice) on such employer, employment agency, labor organization, or joint labor-management committee (hereinafter referred to as the "respondent") within ten days, and shall make an investigation thereof. Charges shall be in writing under oath or affirmation and shall contain such information and be in such form as the Commission requires, Charges shall not be made public by the Commission. If the Commission determines after such investigation that there is not reasonable cause to believe that the charge is true, it shall dismiss the charge and promptly notify the person claiming to be aggrieved and the respondent of its action. In determining whether reasonable cause exists, the Commission shall accord substantial weight to final findings and orders made by State or local authorities in proceedings commenced under State or local law pursuant to the requirements of subsections (c) and (d) of this section. If the Commission determines after such investigation that there is reasonable cause to believe that the charge is true, the Commission shall endeavor to eliminate any such alleged unlawful employment practice by informal methods of conference, conciliation, and persuasion. Nothing said or done during and as a part of such informal endeavors may be made public by the Commission, its officers or employees, or used as evidence in a subsequent proceeding without the written consent of the persons concerned. Any person who makes public information in violation of this subsection shall be fined not more than $1,000 or imprisoned for not more than one year, or both. The Commission shall make its determination on reasonable cause as promptly as possible and, so far as practicable, not later than one hundred and twenty days from the filing of the charge or, where applicable under subsection (c) or (d) of this section, from the date upon which the Commission is authorized to take action with respect to the charge.

(c) State or local enforcement proceedings; notification of State or local authority; time for filing charges with Commission; commencement of proceedings

In the case of an alleged unlawful employment practice occurring in a State, or political subdivision of a State, which has a State or local law prohibiting the unlawful employment practice alleged and establishing or authorizing a State or local authority to grant or seek relief from such practice or to institute criminal proceedings with respect thereto upon receiving notice thereof, no charge may be filed under subsection (b) of this section by the person aggrieved before the expiration of sixty days after proceedings have been commenced under the State or local law, unless such proceedings have been earlier terminated, provided that such sixty-day period shall be extended to one hundred and twenty days during the first year after the effective date of such State or local law. If any requirement for the commencement of such proceedings is imposed by a State or local authority other than a requirement of the filing of a written and signed statement of the facts upon which the proceeding is based, the proceeding shall be deemed to have been commenced for the purposes of this subsection at the time such statement is sent by registered mail to the appropriate State or local authority.

(d) Notification of State or local authority; time for action on charges by Commission

In the case of any charge filed by a member of the Commission alleging an unlawful employment practice occurring in a State or political subdivision of a State which has a State or local law prohibiting the practice alleged and establishing or authorizing a State or local authority to grant or seek relief from such practice or to institute criminal proceedings with respect thereto upon receiving notice thereof, the Commission shall, before taking any action with respect to such charge, notify the appropriate State or local officials and, upon request, afford them a reasonable time, but not less than sixty days (provided that such sixty-day period shall be extended to one hundred and twenty days during the first year after the effective day of such State or local law), unless a shorter period is requested, to act under such State or local law to remedy the practice alleged.

(e) Time for filing charges; time for service of notice of charge on respondent; filing of charge by Commission with State or local agency

(1) A charge under this section shall be filed within one hundred and eighty days after the alleged unlawful employment practice occurred and notice of the charge (including the date, place and circumstances of the

alleged unlawful employment practice) shall be served upon the person against whom such charge is made within ten days thereafter, except that in a case of an unlawful employment practice with respect to which the person aggrieved has initially instituted proceedings with a State or local agency with authority to grant or seek relief from such practice or to institute criminal proceedings with respect thereto upon receiving notice thereof, such charge shall be filed by or on behalf of the person aggrieved within three hundred days after the alleged unlawful employment practice occurred, or within thirty days after receiving notice that the State or local agency has terminated the proceedings under the State or local law, whichever is earlier, and a copy of such charge shall be filed by the Commission with the State or local agency.

       * * *

(f) Civil action by Commission, Attorney General, or person aggrieved; preconditions; procedure; appointment of attorney; payment of fees, costs, or security; intervention; stay of Federal proceedings; action for appropriate temporary or preliminary relief pending final disposition of charge; jurisdiction and venue of United States courts; designation of judge to hear and determine case; assignment of case for hearing; expedition of case; appointment of master

(1) If within thirty days after a charge is filed with the Commission or within thirty days after expiration of any period of reference under subsection (c) or (d) of this section, the Commission has been unable to secure from the respondent a conciliation agreement acceptable to the Commission, the Commission may bring a civil action against any respondent not a government, governmental agency, or political subdivision named in the charge. In the case of a respondent which is a government, governmental agency, or political subdivision, if the Commission has been unable to secure from the respondent a conciliation agreement acceptable to the Commission, the Commission shall take no further action and shall refer the case to the Attorney General who may bring a civil action against such respondent in the appropriate United States district court. The person or persons aggrieved shall have the right to intervene in a civil action brought by the Commission or the Attorney General in a case involving a government, governmental agency, or political subdivision. If a charge filed with the Commission pursuant to subsection (b) of this section is dismissed by the Commission, or if within one hundred and eighty days from the filing of such charge or the expiration of any period of reference under subsection (c) or (d) of this section, whichever is later, the Commission has not filed a civil action under this section or the Attorney General has not filed a civil action in a case involving a government, governmental agency, or political subdivision, or the Commission has not entered into a conciliation agreement to which the person aggrieved is a party, the Commission, or the Attorney General in a case involving a government, governmental agency, or political subdivision, shall so notify the person aggrieved and within ninety days after the giving of such notice a civil action may be brought against the respondent named in the charge (A) by the person claiming to

be aggrieved or (B) if such charge was filed by a member of the Commission, by any person whom the charge alleges was aggrieved by the alleged unlawful employment practice. Upon application by the complainant and in such circumstances as the court may deem just, the court may appoint an attorney for such complainant and may authorize the commencement of the action without the payment of fees, costs, or security. Upon timely application, the court may, in its discretion, permit the Commission, or the Attorney General in a case involving a government, governmental agency, or political subdivision, to intervene in such civil action upon certification that the case is of general public importance. Upon request, the court may, in its discretion, stay further proceedings for not more than sixty days pending the termination of State or local proceedings described in subsections (c) or (d) of this section or further efforts of the Commission to obtain voluntary compliance.

(2) Whenever a charge is filed with the Commission and the Commission concludes on the basis of a preliminary investigation that prompt judicial action is necessary to carry out the purposes of this Act, the Commission, or the Attorney General in a case involving a government, governmental agency, or political subdivision, may bring an action for appropriate temporary or preliminary relief pending final disposition of such charge. Any temporary restraining order or other order granting preliminary or temporary relief shall be issued in accordance with rule 65 of the Federal Rules of Civil Procedure. It shall be the duty of a court having jurisdiction over proceedings under this section to assign cases for hearing at the earliest practicable date and to cause such cases to be in every way expedited.

(3) Each United States district court and each United States court of a place subject to the jurisdiction of the United States shall have jurisdiction of actions brought under this subchapter. Such an action may be brought in any judicial district in the State in which the unlawful employment practice is alleged to have been committed, in the judicial district in which. the employment records relevant to such practice are maintained and administered, or in the judicial district in which the aggrieved person would have worked but for the alleged unlawful employment practice, but if the respondent is not found within any such district, such an action may be brought within the judicial district in which the respondent has his principal office. For purposes of sections 1404 and 1406 of Title 28, the judicial district in which the respondent has his principal office shall in all cases be considered a district in which the action might have been brought.

(5) It shall be the duty of the judge designated pursuant to this subsection to assign the case for hearing at the earliest practicable date and to cause the case to be in every way expedited, If such judge has not scheduled the case for trial within one hundred and twenty days after issue has been joined, that judge may appoint a master pursuant to rule 53 of the Federal Rules of Civil Procedure.

(g) Injunctions; appropriate affirmative action; equitable relief; accrual of back pay; reduction of back pay; limitations on judicial orders

(1) If the court finds that the respondent has intentionally engaged in or is intentionally engaging in an unlawful employment practice charged in the complaint, the court may enjoin the respondent from engaging in such unlawful employment practice, and order such affirmative action as may be appropriate, which may include, but is not limited to, reinstatement or hiring of employees, with or without back pay (payable by the employer, employment agency, or labor organization, as the case may be, responsible for the unlawful employment practice), or any other equitable relief as the court deems appropriate. Back pay liability shall not accrue from a date more than two years prior to the filing of a charge with the Commission. Interim earnings or amounts earnable with reasonable diligence by the person or persons discriminated against shall operate to reduce the back pay otherwise allowable. No order of the court shall require the admission or reinstatement of an individual as a member of a union, or the hiring, reinstatement, or promotion of an individual as an employee, or the payment to him of any back pay, if such individual was refused admission, suspended, or expelled, or was refused employment or advancement or was suspended or discharged for any reason other than discrimination on account of race, color, religion, sex, or national origin or in violation of section 2000e–3(a) of this title.

* * *

(k) Attorney's fee; liability of Commission and United States for costs

In any action or proceeding under this subchapter the court, in its discretion, may allow the prevailing party, other than the Commission or the United States, a reasonable attorney's fee as part of the costs, and the Commission and the United States shall be liable for costs the same as a private person.

§ 2000e–6. (§ 707) Civil Actions by the Attorney General

(a) Complaint

Whenever the Attorney General has reasonable cause to believe that any person or group of persons is engaged in a pattern or practice of resistance to the full enjoyment of any of the rights secured by this subchapter, and that the pattern or practice is of such a nature and is intended to deny the full exercise of the rights herein described, the Attorney General may bring a civil action in the appropriate district court of the United States by filing with it a complaint (1) signed by him (or in his absence the Acting Attorney General), (2) setting forth facts pertaining to such pattern or practice, and (3) requesting such relief, including an application for a permanent or temporary injunction, restraining order or other order against the person or persons responsible for such pattern or practice, as he deems necessary to insure the full enjoyment of the rights herein described.

(b) Jurisdiction; three-judge district court for cases of general public importance: hearing, determination, expedition of action, review by Supreme Court; single-judge district court; hearing, determination, expedition of action

The district courts of the United States shall have and shall exercise jurisdiction of proceedings instituted pursuant to this section, and in any such proceeding the Attorney General may file with the clerk of such court a request that a court of three judges be convened to hear and determine the case. Such request by the Attorney General shall be accompanied by a certificate that, in his opinion, the case is of general public importance. A copy of the certificate and request for a three judge court shall be immediately furnished by such clerk to the chief judge of the circuit (or in his absence, the presiding circuit judge of the circuit) in which the case is pending, Upon receipt of such request it shall be the duty of the chief judge of the circuit or the presiding circuit judge, as the case may be, to designate immediately three judges in such circuit, of whom at least one shall be a circuit judge and another of whom shall be a district judge of the court in which the proceeding was instituted, to hear and determine such case, and it shall be the duty of the judges so designated to assign the case for hearing at the earliest practicable date, to participate in the hearing and determination thereof, and to cause the case to be in every way expedited. An appeal from the final judgment of such court will lie to the Supreme Court.

In the event the Attorney General fails to file such a request in any such proceeding, it shall be the duty of the chief judge of the district (or in his absence, the acting chief judge) in which the case is pending immediately to designate a judge in such district to hear and determine the case. In the event that no judge in the district is available to hear and determine the case, the chief judge of the district, or the acting chief judge, as the case may be, shall certify this fact to the chief judge of the circuit (or in his absence, the acting chief judge) who shall then designate a district or circuit judge of the circuit to hear and determine the case.

It shall be the duty of the judge designated pursuant to this section to assign the case for hearing at the earliest practicable date and to cause the case to be in every way expedited.

(e) Investigation and action by Commission pursuant to filing of charge of discrimination; procedure

Subsequent to March 24, 1972, the Commission shall have authority to investigate and act on a charge of a pattern or practice of discrimination, whether filed by or on behalf of a. person claiming to be aggrieved or by a member of the Commission. All such actions shall be conducted in accordance with the procedures set forth in section 2000e–5 of this title.

§ 2000e–17. (§ 718) Procedure for Denial, Withholding, Termination, or Suspension of Government Contract Subsequent to Acceptance by Government of Affirmative Action Plan of Employer; Time of Acceptance of Plan

No Government contract, or portion thereof, with any employer, shall be denied, withheld, terminated, or suspended, by any agency or officer of the United States under any equal employment opportunity law or order, where such employer has an affirmative action plan which has previously been accepted by the Government for the same facility within the past twelve months without first according such employer full hearing and adjudication under the provisions of section 554 of Title 5, and the following pertinent sections: *Provided*, That if such employer has deviated substantially from such previously agreed to affirmative action plan, this section shall not apply: *Provided further*, That for the purposes of this section an affirmative action plan shall be deemed to have been accepted by the Government at the time the appropriate compliance agency has accepted such plan unless within forty-five days thereafter the Office of Federal Contract Compliance has disapproved such plan.

CIVIL RIGHTS ACTS OF 1991

42 U.S.C.A. § 1981a

§ 1981a. Damages in Cases of Intentional Discrimination in Employment

(a) Right of Recovery—

(1) Civil Rights—In an action brought by a complaining party under section 706 or 717 of the Civil Rights Act of 1964 against a respondent who engaged in unlawful intentional discrimination (not an employment practice that is unlawful because of its disparate impact) prohibited under section 703, 704 or 717 of the Act, and provided that the complaining party cannot recover under 42 U.S.C. § 1981, the complaining party may recover compensatory and punitive damage as allowed in subsection (b), in addition to any relief authorized be section 706(g) of the Civil Rights Act of 1964, from the respondent.

(b) Compensatory and Punitive Damages—

(1) Determination of Punitive Damages—A complaining party may recover punitive damages under this section against a respondent (other than a government, government agency or political subdivision) if the complaining party demonstrates that the respondent engaged in a discriminatory practice or discriminatory practices with malice or with reckless indifference to the federally protected rights of an aggrieved individual.

(2) Exclusions from Compensatory Damages—Compensatory damages awarded under this section shall not include backpay, interest on backpay, or any other type of relief authorized under section 706(g) of the Civil Rights Acts of 1964.

(3) Limitations—The sum of the amount of compensatory damages awarded under this section for future pecuniary losses, emotional pain, suffering, inconvenience, mental anguish, loss of enjoyment of life, and other nonpecuniary losses, and the amount of punitive damages awarded under section, shall not exceed, for each complaining party—

21

(A) in the case of a respondent who has more than 14 and fewer than 101 employees in each of 20 or more calendar weeks in the current or preceding calendar year, $50,000;

(B) in the case of a respondent who has more than 100 and fewer than 201 employees in each of 20 or more calendar weeks in the current or proceeding calendar year, $100,000; and

(C) in the case of a respondent who has more than 200 and fewer than 501 employees in each of 20 or more calendar weeks in the current or preceding calendar year, $200,000; and

(D) in the case of a respondent who has more than 500 employees in each of 20 or more calendar weeks in the current or preceding calendar year, $300,000.

(c) Jury Trial—If a complaining party seeks compensatory or punitive damage under this section—

(1) any party may demand a trial by jury; and

(2) the court shall not inform the jury of the limitations described in subsection (b)(3).

CONVENTION ON THE INTERNATIONAL SALE OF GOODS

Article 11

A contract of sale need not be concluded in or evidenced by writing and is not subject to any other requirement as to form. It may be proved by any means, including witnesses.

Article 16

(1) Until a contract is concluded an offer may be revoked if the revocation reaches the offeree before he has dispatched an acceptance.

(2) However, an offer cannot be revoked:

(a) if it indicates, whether by stating a fixed time for acceptance or otherwise, that it is irrevocable; or

(b) if it was reasonable for the offeree to rely on the offer as being irrevocable and the offeree has acted in reliance on the offer.

Article 19

(1) A reply to an offer which purports to be an acceptance but contains additions, limitations or other modifications is a rejection of the offer and constitutes a counter-offer.

(2) However, a reply to an offer which purports to be an acceptance but contains additional or different terms which do not materially alter the terms of the offer constitutes an acceptance, unless the offeror, without

undue delay, objects orally to the discrepancy or dispatches a notice to that effect. If he does not so object, the terms of the contract are the terms of the offer with the modifications contained in the acceptance.

(3) Additional or different terms relating, among other things, to the price, payment, quality and quantity of the goods, place and time of delivery, extent of one party's liability to the other or the settlement of disputes are considered to alter the terms of the offer materially.

Article 28

If, in accordance with the provisions of this Convention, one party is entitled to require performance of any obligation by the other party, a court is not bound to enter a judgment for specific performance unless the court would do so under its own law in respect of similar contracts of sale not governed by this Convention.

Article 29

(1) A contract may be modified or terminated by the mere agreement of the parties.

(2) A contract in writing which contains a provision requiring any modification or termination by agreement to be in writing may not be otherwise modified or terminated by agreement. However, a party may be precluded by his conduct from asserting such a provision to the extent that the other party has relied on that conduct.

Article 46

(1) The buyer may require performance by the seller of his obligations unless the buyer has resorted to a remedy which is inconsistent with this requirement.

(2) If the goods do not conform with the contract, the buyer may require delivery of substitute goods only if the lack of conformity constitutes a fundamental breach of contract and a request for substitute goods is made either in conjunction with notice given under article 39 or within a reasonable time thereafter.

(3) If the goods do not conform with the contract, the buyer may require the seller to remedy the lack of conformity by repair, unless this is unreasonable having regard to all the circumstances. A request for repair must be made either in conjunction with notice given under article 39 or within a reasonable time thereafter.

Article 62

The seller may require the buyer to pay the price, take delivery or perform his other obligations, unless the seller has resorted to a remedy which is inconsistent with this requirement.

Article 71

(1) A party may suspend the performance of his obligations if, after the conclusion of the contract, it becomes apparent that the other party will not perform a substantial part of obligations as a result of:

(a) a serious deficiency in his ability to perform or in his creditworthiness; or

(b) his conduct in preparing to perform or in performing the contract.

(2) If the seller has already dispatched the goods before the grounds described in the preceding paragraph become evident, he may prevent the handing over of the goods to the buyer even though the buyer holds a document which entitles him to obtain them. The present paragraph relates only to the rights in the goods as between the buyer and the seller.

(3) A party suspending performance, whether before or after dispatch of the goods, must immediately give notice of the suspension to the over the party and must continue. with performance if the other party provides adequate assurance of his performance.

Article 72

(1) If prior to the date for performance of the contract it is clear that one of the parties will commit a fundamental breach of contract, the other party may declare the contract avoided.

(2) If time allows, the party intending to declare the contract avoided must give reasonable notice to the other party in order to permit him to provide adequate assurance of his performance.

(3) The requirements of the preceding paragraph do not apply if the other party has declared that he will not perform his obligations.

Article 74

Damages for breach of contract by one party consist of a sum equal to the loss, including loss of profit, suffered by the other party as a consequence of the breach. Such damages may not exceed the loss which the party in breach foresaw or ought to have foreseen at the time of the conclusion of the contract, in the light of the facts and matters of which he then knew or ought to have known, as a possible consequence of the breach of contract.

———

FEDERAL RULES OF CIVIL PROCEDURE

RULE 23—CLASS ACTIONS

(a) Prerequisites to a Class Action. One or more members of a class may sue or be sued as representative parties on behalf of all only if (1) the class is so numerous that joinder of all members is impracticable, (2) there are questions of law or fact common to the class, (3) the claims or defenses of the representative parties are typical of the claims or defenses of the class, and (4) the representative parties will fairly and adequately protect the interests of the class.

(b) Class Actions Maintainable. An action may be maintained as a class action if the prerequisites of subdivision (a) are satisfied, and in addition:

(1) the prosecution of separate actions by or against individual members of the class would create a risk of

(A) inconsistent or varying adjudications with respect to individual members of the class which would establish incompatible standards of conduct for the party opposing the class, or

(B) adjudications with respect to individual members of the class which would as a practical matter be dispositive of the interests of the other members not parties to the adjudications or substantially impair or impede their ability to protect their interests; or

(2) the party opposing the class has acted or refused to act on grounds generally applicable to the class, thereby making appropriate final injunctive relief or corresponding declaratory relief with respect to the class as a whole; or

(3) the court finds that the questions of law or fact common to the members of the class predominate over any questions affecting only individual members, and that a class action is superior to other available methods for the fair and efficient adjudication of the controversy. The matters pertinent to the findings include: (A) the interest of members of the class in individually controlling the prosecution or defense of separate actions; (B) the extent and nature of any litigation concerning the controversy already commenced by or against members of the class; (C) the desirability or undesirability of concentrating the litigation of the claims in the particular forum; (D) the difficulties likely to be encountered in the management of a class action.

(c) Determination by Order Whether Class Action to be Maintained, Notice; Judgment; Actions Conducted Partially as Class Actions

(1) As soon as practicable after the commencement of an action brought as a class action, the court shall determine by order whether it is to be so maintained. An order under this subdivision may be conditional, and may be altered or amended before the decision on the merits.

(2) In any class action maintained under subdivision (b)(3), the court shall direct to the members of the class the best notice practicable under the circumstances, including individual notice to all members who can be identified through reasonable effort. The notice shall advise each member that (A) the court will exclude him from the class if he so requests by a specified date; (B) the judgment, whether favorable or not, will include all members who do not request exclusion; and (C) any member who does not request exclusion may, if he desires, enter an appearance through his counsel.

(3) The judgment in an action maintained as a class action under subdivision (b)(1) or (b)(2), whether or not favorable to the class, shall

include and describe those whom the court finds to be members of the class. The judgment in an action maintained as a class action under subdivision (b)(3), whether or not favorable to the class, shall include and specify or describe those to whom the notice provided in subdivision (c)(2) was directed, and who have not requested exclusion, and whom the court finds to be members of the class.

(4) When appropriate (A) an action may be brought or maintained as a class action with respect to particular issues, or (B) a class may be divided into subclasses and each subclass treated as a class, and the provisions of this rule shall then be construed and applied accordingly.

(d) Orders in Conduct of Actions. In the conduct of actions to which this rule applies, the court may make appropriate orders: (1) determining the course of proceedings or prescribing measures to prevent undue repetition or complication in the presentation of evidence or argument; (2) requiring, for the protection of the members of the class or otherwise for the fair conduct of the action, that notice be given in such manner as the court may direct to, some or all of the members of any step in the action, or of the proposed extent of the judgment, or of the opportunity of members to signify whether they consider the representation fair and adequate, to intervene and present claims or defenses, or otherwise to come into the action; (3) imposing conditions on the representative parties or on intervenors; (4) requiring that the pleadings be amended to eliminate therefrom allegations as to representation of absent persons, and that the action proceed accordingly; (5) dealing with similar procedural matters. The orders may be combined with an order under Rule 16, and may be altered or amended as may be desirable from time to time.

(e) Dismissal or Compromise. A class action shall not be dismissed or compromised without the approval of the court, and notice of the proposed dismissal or compromise shall be given to all members of the class in such manner as the court directs.

INTERNAL REVENUE CODE OF 1939

26 U.S.C. (1955)

§ 22. Gross income

(a) General definition. "Gross income" includes gains, profits and income derived from salaries, wages, or compensation for personal service (including personal service as an officer or employee of a State, or any political subdivision thereof, or any agency or instrumentality of any one or more of the foregoing), of whatever kind and in whatever form paid, or from professions, vocations, trades, businesses, commerce, or sales, or dealings in property, whether real or personal, growing out of the ownership or use of or interest in such property; also from interest, rent, dividends, securities, or the transaction of any business carried on for gain or profit, or gains or profits and income derived from any source whatever. * * *

(b) Exclusions from gross income. The following items shall not be included in gross income and shall be exempt from taxation under this chapter:

(3) Gifts, bequests, devises, and inheritances. The value of property acquired by gift, bequest, devise, or inheritance. There shall not be excluded from gross income under this paragraph, the income from such property or, in case the gift, bequest, devise, or inheritance is of income from property, the amount of such income. * * *

§ 23. Deductions from Gross Income

In computing net income there shall be allowed as deductions:

(a) Expenses

(1) Trade or business expenses

(A) In general. All the ordinary and necessary expenses paid or incurred during the taxable year in carrying an any trade or business, including a reasonable allowance for salaries or other compensation for personal services actually rendered; * * *

LABOR LEGISLATION

LABOR MANAGEMENT RELATIONS ACT
(Taft Hartley)[2]
29 U.S.C.

§ 172. (§ 201) Federal Mediation and Conciliation Service

(a) Creation—Appointment of director. There is hereby created an independent agency to be known as the Federal Mediation Conciliation Service (herein referred to as the "Service,") * * *

§ 173. (§ 202) Functions of the Service

(a) It shall be the duty of the Service, in order to prevent or minimize interruptions of the free flow of commerce growing out of labor disputes, to assist parties to labor disputes in industries affecting commerce to settle such disputes through conciliation and mediation.

(b) The Service may proffer its services in any labor dispute in any industry affecting commerce, either upon its own motion or upon the request of one or more of the parties to the dispute, whenever in its judgment such dispute threatens to cause a substantial interruption of commerce. The Director and the Service are directed to avoid attempting to mediate disputes which would have only a minor effect on interstate

---

2. Sections of Taft Hartley are usually referred to by the section numbers of the Act, not of the U.S.C. In this excerpt the Act section numbers are set out in parenthesis.

commerce if State or other conciliation services are available to the parties. Whenever the Service does proffer its services in any dispute, it shall be the duty of the Service promptly to put itself in communication with the parties and to use its best efforts, by mediation and conciliation, to bring them to agreement.

(c) If the Director is not able to bring the parties to agreement by conciliation within a reasonable time, he shall seek to induce the parties voluntarily to seek other means of settling the dispute without resort to strike, lock-out, or other coercion, including-submission to the employees in the bargaining unit of the employer's last offer of settlement for approval or rejection in a secret ballot. The failure or refusal of either party to agree to any procedure suggested by the Director shall not be deemed a violation of any duty or obligation imposed by this Act.

(d) Final adjustment by a method agreed upon by the parties is hereby declared to be the desirable method for settlement of grievance disputes arising over the application or interpretation of an existing collective-bargaining agreement. The Service is directed to make its conciliation and mediation services available in the settlement of such grievance disputes only as a last resort and in exceptional cases.

§ 185.   (§ 301) Suits by and Against Labor Organizations

(a) Venue, amount, and citizenship

Suits for violation of contracts between an employer and a labor organization representing employees in an industry affecting commerce as defined in this chapter, or between any such labor organizations, may be brought in any district court of the United States having jurisdiction of the parties, without respect to the amount in controversy or without regard to the citizenship of the parties.

(b) Responsibility for acts of agent; entity for purposes of suit; enforcement of money judgments

Any labor organization which represents employees in an industry affecting commerce as defined in this chapter and any employer whose activities affect commerce as defined in this chapter shall be bound by the acts of its agents. Any such labor organization may sue or be sued as an entity and in behalf of the employees whom it represents in the courts of the United States. Any money judgment against a labor organization in a district court of the United States shall be enforceable only against the organization as an entity and against its assets, and shall not be enforceable against any individual member or his assets. * * *

§ 186.   (§ 302) Restrictions on Payments and Loans to Employee Representatives, Labor Organizations, Officers and Employees of Labor Organizations, and to Employees or Groups or Committees of Employees; Exceptions; Penalties; Jurisdiction; Effective Date; Exception of Certain Trust Funds

(a) It shall be unlawful for any employer or association of employers or any person who acts as a labor relations expert, adviser, or consultant to an employer or who acts in the interest of an employer to pay, lend, or deliver, or agree to pay, lend, or deliver, any money or other thing of value—

(1) to any representative of any of his employees who are employed in an industry affecting commerce; or

(2) to any labor organization, or any officer or employee thereof, which represents, seeks to represent, or would admit to membership, any of the employees of such employer who are employed in an industry affecting commerce; or

(3) to any employee or group or committee of employees of such employer employed in an industry affecting commerce in excess of their normal compensation for the purpose of causing such employee or group or committee directly or indirectly to influence any other employees in the exercise of the right to organize and bargain collectively through representatives of their own choosing; or

(4) to any officer or employee of a labor organization engaged in an industry affecting commerce with intent to influence him in respect to any of his actions, decisions, or duties as a representative of employees or as such officer or employee of such labor organization.

(b)(1) It shall be unlawful for any person to request, demand, receive, or accept, or agree to receive or accept, any payment, loan, or delivery of any money or other thing of value prohibited by subsection (a) of this section. * * *

(c) The provisions of this section shall not be applicable

(5) with respect to money or other thing of value paid to a trust fund established by such representative, for the sole and exclusive benefit of the employees of such employer, and their families and dependents (or of such employees, families, and dependents jointly with the employees of other employers making similar payments, and their families and dependents): *Provided*, That (A) such payments are held in trust for the purpose of paying, either from principal or income or both, for the benefit of employees, their families and dependents, for medical or hospital care, pensions on retirement or death of employees, compensation for injuries or illness resulting from occupational activity or insurance to provide any of the foregoing, or unemployment benefits or life insurance, disability and sickness insurance, or accident insurance; (B) the detailed basis on which such payments are to be made is specified in a written agreement with the employer, and employees and employers are equally represented in the administration of such fund, together with such neutral persons as the representatives of the employers and the representatives of employees may agree upon and in the event the employer and employee groups deadlock on the administration of such fund and there are no neutral persons empowered to break such deadlock, such agreement provides that the two groups shall agree on an impartial umpire to decide such dispute, or in event of their failure to agree within a reasonable length of time, an impartial umpire to decide such dispute shall, on petition of either group, be

appointed by the district court of the United States for the district where the trust fund has its principal office, and shall also contain provisions for an annual audit of the trust fund, a statement of the results of which shall be available for inspection by interested persons at the principal office of the trust fund and at such other places as may be designated in such written agreement; and (C) such payments as are intended to be used for the purpose of providing pensions or annuities for employees are made to a separate trust which provides that the funds held therein cannot be used for any purpose other than paying such pensions or annuities; (6) with respect to money or other thing of value paid by any employer to a trust fund established by such representative for the purpose of pooled vacation, holiday, severance or similar benefits, or defraying costs of apprenticeship or other training programs: *Provided*, That the requirements of clause (B) of the proviso to clause (5) of this subsection shall apply to such trust funds; * * *

LABOR MANAGEMENT REPORTING AND DISCLOSURE ACT

29 U.S.C.

§ 401. Congressional Declaration of Findings, Purposes, and Policy

(a) The Congress finds that, in the public interest, it continues to be the responsibility of the Federal Government to protect employees' rights to organize, choose their own representatives, bargain collectively, and otherwise engage in concerted activities for their mutual aid or protection; that the relations between employers and labor organizations and the millions of workers they represent have a substantial impact on the commerce of the Nation; and that in order to accomplish the objective of a free flow of commerce it is essential that labor organizations, employers, and their officials adhere to the highest standards of responsibility and ethical conduct in administering the affairs of their organizations, particularly as they affect labor-management relations.

(b) The Congress further finds, from recent investigations in the labor and management fields, that there have been a number of instances of breach of trust, corruption, disregard of the rights of individual employees, and other failures to observe high standards of responsibility and ethical conduct which require further and supplementary legislation that will afford necessary protection of the rights and interests of employees and the public generally as they relate to the activities of labor organizations, employers, labor relations consultants, and their officers and representatives.

(c) The Congress, therefore, further finds and declares that the enactment of this chapter is necessary to eliminate or prevent improper practices on the part of labor organizations, employers, labor relations consultants, and their officers and representatives which distort and defeat the policies of the Labor Management Relations Act, 1947, as amended, and the Railway Labor Act, as amended, and have the tendency or necessary effect of burdening or obstructing commerce by (1) impairing the efficiency, safety, or operation of the instrumentalities of commerce; (2) occurring in the current of commerce; (3) materially affecting, restraining, or controlling the flow of raw materials or manufactured or processed goods into or from the channels of commerce, or the prices of such materials or goods in commerce; or (4) causing diminution of employment and wages in such volume as substantially to impair or disrupt the market for goods flowing into or from the channels of commerce.

NATIONAL LABOR RELATIONS ACT[3]

29 U.S.C.

§ 157. (§ 7) Right of Employees as to Organization, Collective Bargaining, etc.

Employees shall have the right to self-organization, to form, join, or assist labor organizations, to bargain collectively through representatives of their own choosing, and to engage in other concerted activities for the purpose of collective bargaining or other mutual aid or protection, and shall also have the right to refrain from any or all of such activities except to the extent that such right may be affected by an agreement requiring membership in a labor, organization as a condition of employment as authorized in section 158(a)(3) of this title.

§ 158. (§ 8) Unfair Labor Practices

(a) It shall be an unfair labor practice for an employer—

(1) to interfere with, restrain, or coerce employees in the exercise of the rights guaranteed in section 157 of this title;

(2) to dominate or interfere with the formation or administration of any labor organization or contribute financial or other support to it: *Provided*, That subject to rules and regulations made and published by the Board pursuant to section 156 of this title, an employer shall not be prohibited from permitting employees to confer with him during working hours without loss of time or pay;

(3) by discrimination in regard to hire or tenure of employment or any term or condition of employment to encourage or discourage membership in any labor organization: *Provided*, That nothing in this subchapter, or in any other statute of the United States, shall preclude

---

3. Sections of the NLRA are usually referred to by the section numbers of the Act, not of the U.S.C. In this excerpt the Act section numbers are set out in parentheses.

an employer from making an agreement with a labor organization (not established, maintained, or assisted by any action defined in this subsection as an unfair labor practice) to require as. a condition of employment membership therein on or after the thirtieth day following the beginning of such employment or the effective date of such agreement, whichever is the later, (i) if such labor organization is the representative of the employees as provided in section 159(a) of this title, in the appropriate collective-bargaining unit covered by such agreement when made; and (ii) unless following an election held as provided in section 159(e) of this title within one year preceding the effective date of such agreement, the Board shall have certified that at least a majority of the employees eligible to vote in such election have voted to rescind the authority of such labor organization to make such an agreement: *Provided further*, That no employer shall justify any discrimination against an employee for nonmembership in a labor organization (A) if he has reasonable grounds for believing that such membership was not available to the employee on the same terms and conditions generally applicable to other members, or (B) if he has reasonable grounds for believing that membership was denied or terminated for reasons other than the failure of the employee to tender the periodic dues and the initiation fees uniformly required as a condition of acquiring or retaining membership;

(4) to discharge or otherwise discriminate against an employee because he has filed charges or given testimony under this subchapter;

(5) to refuse to bargain collectively with the representative of his employees, subject to the provisions of section 159(a) of this title.

(b) It shall be an unfair labor practice for a labor organization or its agents?

(1) to restrain or coerce (A) employees in the exercise of the rights guaranteed in section 157 of this title: *Provided*, That this paragraph shall not impair the right of a labor organization to prescribe its own rules with respect to the acquisition or retention of membership therein; or (B) an employer in the selection of his representatives for the purposes of collective bargaining or the adjustment of grievances;

(2) to cause or attempt to cause an employer to discriminate against an employee in violation of subsection (a)(3) of this section or to discriminate against an employee with respect to whom membership in such organization has been denied or terminated on some ground other than his failure to tender the periodic dues and the initiation fees uniformly required as a condition of acquiring or retaining membership;

(3) to refuse to bargain collectively with an employer, provided it is the representative of his employees subject to the provisions of section 159(a) of this title; * * *

(c) The expressing of any views, argument, or opinion, or the dissemination thereof, whether in written, printed, graphic, or visual form, shall not constitute or be evidence of an unfair labor practice under any of the provisions of this subchapter, if such expression contains no threat of reprisal or force or promise of benefit.

(d) For the purposes of this section, to bargain collectively is the performance of the mutual obligation of the employer and the representative of the employees to meet at reasonable times and confer in good faith with respect to wages, hours, and other terms and conditions of employment, or the negotiation of an agreement, or any question arising thereunder, and the execution of a written contract incorporating any agreement reached if requested by either party, but such obligation does not compel either party to agree to a proposal or require the making of a concession: *Provided*, That where there is in effect a collective bargaining contract covering employees in an industry affecting commerce, the duty to bargain collectively shall also mean that no party to such contract shall terminate or modify such contract, unless the party desiring such termination or modification—

(1) serves a written notice upon the other party to the contract of the proposed termination or modification sixty days prior to the expiration date thereof, or in the event such contract contains no expiration date, sixty days prior to the time it is proposed to make such termination or modification;

(2) offers to meet and confer with the other party for the purpose of negotiating a new contract or a contract containing the proposed modifications;

(3) notifies the Federal Mediation and Conciliation Service within thirty days after such notice of the existence of a dispute, and simultaneously therewith notifies any State or Territorial agency established to mediate and conciliate disputes within the State or Territory where the dispute occurred, provided no agreement has been reached by that time; and

(4) continues in full force and effect, without resorting to strike or lock-out, all the terms and conditions of the existing contract for a period of sixty days after such notice is given or until the expiration date of such contract, whichever occurs later.

The duties imposed upon employers, employees, and labor organizations by paragraphs (2)–(4) of this subsection shall become inapplicable upon an intervening certification of the Board, under which the labor organization or individual, which is a party to the contract, has been superseded as or ceased to be the representative of the employees subject to the provisions of section 159(a) of this title, and the duties so imposed shall not be construed as requiring either party to discuss or agree to any modification of the terms and conditions contained in a contract for a fixed period, if such modification is to become effective before such terms and conditions can be reopened under the provisions of the contract. Any employee who engages in a strike within any notice period specified in this subsection, or who engages in any strike within the appropriate period specified in subsection

(g) of this section, shall lose his status as an employee of the employer engaged in the particular labor dispute, for the purposes of sections 158 to 160 of this title, but such loss of status for such employee shall terminate if and when he is reemployed by such employer. * * *

§ 159.   (§ 9) Representatives and Elections

(a) Exclusive representatives; employees' adjustment of grievances directly with employer

Representatives designated or selected for the purposes of collective bargaining by the majority of the employees in a unit appropriate for such purposes, shall be the exclusive representatives of all the employees in such unit for the purposes of collective bargaining in respect to rates of pay, wages, hours of employment, or other conditions of employment: *Provided*, That any individual employee or a group of employees shall have the right at any time to present grievances to their employer and to have such grievances adjusted, without the intervention of the bargaining representative, as long as the adjustment is not inconsistent with the terms of a collective-bargaining contract or agreement then in effect: *Provided further*, That the bargaining representative has been given opportunity to be present at such adjustment. * * *

§ 160.   (§ 10) Prevention of Unfair Labor Practices

(a) Powers of Board generally

The Board is empowered, as hereinafter provided, to prevent any person from engaging in any unfair labor practice (listed in section 158 of this title) affecting commerce. This power shall not be affected by any other means of adjustment or prevention that has been or may be established by agreement, law, or otherwise: *Provided*, That the Board is empowered by agreement with any agency of any State or Territory to cede to such agency jurisdiction over any cases in any industry (other than mining, manufacturing, communications, and transportation except where predominantly local in character) even though such cases may involve labor disputes affecting commerce, unless the provision of the State or Territorial statute applicable to the determination of such cases by such agency is inconsistent with the corresponding provision of this subchapter or has received a construction inconsistent therewith.

(b) Complaint and notice of hearing; answer; court rules of evidence inapplicable

Whenever it is charged that any person has engaged in or is engaging in any such unfair labor practice, the Board, or any agent or agency designated by the Board for such purposes, shall have power to issue and cause to, be served upon such person a complaint stating the charges in that respect, and containing a notice of hearing before the Board or a member thereof, or before a designated agent or agency, at a place therein fixed, not less than five days after the serving of said complaint: *Provided*, That no complaint shall issue based upon any unfair labor practice occurring more than six months prior to the filing of the charge with the Board and the service of a copy thereof upon the person against whom such charge is made, unless the person aggrieved thereby was prevented from filing such charge by reason of service in the armed forces, in which event the six month period shall be computed from the day of his discharge. Any such complaint may be amended by the member, agent, or agency conducting the hearing or the Board in its discretion at any time prior to the issuance of an order based thereon. The person so complained of shall have the right to file an answer to the original or amended complaint and to appear in person or otherwise and give testimony at the place and time fixed in the complaint. In the discretion of the member, agent, or agency conducting the hearing or the Board, any other person may be allowed to intervene in the said proceeding and to present testimony. Any such proceeding shall, so far as practicable, be conducted in accordance with the rules of evidence applicable in the district courts of the United States under the rules of civil procedure for the district courts of the United States, adopted by the Supreme Court of the United States pursuant to section 2072 of Title 28.

(c) Reduction of testimony to writing; findings and orders of Board

The testimony taken by such member, agent, or agency or the Board shall be reduced to writing and filed with the Board. Thereafter, in its discretion, the Board upon notice may take further testimony or hear argument. If upon the preponderance of the testimony taken the Board shall be of the opinion that any person named in the complaint has engaged in or is engaging in any such unfair labor practice, then the Board shall state its findings of fact and shall issue and cause to be served on such person an order requiring such person to cease and desist from such unfair labor practice, and to take such affirmative action including reinstatement of employees with or without back pay, as will effectuate the policies of this subchapter: *Provided*, That where an order directs reinstatement of an employee, back pay may be required of the employer or labor organization, as the case may be, responsible for the discrimination suffered by him: And provided further, That in determining whether a complaint shall issue alleging a violation of subsection (a)(1) or (a)(2) of section 158 of this title, and in deciding such cases, the same regulations and rules of decision shall apply irrespective of whether or not the labor organization affected is affiliated with a labor organization national or international in scope. Such order may further require such person to make reports from time to time showing the extent to which it has complied with the order. If upon the preponderance of the testimony taken the Board shall not be of the opinion that the person named in the complaint has engaged in or is engaging in any such unfair labor practice, then the Board shall state its findings of fact and shall issue an order dismissing the said complaint. No order of the Board shall require the reinstatement of any individual as an employee who has been suspended or discharged, or the payment to him of any back pay, if such individual was suspended or discharged for cause. In case the evidence is presented before a member of the Board, or before an examiner or examiners thereof, such member, or such examiner or examiners as the case may be, shall issue and cause to be served on the parties to the proceeding a proposed report, together with a recommended order, which shall be, filed with the Board, and if no exceptions are filed within twenty days after service thereof upon such parties, or within such further period as the Board may authorize, such recommended order shall become the order of the Board and become effective as therein prescribed. * * *

(e) Petition to court for enforcement of orders; proceedings; review of judgment

The Board shall have power to petition any court of appeals of the United States, or if all the courts of appeals to which application may be made are in vacation, any district court of the United States, within any circuit or district, respectively, wherein the unfair labor practice in question occurred or wherein such person resides or transacts business, for the enforcement of such order and for appropriate temporary relief or restraining order, and shall file in the court the record in the proceedings, as provided in section 2112 of Title 28. Upon the filing of such petition, the court shall cause notice thereof to be served upon such person, and thereupon shall have jurisdiction of the proceeding and of the question determined therein, and shall have power to grant such temporary relief or restraining order as it deems just and proper, and to make and enter a decree enforcing, modifying, and enforcing as so modified, or setting aside in whole or in part the order of the Board. No objection that has not been urged before the Board, its member, agent, or agency, shall be considered by the court, unless the failure or neglect to urge such objection shall be excused because of extraordinary circumstances. The findings of the Board with respect to questions of fact if supported by substantial evidence on the record considered as a whole shall be conclusive. If either party shall apply to the court for leave to adduce additional evidence and shall show to the satisfaction of the court that such additional evidence is material and that there were reasonable grounds for the failure to adduce such evidence in the hearing before the Board, its member, agent, or agency, the court may order such additional evidence to be taken before the Board, its member, agent, or agency, and to be made a part of the record. The Board may modify its findings as to the facts, or make new findings by reason of additional evidence so taken and filed, and it shall file such modified or new findings, which findings with respect to questions of fact if supported by substantial evidence on the record considered as a whole shall be conclusive, and shall file its recommendations, if any, for the modification or setting aside of its original order. Upon the filing of the record with it the jurisdiction of the court shall be exclusive and its judgment and decree shall be final, except that the same shall be subject to review by the appropriate United States court of appeals if application was made to the district court as hereinabove provided, and by the Supreme Court of the United States upon writ of certiorari or certification as provided in section 1254 of Title 28.

(f) Review of final order of Board on petition to court

Any person aggrieved by a final order of the Board granting or denying in whole or in part the relief sought may obtain a review of such order in any United States court of appeals in the circuit wherein the unfair labor practice in question was alleged to have been engaged in or wherein such person resides or transacts business, or in the United States Court of Appeals for the District of Columbia, by filing in such a court a written petition praying that the order of the Board be modified or set aside. A copy of such petition shall be forthwith transmitted by the clerk of the court to the Board, and thereupon the aggrieved party shall file in the court the record in the proceeding, certified by the Board, as provided in section 2112 of Title 28. Upon the filing of such petition, the court shall proceed in the same manner as in the case of an application by the Board under subsection (e) of this section, and shall have the same jurisdiction to grant to the Board such temporary relief or restraining order as it deems just and proper, and in like manner to make and enter a decree enforcing, modifying, and enforcing as so modified, or setting aside in whole or in part the order of the Board; the findings of the Board with respect to questions of fact if supported by substantial evidence on the record considered as a whole shall in like manner be conclusive.

(g) Institution of court proceedings as stay of Board's order

The commencement of proceedings under subsection (e) or (f) of this section shall not, unless specifically ordered by the court, operate as a stay of the Board's order.

(h) Jurisdiction of courts unaffected by limitations prescribed in sections 101–115 of this title

When granting appropriate temporary relief or a restraining order, or making and entering a decree enforcing, modifying, and enforcing as so modified or setting aside in whole or in part an order of the Board, as provided in this section, the jurisdiction of courts sitting in equity shall not be limited by sections 101–115 of this title.

(i) Expeditious hearings on petitions

Petitions filed under this subchapter shall be heard expeditiously, and if possible within ten days after they have been docketed.

(j) Injunctions

The Board shall have power, upon issuance of a complaint as provided in subsection (b) of this section charging that any person has engaged in or is engaging in an unfair labor practice, to petition any United States district court, within any district wherein the unfair labor practice in question is alleged to have occurred or wherein such person resides or transacts business, for appropriate temporary relief or restraining order. Upon the filing of any such petition the court shall cause notice thereof to be served upon such person, and thereupon shall have jurisdiction to grant to the Board such temporary relief or restraining order as it deems just and proper. * * *

37

NORRIS LAGUARDIA ACT

29 U.S.C.

§ 104. Enumeration of Specific Acts not Subject to Restraining Orders or Injunctions

No court of the United States shall have jurisdiction to issue any restraining order or temporary or permanent injunction in any case involving or growing out of any labor dispute to prohibit any person or persons participating or interested in such dispute (as these terms are herein defined) from doing, whether singly or in concert, any of the following acts:

(a) Ceasing or refusing to perform any work or to remain in any relation of employment;

(b) Becoming or remaining a member of any labor organization or of any employer organization, regardless of any such undertaking or promise as is described in section 103 of this title;

(c) Paying or giving to, or withholding from, any person participating or interested in such labor dispute any strike or unemployment benefits or insurance, or other moneys or things of value;

(d) By all lawful means aiding any person participating or interested in any labor dispute who is being proceeded against in, or is prosecuting, any action or suit in any court of the United States or of any State;

(e) Giving publicity to the existence of, or the facts involved in, any labor dispute, whether by advertising, speaking, patrolling, or by any other method not involving fraud or violence;

(f) Assembling peaceably to act or to organize to act in promotion of their interests in a labor dispute;

(g) Advising or notifying any person of an intention to do any of the acts heretofore specified;

(h) Agreeing with other persons to do or not to do any of the acts heretofore specified; and

(i) Advising, urging, or otherwise causing or inducing without fraud or violence the acts heretofore specified, regardless of any such undertaking or promise as is described in section 103 of this title.

§ 105. Doing in Concert of Certain Acts as Constituting Unlawful Combination or Conspiracy Subjecting Person to Injunctive Remedies

No court of the United States shall have jurisdiction to issue a restraining order or temporary or permanent injunction upon the ground that any of the persons participating or interested in a labor dispute constitute or are engaged in an unlawful combination or conspiracy because of the doing in concert of the acts enumerated in section 104 of this title.

MILLER ACT
40 U.S.C.

§ 270a. Bonds of contractors for public buildings or works

(a) *Type of bonds required.* Before any contract, exceeding $25,000 in amount, for the construction, alteration, or repair of any public building or public work of the United States is awarded to any person, such person shall furnish to the United States the following bonds, which shall become binding upon the award of the contract to such person, who is hereinafter designated as, "contractor":

    (1) A performance bond with a surety or sureties satisfactory to the officer awarding such contract, and in such amount as he shall deem adequate, for the protection of the United States,.

    (2) A payment bond with a surety or sureties satisfactory to such officer for the protection of all persons supplying labor and material in the prosecution of the work provided for in said contract for the use of each such person. The amount of the payment bond shall be equal to the total amount payable by the terms of the contract unless the contracting officer awarding the contract makes a written determination supported by specific findings that a payment bond in that amount is impractical, in which case the amount of the payment bond shall be set by the contracting officer. In no case shall the amount of the payment bond be less than the amount of the performance bond.

(c) *Authority to require additional bonds.* Nothing in this section shall be construed to limit the authority of any contracting officer to require a performance bond or other security in addition to, those, or in cases other than the cases specified in subsection (a) of this section.

(d) *Coverage for taxes on performance bond.* Every performance bond required under this section shall specifically provide coverage for taxes imposed by the United States which are collected, deducted, or withheld from wages paid by the contractor in carrying out the contract with respect to which such bond is furnished. However, the United States shall give the surety or sureties on such bond written notice, with respect to any such unpaid taxes attributable to any period, within ninety days after the date when such contractor files a return for such period, except that no such notice shall be given more than one hundred and eighty days from the date when a return for the period was required to be filed under the Internal Revenue Code of 1954. No suit on such bond for such taxes shall be commenced by the United States unless notice is given as provided in the preceding sentence, and no such suit shall be commenced after the expiration of one year after the day on which such notice is given.

§ 270b. Rights of persons furnishing labor or material

(a) Every person who has furnished labor or material in the prosecution of the work provided for in such contract, in respect of which a payment bond is furnished under this Act and who, has not been paid in full therefor before the expiration of a period of ninety days after the day on which the last of the labor was done or performed by him or material was furnished or supplied by him for which such claim is made, shall have the right to sue on such payment bond for the amount, or the balance thereof, unpaid at the time of institution of such suit and to prosecute said action to final execution and judgment for the sum or sums justly due him: *Provided*, however, That any person having direct contractual relationship with a subcontractor but no contractual relationship express or implied with the contractor furnishing said payment bond shall have a right of action upon the said payment bond upon giving written notice to said contractor within ninety days from the date on which such person did or performed the last of the labor or furnished or supplied the last of the material for which such claim is made, stating with substantial accuracy the amount claimed and the name of the party to whom the material was, furnished or supplied or for whom the labor was done or performed. Such notice shall be served by any means which provides written, third-party verification of delivery to the contractor at any place he maintains an office or conducts his business, or his residence, or in any manner in which the United States marshal of the district in which the public improvement is situated is authorized by law to serve summons.

(b) Every suit instituted under this section shall be brought in the name of the United States for the use of the person suing in the United States District Court for any district in which the contract was to be performed and executed and not elsewhere, irrespective of the amount in controversy in such suit, but no such suit shall be commenced after the expiration of one year after the day on which the last of the labor was performed or material was supplied by him. The United States shall not be liable for the payment of any costs or expenses of any such suit.

(c) Any waiver of the right to sue on the payment bond required by the Act shall be void unless it is in writing signed by the person whose right is waived, and executed after such person has furnished labor or material for use in the performance of the contract.

PART II: NATIONAL, NON–FEDERAL

MODEL RULES OF PROFESSIONAL CONDUCT

PREAMBLE, SCOPE, AND TERMINOLOGY

Preamble: A Lawyer's Responsibilities

[1]   A lawyer is a representative of clients, an officer of the legal system and a public citizen having special responsibility for the quality of justice.

[2]   As a representative of clients, a lawyer performs various functions. As advisor, a lawyer provides a client with an informed understanding of the client's legal rights and obligations and explains their practical implications. As advocate, a lawyer zealously asserts the client's position under the rules of the adversary system. As negotiator, a lawyer seeks a result advantageous to the client but consistent with requirements of honest dealing with others. As intermediary between clients, a lawyer seeks to reconcile their divergent interests as an advisor and, to a limited extent, as a spokesperson for each client. A lawyer acts as evaluator by examining a client's legal affairs and reporting about them to the client or to others.

[3]   In all professional functions a lawyer should be competent, prompt and diligent. A lawyer should maintain communication with a client concerning the representation. A lawyer should keep in confidence information relating to representation of a client except so far as disclosure is required or permitted by the Rules of Professional Conduct or other law.

[4]   A lawyer's conduct should conform to the requirements of the law, both in professional service to clients and in the lawyer's business and personal affairs. A lawyer should use the law's procedures only for legitimate purposes and not to harass or intimidate others. A lawyer should demonstrate respect for the legal system and for those who serve it, including judges, other lawyers and public officials. While it is a lawyer's duty, when necessary, to challenge the rectitude of official action, it is also a lawyer's duty to uphold legal process.

[5]   As a public citizen, a lawyer should seek improvement of the law, the administration of justice and the quality of service rendered by the legal profession. As a member of a learned profession, a lawyer should cultivate knowledge of the law beyond its use for clients, employ that knowledge in reform of the law and work to strengthen legal education. A lawyer should be mindful of deficiencies in the administration of justice and of the fact that the poor, and sometimes persons who are not poor, cannot afford adequate legal assistance, and should therefore devote professional time and civic influence in their behalf. A lawyer should aid the legal profession in pursuing these objectives and should help the bar regulate itself in the public interest.

41

[6]   Many of a lawyer's professional responsibilities are prescribed in the Rules of Professional Conduct, as well as substantive and procedural law. However, a lawyer is also guided by personal conscience and the approbation of professional peers. A lawyer should strive to attain the highest level of skill, to improve the law and the legal profession and to exemplify the legal profession's ideals of public service.

[7]   A lawyer's responsibilities as a representative of clients, an officer of the legal system and a public citizen are usually harmonious. Thus, when an opposing party is well represented, a lawyer can be a zealous advocate on behalf of a client and at the same time assume that justice is being done. So also, a lawyer can be sure that preserving client confidences ordinarily serves the public interest because people are more likely to seek legal advice, and thereby heed their legal obligations, when they know their communications will be private.

[8]   In the nature of law practice, however, conflicting responsibilities are encountered. Virtually all difficult ethical problems arise from conflict between a lawyer's responsibilities to clients, to the legal system and to the lawyer's own interest in remaining an upright person while earning a satisfactory living. The Rules of Professional Conduct prescribe terms for resolving such conflicts. Within the framework of these Rules many difficult issues of professional discretion can arise. Such issues must be resolved through the exercise of sensitive professional and moral judgment guided by the basic principles underlying the Rules.

[9]   The legal profession is largely self-governing. Although other professions also have been granted powers of self-government, the legal profession is unique in this respect because of the close relationship between the profession and the processes of government and law enforcement. This connection is manifested in the fact that ultimate authority over the legal profession is vested largely in the courts.

[10]   To the extent that lawyers meet the obligations of their professional calling, the occasion for government regulation is obviated. Self-regulation also helps maintain the legal profession's independence from government domination. An independent legal profession is an important force in preserving government under law, for abuse of legal authority is more readily challenged by a profession whose members are not dependent on government for the right to practice.

[11]   The legal profession's relative autonomy carries with it special responsibilities of self-government. The profession has a responsibility to assure that its regulations are conceived in the public interest and not in furtherance of parochial or self-interested concerns of the bar. Every lawyer is responsible for observance of the Rules of Professional Conduct. A lawyer should also aid in securing their observance by other lawyers. Neglect of these responsibilities compromises the independence of the profession and the public interest which it serves.

[12]   Lawyers play a vital role in the preservation of society. The fulfillment of this role requires an understanding by lawyers of their

relationship to our legal system. The Rules of Professional Conduct, when properly applied, serve to define that relationship.

Scope

[1]   The Rules of Professional Conduct are rules of reason. They should be interpreted with reference to the purposes of legal representation and of the law itself. Some of the Rules are imperatives, cast in the terms "shall" or "shall not." These define proper conduct for purposes of professional discipline. Others, generally cast in the term "may," are permissive and define areas under the Rules in which the lawyer has professional discretion. No disciplinary action should be taken when the lawyer chooses not to act or acts within the bounds of such discretion. Other Rules define the nature of relationships between the lawyer and others. The Rules are thus partly obligatory and disciplinary and partly constitutive and descriptive in that they define a lawyer's professional role. Many of the Comments use the term "should." Comments do not add obligations to the Rules but provide guidance for practicing in compliance with the Rules.

[2]   The Rules presuppose a larger legal context shaping the lawyer's role. That context includes court rules and statutes relating to matters of licensure, laws defining specific obligations of lawyers and substantive and procedural law in general. Compliance with the Rules, as with all law in an open society, depends primarily upon understanding and voluntary compliance, secondarily upon reinforcement by peer and public opinion and finally, when necessary, upon enforcement through disciplinary proceedings. The Rules do not, however, exhaust the moral and ethical considerations that should inform a lawyer, for no worthwhile human activity can be completely defined by legal rules. The Rules simply provide a framework for the ethical practice of law.

[3]   Furthermore, for purposes of determining the lawyer's authority and responsibility, principles of substantive law external to these Rules determine whether a client-lawyer relationship exists. Most of the duties flowing from the client-lawyer relationship attach only after the client has requested the lawyer to render legal services and the lawyer has agreed to do so. But there are some duties, such as that of confidentiality under Rule 1.6, that may attach when the lawyer agrees to consider whether a client-lawyer relationship shall be established. Whether a client-lawyer relationship exists for any specific purpose can depend on the circumstances and may be a question of fact.

[4]   Under various legal provisions, including constitutional, statutory and common law, the responsibilities of government lawyers may include authority concerning legal matters that ordinarily reposes in the client in private client-lawyer relationships. For example, a lawyer for a government agency may have authority on behalf of the government to decide upon settlement or whether to appeal from an adverse judgment. Such authority in various respects is generally vested in the attorney general and the state's attorney in state government, and their federal counterparts, and the same may be true of other government law officers. Also, lawyers under the supervision of these officers may be authorized to represent several

government agencies in intragovernmental legal controversies in circumstances where a private lawyer could not represent multiple private clients. They also may have authority to represent the "public interest" in circumstances where a private lawyer would not be authorized to do so. These Rules do not abrogate any such authority.

[5] Failure to comply with an obligation or prohibition imposed by a Rule is a basis for invoking the disciplinary process. The Rules presuppose that disciplinary assessment of a lawyer's conduct will be made on the basis of the facts and circumstances as they existed at the time of the conduct in question and in recognition of the fact that a lawyer often has to act upon uncertain or incomplete evidence of the situation. Moreover, the Rules presuppose that whether or not discipline should be imposed for a violation, and the severity of a sanction, depend on all the circumstances, such as the willfulness and seriousness of the violation, extenuating factors and whether there have been previous violations.

[6] Violation of a Rule should not give rise to a cause of action nor should it create any presumption that a legal duty has been breached. The Rules are designed to provide guidance to lawyers and to provide a structure for regulating conduct through disciplinary agencies. They are not designed to be a basis for civil liability. Furthermore, the purpose of the Rules can be subverted when they are invoked by opposing parties as procedural weapons. The fact that a Rule is a just basis for a lawyer's self-assessment, or for sanctioning a lawyer under the administration of a disciplinary authority, does not imply that an antagonist in a collateral proceeding or transaction has standing to seek enforcement of the Rule. Accordingly, nothing in the Rules should be deemed to augment any substantive legal duty of lawyers or the extra-disciplinary consequences of violating such a duty.

[7] Moreover, these Rules are not intended to govern or affect judicial application of either the attorney-client or work product privilege. Those privileges were developed to promote compliance with law and fairness in litigation. In reliance on the attorney-client privilege, clients are entitled to expect that communications within the scope of the privilege will be protected against compelled disclosure. The attorney-client privilege is that of the client and not of the lawyer. The fact that in exceptional situations the lawyer under the Rules has a limited discretion to disclose a client confidence does not vitiate the proposition that, as a general matter, the client has a reasonable expectation that information relating to the client will not be voluntarily disclosed and that disclosure of such information may be judicially compelled only in accordance with recognized exceptions to the attorney-client and work product privileges.

[8] The lawyer's exercise of discretion not to disclose information under Rule 1.6 should not be subject to reexamination. Permitting such reexamination would be incompatible with the general policy of promoting compliance with law through assurances that communications will be protected against disclosure.

[9] The Comment accompanying each Rule explains and illustrates the meaning and purpose of the Rule. The Preamble and this note on Scope

provide general orientation. The Comments are intended as guides to interpretation, but the text of each Rule is authoritative. Research notes were prepared to compare counterparts in the ABA Model Code of Professional Responsibility (adopted 1969, as amended) and to provide selected references to other authorities. The notes have not been adopted, do not constitute part of the Model Rules, and are not intended to affect the application or interpretation of the Rules and Comments.

Terminology

[1] "Belief" or "Believes" denotes that the person involved actually supposed the fact in question to be true. A person's belief may be inferred from circumstances.

[2] "Consult" or "Consultation" denotes communication of information reasonably sufficient to permit the client to appreciate the significance of the matter in question.

[3] "Firm" or "Law firm" denotes a lawyer or lawyers in a private firm, lawyers employed in the legal department of a corporation or other organization and lawyers employed in a legal services organization. See Comment, Rule 1.10.

[4] "Fraud" or "Fraudulent" denotes conduct having a purpose to deceive and not merely negligent misrepresentation, or failure to apprize another of relevant information.

[5] "Knowingly," "Known," or "Knows" denotes actual knowledge of the fact in question. A person's knowledge may be inferred from circumstances.

[6] "Partner" denotes a member of a partnership and a shareholder in a law firm organized as a professional corporation.

[7] "Reasonable" or "Reasonably" when used in relation to conduct by a lawyer denotes the conduct of a reasonably prudent and competent lawyer.

[8] "Reasonable belief" or "Reasonably believes" when used in reference to a lawyer denotes that the lawyer believes the matter in question and that the circumstances are such that the belief is reasonable.

[9] "Reasonably should know" when used in reference to a lawyer denotes that a lawyer of reasonable prudence and competence would ascertain the matter in question.

[10] "Substantial" when used in reference to degree or extent denotes a material matter of clear and weighty importance.

MODEL RULES OF PROFESSIONAL CONDUCT
CLIENT–LAWYER RELATIONSHIP

RULE 1.1 Competence

A Lawyer shall provide competent representation to a client. Competent representation requires the legal knowledge, skill, thoroughness and preparation reasonably necessary for the representation.

COMMENT:

Legal Knowledge and Skill

[1] In determining whether a lawyer employs the requisite knowledge and skill in a particular matter, relevant factors include the relative complexity and specialized nature of the matter, the lawyer's general experience, the lawyer's training and experience in the field in question, the preparation and study the lawyer is able to give the matter and whether it is feasible to refer the matter to, or associate or consult with, a lawyer of established competence in the field in question. In many instances, the required proficiency is that of a general practitioner. Expertise in a particular field of law may be required in some circumstances.

* * *

RULE 1.3   Diligence

A lawyer shall act with reasonable diligence and promptness in representing a client.

COMMENT:

[1] A lawyer should pursue a matter on behalf of a client despite opposition, obstruction or personal inconvenience to the lawyer, and may take whatever lawful and ethical measures are required to vindicate a client's cause or endeavor. A lawyer should act with commitment and dedication to the interests of the client and with zeal in advocacy upon the client's behalf. However, a lawyer is not bound to press for every advantage that might be realized for a client. A lawyer has professional discretion in determining the means by which a matter should be pursued. See Rule 1.2. A lawyer's workload should be controlled so that each matter can be handled adequately. * * *

[3] Unless the relationship is terminated as provided in Rule 1.16, a lawyer should carry through to conclusion all matters undertaken for a client. If a lawyer's employment is limited to a specific matter, the relationship terminates when the matter has been resolved. If a lawyer has served a client over a substantial period in a variety of matters, the client sometimes may assume that the lawyer will continue to serve on a continuing basis unless the lawyer gives notice of withdrawal. Doubt about whether a client-lawyer relationship still exists should be clarified by the lawyer, preferably in writing, so that the client will not mistakenly suppose the lawyer is looking after the client's affairs when the lawyer has ceased to do so. For example, if a lawyer has handled a judicial or administrative proceeding that produced a result adverse to the client but has not been specifically instructed concerning pursuit of an appeal, the lawyer should advise the client of the possibility of appeal before relinquishing responsibility for the matter.

* * *

RULE 1.4   Communication

(a) A lawyer shall keep a client reasonably informed about the status of a matter and promptly comply with reasonable requests for information.

(b) A lawyer shall explain a matter to the extent reasonably necessary to permit the client to make informed decisions regarding the representation.

COMMENT:

[1] The client should have sufficient information to participate intelligently in decisions concerning the objectives of the representation and the means by which they are to be pursued, to the extent the client is willing and able to do so. For example, a lawyer negotiating on behalf of a client should provide the client with facts relevant to the matter, inform the client of communications from another party and take other reasonable steps that permit the client to make a decision regarding a serious offer from another party. A lawyer who receives from opposing counsel an offer of settlement in a civil controversy or a proffered plea bargain in a criminal case should promptly inform the client of its substance unless prior discussions with the client have left it clear that the proposal will be unacceptable. See Rule 1.2(a). Even when a client delegates authority to the law-

yer, the client should be kept advised of the status of the matter.

[2] Adequacy of communication depends in part on the kind of' advice or assistance involved. For example, in negotiations where there is time to explain a proposal the lawyer should review all important provisions with the client before proceeding to an agreement. In litigation a lawyer should explain the general strategy and prospects of success and ordinarily should consult the client on tactics that might injure or coerce others. On the other hand, a lawyer ordinarily cannot be expected to describe trial or negotiation strategy in detail. The guiding principle is that the lawyer should fulfill reasonable client expectations for information consistent with the duty to act in the client's best interests, and the client's overall requirements as to the character of representation.

* * *

RULE 1.6   Confidentiality of Information

(a) A lawyer shall not reveal information relating to representation of a client unless the client consents after consultation, except for disclosures that are impliedly authorized in order to carry out the representation, and except as stated in paragraph (b).

(b) A lawyer may reveal such information to the extent the lawyer reasonably believes necessary:

(1) to prevent the client from committing a criminal act that the lawyer believes is likely to result in imminent death or substantial bodily harm; or

(2) to establish a claim or defense on behalf of the lawyer in a controversy between the lawyer and the client, to establish a defense to a criminal charge or civil claim against the lawyer based upon conduct in which the client was involved, or to respond to allegations in any proceeding concerning the lawyer's representation of the client.

47

COMMENT:

[1] The lawyer is part of a judicial system charged with upholding the law. One of the lawyer's functions is to advise clients so that they avoid any violation of the law in the proper exercise of their rights.

[2] The observance of the ethical obligation of a lawyer to hold inviolate confidential information of the client not only facilitates the full development of facts essential to proper representation of the client but also encourages people to seek early legal assistance.

[3] Almost without exception, clients come to lawyers in order to determine what their rights are and what is, in the maze of laws and regulations, deemed to be legal and correct. The common law recognizes that the client's confidences must be protected from disclosure. Based upon experience, lawyers know that almost all clients follow the advice given, and the law is upheld.

[4] A fundamental principle in the client-lawyer relationship is that the lawyer maintain confidentiality of information relating to the representation. The client is thereby encouraged to communicate fully and frankly with the lawyer even as to embarrassing or legally damaging subject matter.

* * *

Former Client

[21] The duty of confidentiality continues after the client-lawyer relationship has terminated.

* * *

RULE 1.7 Conflict of Interest: General Rule

(a) A lawyer shall not represent a client if the representation of that client will be directly adverse to another client, unless:

(1) the lawyer reasonably believes the representation will not adversely affect the relationship with the other client; and

(2) each client consents after consultation.

(b) A lawyer shall not represent a client if the representation of that client may be materially limited by the lawyer's responsibilities to another client or to a third person, or by the lawyer's own interests, unless:

(1) the lawyer reasonably believes the representation will not be adversely affected; and

(2) the client consents after consultation. When representation of multiple clients in a single matter is undertaken, the consultation shall include explanation of the implications of the common representation and the advantages and risks involved.

COMMENT:

Loyalty to a Client

[1] Loyalty is an essential element in the lawyer's relationship to a client. An impermissible conflict of interest may exist before representation is undertaken, in which event the representation should be declined. The lawyer should adopt reasonable procedures, appropriate for the size and type of firm and practice, to determine in both litigation and nonlitigation matters the parties and issues involved and to determine whether there are actual or potential conflicts of interest.

[2] If such a conflict arises after representation has been undertaken, the lawyer should withdraw from the representation. See Rule 1.16. Where more than one client is involved and the lawyer withdraws because a conflict arises after representation, whether the lawyer may continue to represent any of the clients is determined by Rule 1.9. See also Rule 2.2(c). As to whether a client-lawyer relationship exists or, having once been established, is continuing, see Comment to Rule 1.3 and Scope.

[3] As a general proposition, loyalty to a client prohibits undertaking representation directly adverse to that client without that client's consent. Paragraph (a) expresses that general rule. Thus, a lawyer ordinarily may not act as advocate against a person the lawyer represents in some other matter, even if it is wholly unrelated. On the other hand, simultaneous representation in unrelated matters of clients whose interests are only generally adverse, such as competing economic enterprises, does not require consent of the respective clients. Paragraph (a) applies only when the representation of one client would be directly adverse to the other.

[4] Loyalty to a client is also impaired when a lawyer cannot consider, recommend or carry out an appropriate course of action for the client because of the lawyer's other responsibilities or interests. The conflict in effect forecloses alternatives that would otherwise be available to the client. Paragraph (b) addresses such situations. A possible conflict does not itself preclude the representation. The critical questions are the likelihood that a conflict will eventuate and, if it does, whether it will materially interfere with the lawyer's independent professional judgment in considering alternatives or foreclose courses of action that reasonably should be pursued on behalf of the client. Consideration should be given to whether the client wishes to accommodate the other interest involved.

Consultation and Consent

[5] A client may consent to representation notwithstanding a conflict. However, as indicated in paragraph (a)(1) with respect to representation directly adverse to a client, and paragraph (b)(1) with respect to material limitations on representation of a client, when a disinterested lawyer would conclude that the client should not agree to the representation under the circumstances, the lawyer involved cannot properly ask for such agreement or provide representation on the basis of the client's consent. When more than once client is involved, the question of conflict must be resolved as to each client. Moreover, there may be circumstances where it is impossible to make the disclosure

49

necessary to obtain consent. For example, when the lawyer represents different clients in related matters and one of the clients refuses to consent to the disclosure necessary to permit the other client to make an informed decision, the lawyer cannot properly ask the latter to consent.

Lawyer's Interests

[6] The lawyer's own interests should not be permitted to have adverse effect on representation of a client. For example, a lawyer's need for income should not lead the lawyer to undertake matters that cannot be handled competently and at a reasonable fee. See Rules 1.1 and 1.5. If the probity of a lawyer's own conduct in a transaction is in serious question, it may be difficult or impossible for the lawyer to give a client detached advice. A lawyer may not allow related business interests to affect representation, for example, by referring clients to an enterprise in which the lawyer has an undisclosed interest.

Conflicts in Litigation

[7] Paragraph (a) prohibits representation of opposing parties in litigation. Simultaneous representation of parties whose interests in litigation may conflict, such as co-plaintiffs or co-defendants, is governed by paragraph (b). An impermissible conflict may exist by reason of substantial discrepancy in the parties' testimony, incompatibility in positions in relation to an opposing party or the fact that there are substantially different possibilities of settlement of the claims or liabilities in question. Such conflicts can arise in criminal cases as well as civil. The potential for conflict of interest in representing multiple defendants in a criminal case is so grave that ordinarily a lawyer should decline to represent more than one codefendant. On the other hand, common representation of persons having similar interests is proper if the risk of adverse effect is minimal and the requirements of paragraph (b) are met. Compare Rule 2.2 involving intermediation between clients.

[8] Ordinarily, a lawyer may not act as advocate against a client the lawyer represents in some other matter, even if the other matter is wholly unrelated. However, there are circumstances in which a lawyer may act as advocate against a client. For example, a lawyer representing an enterprise with diverse operations may accept employment as an advocate against the enterprise in an unrelated matter if doing so will not adversely affect the lawyer's relationship with the enterprise or conduct of the suit and if both clients consent upon consultation. By the same token, government lawyers in some circumstances may represent government employees in proceedings in which a government agency is the opposing party. The propriety of concurrent representation can depend on the nature of the litigation. For example, a suit charging fraud entails conflict to a degree not involved in a suit for a declaratory judgment concerning statutory interpretation.

[9] A lawyer may represent parties having antagonistic positions on a legal question that has arisen in different cases, unless representation of either client would be adversely affected. Thus, it is ordinarily not improper to assert such positions in cases pending in different trial courts, but it may be improper to do so in cases pending

at the same time in an appellate court.

Interest of Person Paying for a Lawyer's Service

[10] A lawyer may be paid from a source other than the client, if the client is informed of that fact and consents and the arrangement does not compromise the lawyer's duty of loyalty to the client. See Rule 1.8(f). For example, when an insurer and its insured have conflicting interests in a matter arising from a liability insurance agreement, and the insurer is required to provide special counsel for the insured, the arrangement should assure the special counsel's professional independence. So also, when a corporation and its directors or employees are involved in a controversy in which they have conflicting interests, the corporation may provide funds for separate legal representation of the directors or employees, if the clients consent after consultation and the arrangement ensures the lawyer's professional independence.

Other Conflict Situations

[11] Conflicts of interest in contexts other than litigation sometimes may be difficult to assess. Relevant factors in determining whether there is potential for adverse effect include the duration and intimacy of the lawyer's relationship with the client or clients involved, the functions being performed by the lawyer, the likelihood that actual conflict will arise and the likely prejudice to the client from the conflict if it does arise. The question is often one of proximity and degree.

[12] For example, a lawyer may not represent multiple parties to a negotiation whose interests are fundamentally antagonistic to each other, but common representation is permissible where the clients are generally aligned in interest even though there is some difference of interest among them.

[13] Conflict questions may also arise in estate planning and estate administration. A lawyer may be called upon to prepare wills for several family members, such as husband and wife, and, depending upon the circumstances, a conflict of interest may arise. In estate administration the identity of the client may be unclear under the law of a particular jurisdiction. Under one view, the client is the fiduciary; under another view the client is the estate or trust, including its beneficiaries. The lawyer should make clear the relationship to the parties involved.

[14] A lawyer for a corporation or other organization who is also a member of its board of directors should determine whether the responsibilities of the two roles may conflict. The lawyer may be called on to advise the corporation in matters involving actions of the directors. Consideration should be given to the frequency with which such situations may arise, the potential intensity of the conflict, the effect of the lawyer's resignation from the board and the possibility of the corporation's obtaining legal advice from another lawyer in such situations. If there is material risk that the dual role will compromise the lawyer's independence of professional judgment, the lawyer should not serve as a director.

51

Conflict Charged by an Opposing Party

[15] Resolving questions of conflict of interest is primarily the responsibility of the lawyer undertaking the representation. In litigation, a court may raise the question when there is reason to infer that the lawyer has neglected the responsibility. In a criminal case, inquiry by the court is generally required when a lawyer represents multiple defendants. Where the conflict is such as clearly to call in question the fair or efficient administration of justice, opposing counsel may properly raise the question. Such an objection should be viewed with caution, however, for it can be misused as a technique of harassment. See Scope. * * *

RULE 1.9   Conflict of Interest: Former Client

(a) A lawyer who has formerly represented a client in a matter shall not thereafter represent another person in the same or a substantially related matter in which that person's interests are materially adverse to the interests of the former client unless the former client consents after consultation.

(b) A lawyer shall not knowingly represent a person in the same or a substantially related matter in which a firm with which the lawyer formerly was associated had previously represented a client,

（1) whose interests are materially adverse to that person; and

(2) about whom the lawyer had acquired information protected by Rules 1.6 and 1.9(c) that is material to the matter;

unless the former client consents after consultation.

(c) A lawyer who has formerly represented a client in a matter or whose present or former firm has formerly represented a client in a matter shall not thereafter:

(1) use information relating to the representation to the disadvantage of the former client except as Rule 1.6 or Rule 3.3 would permit or require with respect to a client, or when the information has become generally known; or

(2) reveal information relating to the representation except as Rule 1.6 or Rule 3.3 would permit or require with respect to a client.

COMMENT:

[1] After termination of a client-lawyer relationship, a lawyer may not represent another client except in conformity with this Rule. The principles in Rule 1.7 determine whether the interests of the present and former client are adverse. Thus, a lawyer could not properly seek to rescind on behalf of a new client a contract drafted on behalf of the former client. So also a lawyer who has prosecuted an accused person could not properly represent the accused in a subsequent civil action against the government concerning the same transaction.

[2] The scope of a "matter" for purposes of this Rule may depend on the facts of a particular situation or transaction. The lawyer's involvement in a matter can also be a question of

degree. When a lawyer has been directly involved in a specific transaction, subsequent representation of other clients with materially adverse interests clearly is prohibited. On the other hand, a lawyer who recurrently handled a type of problem for a former client is not precluded from later representing another client in a wholly distinct problem of that type even though the subsequent representation involves a position adverse to the pri-

Confidentiality

[6] Preserving confidentiality is a question of access to information. Access to information, in turn, is essentially a question of fact in particular circumstances, aided by inferences, deductions or working presumptions that reasonably may be made about the way in which lawyers work together. A lawyer may have general access to files of all clients of a law firm and may regularly participate in discussions of their affairs; it should be inferred that such a lawyer in fact is privy to all information about all the firm's clients. In contrast, another lawyer may have access to the files of only a limited number of clients and participate in discussions of the affairs of no other clients; in the absence of information to the contrary, it should be inferred that such a lawyer in fact is privy to information about the clients actually served but not those of other clients.

[7] Application of paragraph (b) depends on a situation's particular facts. In such an inquiry, the burden

Adverse Positions

[10] The second aspect of loyalty to a client is the lawyer's obligation to decline subsequent representations involving positions adverse to a former client arising in substantially related matters. This obligation requires ab-

or client. Similar considerations can apply to the reassignment of military lawyers between defense and prosecution functions within the same military jurisdiction. The underlying question is whether the lawyer was so involved in the matter that the subsequent representation can be justly regarded as a changing of sides in the matter in question.

* * *

of proof should rest upon the firm whose disqualification is sought.

[8] Paragraph (b) operates to disqualify the lawyer only when the lawyer involved has actual knowledge of information protected by Rules 1.6 and 1.9(b). Thus, if a lawyer while with one firm acquired no knowledge or information relating to a particular client of the firm, and that lawyer later joined another firm, neither the lawyer individually nor the second firm is disqualified from representing another client in the same or a related matter even though the interests of the two clients conflict. See Rule 1.10(b) for the restrictions on a firm once a lawyer has terminated association with the firm.

[9] Independent of the question of disqualification of a firm, a lawyer changing professional association has a continuing duty to preserve confidentiality of information about a client formerly represented. See Rules 1.6 and 1.9.

stention from adverse representation by the individual lawyer involved, but does not properly entail abstention of other lawyers through imputed disqualification. Hence, this aspect of the problem is governed by Rule 1.9(a).

53

Thus, if a lawyer left one firm for another, the new affiliation would not preclude the firms involved from continuing to represent clients with adverse interests in the same or related matters, so long as the conditions of paragraphs (b) and (c) concerning confidentiality have been met.

[11] Information acquired by the lawyer in the course of representing a client may not subsequently be used or revealed by the lawyer to the disadvantage of the client. However, the fact that a lawyer has once served a client does not preclude the lawyer from using generally known information about that client when later representing another client.

[12] Disqualification from subsequent representation is for the protection of former clients and can be waived by them. A waiver is effective only if there is disclosure of the circumstances, including the lawyer's intended role in behalf of the new client.

[13] With regard to an opposing party's raising a question of conflict of interest, see Comment to Rule 1.7. With regard to disqualification of a firm with which a lawyer is or was formerly associated, see Rule 1.10.

* * *

COUNSELOR

RULE 2.1 Advisor

In representing a client, a lawyer shall exercise independent professional judgment and render candid advice. In rendering advice, a lawyer may refer not only to law but to other considerations such as moral, economic, social and political factors, that may be relevant to the client's situation.

COMMENT:

Scope of Advice

[1] A client is entitled to straightforward advice expressing the lawyer's honest assessment. Legal advice often involves unpleasant facts and alternatives that a client may be disinclined to confront. In presenting advice, a lawyer endeavors to sustain the client's morale and may put advice in as acceptable a form as honesty permits. However, a lawyer should not be deterred from giving candid advice by the prospect that the advice will be unpalatable to the client.

[2] Advice couched in narrowly legal terms may be of little value to a client, especially where practical considerations, such as cost or effects on other people, are predominant. Purely technical legal advice, therefore, can sometimes be inadequate. It is proper for a lawyer to refer to relevant moral and ethical considerations in giving advice. Although a lawyer is not a moral advisor as such, moral and ethical considerations impinge upon most legal questions and may decisively influence how the law will be applied.

[3] A client may expressly or impliedly ask the lawyer for purely technical advice. When such a request is made by a client experienced in legal matters, the lawyer may accept it at face value. When such a request is made by a client inexperienced in legal matters, however, the lawyer's responsibility as advisor may include indicating that more may be involved than strictly legal considerations.

[4] Matters that go beyond strictly legal questions may also be in the domain of another profession. Family matters can involve problems within the professional competence of psychiatry, clinical psychology or social work; business matters can involve problems within the competence of the accounting profession or of financial specialists. Where consultation with a professional in another field is itself something a competent lawyer would recommend, the lawyer should make such a recommendation. At the same time, a lawyer's advice at its best often consists of recommending a course of action in the face of conflicting recommendations of experts.

Offering Advice

[5] In general, a lawyer is not expected to give advice until asked by the client. However, when a lawyer knows that a client proposes a course of action that is likely to result in substantial adverse legal consequences to the client, duty to the client under Rule 1.4 may require that the lawyer act if the client's course of action is related to the representation. A lawyer ordinarily has no duty to initiate investigation of a client's affairs or to give advice that the client has indicated is unwanted, but a lawyer may initiate advice to a client when doing so appears to be in the client's interest.

* * *

RULE 2.2 Intermediary

(a) A lawyer may act as intermediary between clients if:

(1) the lawyer consults with each client concerning the implications of the common representation, including the advantages and risks involved, and the effect on the attorney-client privileges, and obtains each client's consent to the common representation;

(2) the lawyer reasonably believes that the matter can be resolved on terms compatible with the clients' best interests, that each client will be able to make adequately informed decisions in the matter and that there is little risk of material prejudice to the interest of any of the clients if the contemplated resolution is unsuccessful; and

(3) the lawyer reasonably believes that the common representation can be undertaken impartially and without improper effect on other responsibilities the lawyer has to any of the clients.

(b) While acting as intermediary, the lawyer shall consult with each client concerning the decisions to be made and the considerations relevant in making them, so that each client can make adequately informed decisions.

(c) A lawyer shall withdraw as intermediary if any of the clients so request, or if any of the conditions stated in paragraph (a) is no longer satisfied. Upon withdrawal, the lawyer shall not continue to represent any of the clients in the matter that was the subject of the intermediation.

COMMENT:

[1] A lawyer acts as intermediary under this Rule when the lawyer represents two or more parties with potentially conflicting interests. A key factor in defining the relationship is whether the parties share responsibility for the lawyer's fee, but the common representation may be inferred from other circumstances. Because confusion can arise as to the lawyer's role where each party is not separately represented, it is important that the lawyer make clear the relationship.

[2] The Rule does not apply to a lawyer acting as arbitrator or mediator between or among parties who are not clients of the lawyer, even where the lawyer has been appointed with the concurrence of the parties. In performing such a role the lawyer may be subject to applicable codes of ethics, such as the Code of Ethics for Arbitration in Commercial Disputes prepared by a joint Committee of the American Bar Association and the American Arbitration Association.

[3] A lawyer acts as intermediary in seeking to establish or adjust a relationship between clients on an amicable and mutually advantageous basis; for example, in helping to organize a business in which two or more clients are entrepreneurs, working out the financial reorganization of an enterprise in which two or more clients have an interest, arranging a property distribution in settlement of an estate or mediating a dispute between clients. The lawyer seeks to resolve potentially conflicting interests by developing the parties' mutual interests. The alternative can be that each party may have to obtain separate representation, with the possibility in some situations of incurring additional cost, complication or even litigation. Given these and other relevant factors, all the clients may prefer that the lawyer act as intermediary.

[4] In considering whether to act as intermediary between clients, a lawyer should be mindful that if the intermediation fails the result can be additional cost, embarrassment and recrimination. In some situations the risk of failure is so great that intermediation is plainly impossible. For example, a lawyer cannot undertake common representation of clients between whom contentious litigation is imminent or who contemplate contentious negotiations. More generally, if the relationship between the parties has already assumed definite antagonism, the possibility that the clients' interests can be adjusted by intermediation ordinarily is not very good.

[5] The appropriateness of intermediation can depend on its form. Forms of intermediation range from informal arbitration, where each client's case is presented by the respective client and the lawyer decides the outcome, to mediation, to common representation where the clients' interests are substantially though not entirely compatible. One form may be appropriate in circumstances where another would not. Other relevant factors are whether the lawyer subsequently will represent both parties on a continuing basis and whether the situation involves creating a relationship between the parties or terminating one.

Confidentiality and Privilege

[6] A particularly important factor in determining the appropriateness of intermediation is the effect on client-lawyer confidentiality and the

attorney-client privilege. In a common representation, the lawyer is still required both to keep each client adequately informed and to maintain confidentiality of information relating to the representation. See Rules 1.4 and 1.6. Complying with both requirements while acting as intermediary requires a delicate balance. If the balance cannot be maintained, the common representation is improper. With regard to the attorney-client privilege, the prevailing rule is that as between commonly represented clients the privilege does not attach. Hence, it must be assumed that if litigation eventuates between the clients, the privilege will not protect any such communications, and the clients should be so advised.

[7] Since the lawyer is required to be impartial between commonly represented clients, intermediation is improper when that impartiality cannot be maintained. For example, a lawyer who has represented one of the clients for a long period and in a variety of matters might have difficulty being impartial between that client and one to whom the lawyer has only recently been introduced.

Consultation

[8] In acting as intermediary between clients, the lawyer is required to consult with the clients on the implications of doing so, and proceed only upon consent based on such a consultation. The consultation should make clear that the lawyer's role is not that of partisanship normally expected in other circumstances.

[9] Paragraph (b) is an application of the principle expressed in Rule 1.4. Where the lawyer is intermediary, the clients ordinarily must assume greater responsibility for decisions than when each client is independently represented.

Withdrawal

[10] Common representation does not diminish the rights of each client in the client-lawyer relationship. Each has the right to loyal and diligent representation, the right to discharge the lawyer as stated in Rule 1.16, and the protection of Rule 1.9 concerning obligations to a former client.

* * *

RULE 4.3 Dealing With Unrepresented Person

In dealing on behalf of a client with a person who is not represented by counsel, a lawyer shall not state or imply that the lawyer is disinterested. When the lawyer knows or reasonably should know that the unrepresented person misunderstands the lawyer's role in the matter, the lawyer shall make reasonable efforts to correct the misunderstanding.

COMMENT:

An unrepresented person, particularly one not experienced in dealing with legal matters, might assume that a lawyer is disinterested in loyalties or is a disinterested authority on the law even when the lawyer represents a client. During the course of a lawyer's representation of a client, the lawyer should not give advice to an unrepresented person other than the advice to obtain counsel.

* * *

_____

MODEL WRITTEN OBLIGATIONS ACT[1]

§ 1. Written Release or Promise Valid Without Consideration

A written release or promise hereafter made and signed by the person releasing or promising shall not be invalid or unenforceable for lack of consideration, if the writing also contains an additional express statement, in any form of language, that the signer intends to be legally bound.

_____

NATIONAL CONSUMER ACT[2]

Section 5.107 Unconscionability

(1) If it is found as a matter of fact that a consumer credit transaction, any aspect of the transaction, any conduct directed against the consumer by a party to the transaction, or any result of the transaction is unconscionable, the court shall, in addition to the penalty authorized in Subsection (4), either refuse to enforce the transaction against the consumer or so limit the application of any unconscionable aspect or conduct to avoid any unconscionable result.

(2) Specific practices forbidden by the Administrator in regulations promulgated pursuant to Section 6.109 shall be presumed to be unconscionable.

(3) Without limiting the scope of Subsection (1), the trier of fact shall be entitled to consider, among other things, the following as pertinent to the issue of unconscionability:

(a) The degree to which the practice unfairly takes advantage of the lack of knowledge, ability, experience, or capacity of consumers;

(b) Knowledge by those engaging in the practice of the inability of consumers to receive benefits properly anticipated from the goods or services involved;

(c) Gross disparity between the price of goods or services and their value as measured by the price at which similar goods or services are readily obtainable by other consumers, or by other tests of true value;

---

1. In effect only in Pennsylvania.

2. Proposed in 1970 by the National Consumer Law Center at Boston College Law School.

(d) The fact that the practice may enable merchants to take advantage of the inability of consumers reasonably to protect their interests by reason of physical or mental infirmities, illiteracy or inability to understand the language of the agreement, ignorance or lack of education or similar factors;

(e) The degree to which terms of the transaction require consumers to waive legal rights;

(f) The degree to which terms of the transaction require consumers to jeopardize money or property beyond the money or property immediately at issue in the transaction;

(g) The degree to which the natural effect of the practice is to cause or aid in causing consumers to misunderstand the true nature of the transaction or their rights and duties thereunder;

(h) The extent or degree to which the writing purporting to evidence the obligation of the consumer in the transaction contains terms or provisions or authorizes practices prohibited by law; and

(i) Definitions of unconscionability in statutes, regulations, rulings and decisions of legislative, administrative or judicial bodies in this state or elsewhere.

(4) In addition to the protections afforded in Subsection (1), the consumer shall be entitled upon a finding of unconscionability to recover from the creditor or the person responsible for the unconscionable conduct a penalty in accordance with the provisions of Section 5.304.

Section 5.304 Remedy for Certain Violations

A consumer may recover from the person violating this Act actual and punitive damages, thirty percent of the transaction total, if applicable, or $300, whichever is greater, for violations to which this section applies.

Section 5.307 Consumer's Attorney's Fees; Time Limitations

(1) In any action to enforce a consumer's remedy under this Part, or to enforce any other consumer's right with respect to any transaction subject to this Act, whether as an original claim, set-off or counter-claim, a consumer who prevails shall be awarded a reasonable attorney's fees incurred. Fees shall be measured by the amount of time reasonably expended by the consumer's attorney and not by the amount of the recovery. If the consumer is represented by a non-profit organization in such a case, the organization shall be awarded a service fee in lieu of attorney's fees, equal to the amount of fees which a private attorney would be awarded for the same work.

(2) Any action brought by a consumer to enforce rights pursuant to this Act may be commenced within one year after the due date of the last scheduled payment of the transaction in question or four years after consummation of the agreement, whichever is later. Rights under this Act

may be asserted as a defense, set-off or counter-claim to an action against the consumer without regard to this time limitation.

* * *

The Administrator referred to in some of the above sections would be required to promulgate regulations declaring specific practices in consumer transaction and consumer debt collection to be unconscionable and prohibiting their use (§ 6.109).

UNIFORM ARBITRATION ACT (1955)[3]

§ 1. Validity of Arbitration Agreement

A written agreement to submit any existing controversy to arbitration or a provision in a written contract to submit to arbitration any controversy thereafter arising between the parties is valid, enforceable and irrevocable, save upon such grounds as exist at law or in equity for the revocation of any contract. This act also applies to arbitration agreements between employers and employees or between their respective representatives [unless otherwise provided in the agreement].

§ 2. Proceedings to Compel or Stay Arbitration

(a) On application of a party showing an agreement described in Section 1, and the opposing party's refusal to arbitrate, the Court shall order the parties to proceed with arbitration, but if the opposing party denies the existence of the agreement to arbitrate, the Court shall proceed summarily to the determination of the issue so raised and shall order arbitration if found for the moving party, otherwise, the application shall be denied.

(b) On application, the court may stay an arbitration proceeding commenced or threatened on a showing that there is no agreement to arbitrate. Such an issue, when in substantial and bona fide dispute, shall be forthwith and summarily tried and the stay ordered if found for the moving party. If found for the opposing party, the court shall order the parties to proceed to arbitration.

(c) If an issue referable to arbitration under the alleged agreement is involved in an action or proceeding pending in a court having jurisdiction to hear applications under subdivision (a) of this Section, the application

---

3. Enacted in Alaska, Arizona, Arkansas, Colorado, Delaware, District of Columbia, Florida, Idaho, Illinois, Indiana, Iowa, Kansas, Kentucky, Maine, Maryland, Massachusetts, Michigan, Minnesota, Missouri, Montana, Nebraska, Nevada, New Mexico, North Carolina, North Dakota, Oklahoma, Pennsylvania, South Carolina, Utah, Vermont, Virginia, South Dakota, Tennessee, Texas, Utah, Vermont, Virginia and Wyoming. A new Uniform Arbitration Act, replacing the 1955 Act, was approved by the National Conference of Commissioners on Uniform State Laws in 2000.

shall be made therein. Otherwise and subject to Section 18, the application may be made in any court of competent jurisdiction.

(d) Any action or proceeding involving an issue subject to arbitration shall be stayed if an order for arbitration or an application therefor has been made under this section or, if the issue is severable, the stay may be with respect thereto only. When the application is made in such action or proceeding, the order for arbitration shall include such stay.

(e) An order for arbitration shall not be refused on the ground that the claim in issue lacks merit or bona fides or because any fault or grounds for the claim sought to be arbitrated have not been shown.

§ 3. Appointment of Arbitrators by Court

If the arbitration agreement provides a method of appointment of arbitrators, this method. shall be followed. In the absence thereof, or if the agreed method fails or for any reason cannot be followed, or when an arbitrator appointed fails or is unable to act and his successor has not been duly appointed, the court on application of a party shall appoint one or more arbitrators. An arbitrator so appointed has all the powers of one specifically named in the agreement.

§ 4. Majority Action by Arbitrators

The powers of the arbitrators may be exercised by a majority unless otherwise provided by the agreement or by this act.

§ 5. Hearing

Unless otherwise provided by the agreement:

(a) The arbitrators shall appoint a time and place for the hearing and cause notification to the parties to be served personally or by registered mail not less than five days before the hearing. Appearance at the hearing waives such notice. The arbitrators may adjourn the hearing from time to time as necessary and, on request of a party and for good cause, or upon their own motion may postpone the hearing to a time not later than the date fixed by the agreement for making the award unless the parties consent to a later date. The arbitrators may hear and determine the controversy upon the evidence produced notwithstanding the failure of a party duly notified to appear. The court on application may direct the arbitrators to proceed promptly with the hearing and determination of the controversy.

(b) The parties are entitled to be heard, to, present evidence material to the controversy and to cross-examine witnesses appearing at the hearing,

(c) The hearing shall be conducted by all the arbitrators but a majority may determine any question and render a final award. If, during the course of the hearing, an arbitrator for any reason ceases to act, the remaining arbitrator or arbitrators appointed to act as neutrals, may continue with the hearing and determination of the controversy.

§ 6. Representation by Attorney

A party has the right to be represented by an attorney at any proceeding or hearing under this act. A waiver thereof prior to the proceeding or hearing is ineffective.

§ 7. Witnesses, Subpoenas, Depositions.

(a) The arbitrators may issue (cause to be issued) subpoenas for the attendance of witnesses and for the production of books, records, documents and other evidence, and shall have the power to administer oaths. Subpoenas so issued shall be served, and upon application to the Court by a party or the arbitrators, enforced, in the manner provided by law for the service and enforcement of subpoenas in a civil action.

(b) On application of a party and for use as evidence, the arbitrators may permit a deposition to be taken, in the manner and upon the terms designated by the arbitrators, of a witness who cannot be subpoenaed or is unable to attend the hearing.

(c) All provisions of law compelling a person under subpoena to testify are applicable.

(d) Fees for attendance as a witness, shall be the same as for a witness in the * * * Court.

§ 8. Award

(a) The award shall be in writing and signed by the arbitrators joining in the award. The arbitrators shall deliver a copy to each party personally or by registered mail, or as provided in the agreement.

(b) An award shall be made within the time fixed therefor by the agreement or, if not so fixed, within such time as the court orders on application of a party. The parties may extend the time in writing either before or after the expiration thereof. A party waives the objection that an award was not made within the time required unless he notifies the arbitrators of his objection prior to the delivery of the award to him.

§ 9. Change of Award by Arbitrators

On application of a party or, if an application to, the court is pending under Sections 11, 12 or 13, on submission to the arbitrators by the court under such conditions as the court may order, the arbitrators may modify or correct the award upon the grounds stated in paragraphs (1) and (3) of subdivision (a) of Section 13, or for the purpose of clarifying the award. The application shall be made within twenty days after delivery of the award to the applicant. Written notice thereof shall be given forthwith to the opposing party, stating he must serve his objections thereto, if any, within ten days from the notice. The award so modified or corrected is subject to the provisions of Sections 11, 12 and 13.

§ 10. Fees and Expenses of Arbitration

Unless otherwise provided in the agreement to arbitrate, the arbitrators' expenses and fees, together with other expenses, not including counsel fees, incurred in the conduct of the arbitration, shall be paid as provided in the award.

§ 11. Confirmation of an Award

Upon application of a party, the Court shall confirm an award, unless within the time limits hereinafter imposed grounds are urged for vacating or modifying or correcting the award, in which case the court shall proceed as provided in Sections 12 and 13.

§ 12. Vacating an Award

(a) Upon application of a party, the court shall vacate an award where:

(1) The award was procured by corruption, fraud or other undue means;

(2) There was evident partiality by an arbitrator appointed as a neutral or corruption in any of the arbitrators or misconduct prejudicing the rights of any party;

(3) The arbitrators exceeded their powers;

(4) The arbitrators refused to postpone the hearing upon sufficient cause being shown therefor or refused to hear evidence material to the controversy or otherwise so conducted the hearing, contrary to the provisions of Section 5, as to prejudice substantially the rights of a party; or

(5) There was no arbitration agreement and the issue was not adversely determined in proceedings under Section 2 and the party did not participate in the arbitration hearing without raising the objection;

but the fact that the relief was such that it could not or would not be granted by a court of law or equity is not ground for vacating or refusing to confirm the award.

(b) An application under this Section shall be made within ninety days after delivery of a copy of the award to the applicant, except that, if predicated upon corruption, fraud or other undue means, it shall be made within ninety days after such grounds are known or should have been known.

(c) In vacating the award on grounds other than stated in clause (5) of Subsection (a) the court may order a rehearing before new arbitrators chosen as provided in the agreement, or in the absence thereof, by the court in accordance with Section 3, or if the award is vacated on grounds set forth in clauses (3) and (4) of Subsection (a) the court may order a rehearing before the arbitrators who made the award or their successors appointed in accordance with Section 3. The time within which the agreement requires the award to be made is applicable to the rehearing and commences from the date of the order.

(d) If the application to vacate is denied and no motion to modify or correct the award is pending, the court shall confirm the award. As amended Aug. 1956.

Historical Note

The 1956 amendment omitted "or rendered an award contrary to public policy" from subd. 3, and omitted provisions authorizing vacation of award where it is so indefinite or incomplete that it cannot be performed, or is so grossly erroneous as to imply bad faith on the part of the arbitrators.

§ 13. Modification or Correction of Award

(a) Upon application made within ninety days after delivery of a copy of the award to the applicant, the court shall modify or correct the award where:

(1) There was an evident miscalculation of figures or an evident mistake in the description of any person, thing or property referred to in the award;

(2) The arbitrators have awarded upon a matter not submitted to them and the award may be corrected without affecting the merits of the decision upon the issues submitted; or

(3) The award is imperfect in a matter of form, not affecting the merits of the controversy.

(b) If the application is granted, the court shall modify and correct the award so as to effect its intent and shall confirm the award as so modified and corrected. Otherwise, the court shall confirm the award as made.

(c) An application to modify or correct an award may be joined in the alternative with an application to vacate the award.

§ 14. Judgment or Decree on Award

Upon the granting of an order confirming, modifying or correcting an award, judgment or decree shall be entered in conformity therewith and be enforced as. any other judgment or decree. Costs of the application and of the proceedings subsequent thereto, and disbursements may be awarded by the court.

§ 15. Judgment Roll, Docketing

(a) On entry of judgment or decree, the clerk shall prepare the judgment roll consisting, to the extent filed, of the following:

(1) The agreement and each written extension of the time within which to make the award;

(2) The award;

(3) A copy of the order confirming, modifying or correcting the award; and

(4) A copy of the judgment or decree.

(b) The judgment or decree may be docketed as if rendered in an action.

§ 16. Applications to Court

Except as otherwise provided, an application to the court under this act shall be by motion and shall be heard in the manner and upon the notice provided by law or rule of court for the making and hearing of motions. Unless the parties have agreed otherwise, notice of an initial application for an order shall be served in the manner provided by law for the service of a summons in an action.

§ 17. Court, Jurisdiction

The term "court" means any court of competent jurisdiction of this State. The making of an agreement described in Section 1 providing for arbitration in this State confers jurisdiction on the court to enforce the agreement under this Act and to enter judgment on an award thereunder.

§ 18. Venue

An initial application shall be made to the court of the [county] in which the agreement provides the arbitration hearing shall be held or, if the hearing has been held, in the county in which it was held. Otherwise the application shall be made in the [county] where the adverse party resides or has a place of business or, if he has no residence or place of business in this State, to the court of any [county]. All subsequent applications shall be made to the court hearing the initial application unless the court otherwise directs.

§ 19. Appeals

(a) An appeal may be taken from:

(1) An order denying an application to compel arbitration made under Section 2;

(2) An order granting an application to stay arbitration made under Section 2(b);

(3) An order confirming or denying confirmation of an award;

(4) An order modifying or correcting an award;

(5) An order vacating an award without directing a rehearing; or

(6) A judgment or decree entered pursuant to the provisions of this act.

(b) The appeal shall be taken in the manner and to the same extent as, from orders or judgments in a civil action.

§ 20. Act Not Retroactive

This act applies only to agreements made subsequent to the taking effect of this act. * * *

———

UNIFORM COMMERCIAL CODE

This supplement does not contain the sections of the UCC needed for use of the principal book. It contains only selected State Comments and Notes of Decision from Uniform Laws Annotated for UCC 2–708, for use in connection with the Problem on p. 97 of the principal book.

UCC 2–708

UNIFORM COMMERCIAL CODE

This supplement does *not* contain the sections of the sections of the UCC needed for use of the principal book. It contains only selected State Comments, and Notes of Decision from Uniform Laws Annotated for UCC 2–708, for use in connection with the Problem on p. 97 of the principal book.

UCC 2–708

STATE COMMENTS

California Code Comment

By John A. Bohn and Charles J. Williams

Prior California Law

1. Subdivision (1) is the counterpart of former Civil Code § 1784(3). Both use the current market price of the goods as the standard for fixing damages for non-acceptance.

2. Where the goods had a fixed price, the measure of damages (difference between contract price and market price) under former Civil Code § 1784 did not give the seller adequate protection. Although the seller could recover prospective damages, the courts refused to award uncertain and speculative damages. Phillips v. Mathews, 90 Cal.App.2d 161, 202 P.2d 798 (1949); Los Angeles Coin–0–Matic Laundries v. Harow, 195 Cal.App.2d 324, 15 Cal.Rptr. 693 (1961).

Subdivision (2) changes this measure of damages when it is inadequate and substitutes the measure of the seller's expected profit.

3. A measure of damages can be based upon a theory of restitution (putting the parties in the position they were in before the contract was made), reliance (putting the innocent party in a position as if he had not relied on the breaching party's performance), and expectation (putting the innocent party in as good a position as if the breaching party had performed).

The theory behind both measures in this section is to allow the seller to recover an amount equal to the expected performance of the buyer.

Illinois Code Comment

By William B. Davenport

This is § 2–708 of the 1958 Official Text without change.

Subsection (1)

This subsection is an amplification of USA § 64(3). Numerous prior decisions, both prior and subsequent to the Uniform Sales Act, support the rule: Murray v. Doud, 167 Ill. 368, 47 N.E. 717 (1897); Kadish v. Young, 108 Ill. 170 (1883); Foos v. Sabin, 84 Ill. 564 (1877); Mc Neff v. White Eagle Brewing Co., 294 Ill. App. 37, 13 N.E.2d 493 (1st Dist. 1938). In Sloss–Sheffield Steel & Iron Co. v. Stover Mfg. & Engine Co., 37 F.2d 876 (7th Cir. 1930), a seller of pig iron was held entitled to no damages for the buyer's wrongful refusal to accept where the seller eventually sold the pig iron at a price in excess of the contract price, although at the time of the breach the market price was less than the contract price.

Subsection (2)

This subsection is an amplification of USA § 64(2). Numerous decisions have given the seller as his measure of damages the anticipated profit on the unperformed portion of the contract where the buyer has wrongfully repudiated it: Kingman & Co. v. Hanna Wagon Co., 176 Ill. 545, 52 N.E. 328 (1898) (difference between the cost of manufacture and delivery and the contract price was the proper measure of the seller's damages for wagons to be manufactured where the purchaser had the exclusive right to market the wagons in the state where they were manufactured); Capitol Paper Box, Inc. v. Belden Hosiery Mills, Inc., 350 Ill.App. 68, 111 N.E.2d 858 (1st Dist. 1953), petition for leave to appeal denied, 351 Ill.App. xv (buyer's repudiation of partially performed contract to purchase 500,000 hosiery boxes entitled the seller to damages of the full contract price for boxes on hand and partially completed, of cost of unused labels, and of profit on unordered balance); Larson v. Material Service Corp., 881 Ill.App. 430, 73 N.E.2d 444 (2d Dist. 1947) (seller was entitled to contract price less costs of producing and hauling sand and gravel); Nestler v. Pure Silk Hosiery Mills, Inc., 242 Ill.App. 151 (1st Dist. 1926) (seller's damages were contract price less cost of performance); Anderson v. Pan–American Motors Corp., 232 Ill. App. 27 (3rd Dist. 1924) (seller was entitled to damages for prospective profits on sale of 824 motors still to be manufactured, taking into consideration reasonable overhead costs).

New York Annotations

The fundamental rule of measuring damages approximates that of Personal Property Law, § 145. But the limitations imposed by present New York law on the right to recover profits are omitted. See, e.g., A. Lenobel, Inc. v. Senif, 252 App.Div. 533, 300 N.Y.S. 226 (1937) (profit not recovered by dealer in fixed price articles). As to seller's damages for anticipatory repudiation, see Section 2–723.

Historical Note: The section was revised in Supp. No. 1 to extend the rule clearly to cases of repudiation and to clarify the privilege of the seller to realize junk value when it is manifestly useless to complete the operation of manufacture. Further changes, made for clarification to meet criticisms of the Law Revision Commission, divided the section into two subsections, inserted cross-references to Sections 2–710 and 2–723, substituted "market" for "current" price, and inserted the provision for credit for payments in new subsection (2). As to "expenses", see Section 2–706 (1956 Recommendations, p. 77: Excerpts, p. 397.)

Wisconsin Annotations

Wisconsin Legislative Council—1961 Report

Cross references

(1) Wis.Stat. § 121.64(1), (2), (3) USA § 64(1), (2), (3). See point 1 of official UCC comment to § 2–708. Accord, as to the measure of damages: Sloss–Sheffield S. & I. Co. v. Wis. F. & M, Co., 187 Wis. 34, 203 N.W. 746, (1925) and Saveland v. Western Wis. R. Co., 118 Wis. 267, 95 N.W. 130 (1903) to the effect that the general rule of damages for breach of an executory sales contract is the difference between the contract price and the market value of the goods at the time the contract should have been performed. Accord, as to the right to recover incidental damages: William M. Roylance Co. v. Jewett & Sherman Co., 191 Wis. 490, 210 N.W. 376 (1927) (expenses of resale, storage, demurrage and interest were recoverable under § 121.64(2)).

(2) Wis.Stat. § 121.64(1), (2), (3); USA § 64(1), (2), (3). See point 2 of official UCC comment to § 2–707. The applicability of this subsection's rule of damages under present law appears to depend on whether the seller has elected to resell the goods and liquidate his damages or whether he still holds the goods for the original buyer. This is illustrated in 2 cases involving repudiation of contracts to purchase new automobiles. In Schuenemann v. John G. Wollaeger Co., 170 Wis. 616, 176 N.W. 59 (1920), the seller resold the car to a third party. The court said that since seller had elected to liquidate his damages, he waived his other remedies and could recover only the difference between the contract price and the amount obtained on resale; he could not recover the profit he would have made on the original sale.

In Popp v. Yuenger, 229 Wis. 189, 282 N.W. 55 (1938), seller had not resold the auto. On that basis, the court distinguished this case from the Schuenemann case, and said that the difference between the contract price and the manufacturer's suggested retail price would be inadequate damages and seller could recover the contract price minus the cost of the auto to him, thus in effect allowing the seller his expected profit on the original sale. Note that the measure of damages under the Code may be slightly be slightly broader even than that used in the Popp case, in that a portion of overhead expenses may also be charged as damages.

Summary of changes or clarifications

1. Makes minor variations in the standard measure of damages (contract price minus market price), by emphasizing market price at the time and place of tender rather than at the time and place of acceptance, and by placing greater emphasis than present law on methods of proving market price (§ 2–723).

2. In cases where the standard measure of damages (contract price minus market price) is inadequate, the Code broadens seller's measure of damages by permitting recovery of the expected profit on the sale, together with reasonable overhead expenses, regardless of whether the seller has resold the goods to a third party; under present law the doctrine of election of remedies bars recovery of such expected profit and expenses if seller has elected to liquidate damages by reselling the goods.

UNIFORM LAWS ANNOTATED—NOTES OF DECISION

3. Availability of market

In attempting to fix damages for breach of sales contract, where there is no market available at time and place of performance, resort may be had to market value of the goods at nearest available market, and in absence of such a market the measure of damages may be the difference between contract price and value of goods as best can be ascertained or the difference between contract price and best offer that can be obtained for the goods, or the difference between contract price and price obtained on a resale, or the actual damages naturally and directly resulting from buyer's breach. Sackett v. Spindler, App.1967, 56 Cal.Rptr. 435, 248 C.A.2d 220.

Provision of this section entitling seller to damages based on difference between contract price and market price on date of breach is applicable only when there is an available market for the goods and there Is an absence of special circumstances showing approximate damages of a greater amount. Irving Tier Co. v. Griffin, 1966, 53 Cal.Rptr. 469, 244 C.A.2d 852.

Within rule that loss of profits rather than difference between contract price and market price is measure of damages for breach of contract when there is no market for the goods, "market" means a market which, if availed of, would have substantially mitigated seller's damages. Timber Access Industries Co. v. U.S. Plywood–Champion Papers, Inc., 1972, 503 P.2d 482, 263 Or. 509.

Where buyer wrongfully refuses to accept and pay for goods ordered, seller is not entitled to recover contract price if he has an available market to dispose of the goods without loss. James Mfg. Co. v. Stovner, 1969, 459 P.2d 51, 1 Wash.App. 27.

Where buyers wrongfully refused to accept four-unit pipeline milker but milker which could have been sold to another had reasonable market value equivalent to contract price at time of buyer's breach of contract, seller was not entitled to recover any damages for the breach. Id.

5. Difference between market and contract price

Rule in Pennsylvania for measuring damages for buyer's breach of contract for the purchase of stock generally is the difference between the market value of the stock at the time and place of delivery and the contract price. American Electronic Laboratories, Inc. v. Dopp, D.C.Del. 1974, 369 F.Supp. 1245.

"Market value" of stock, for purposes of computing damages for buyer's breach of contract to purchase the same, can be defined generally as the price that a willing buyer and a willing seller would agree upon in the market place at the relevant time. Id.

In suit to recover damages for breach of a tender offer to purchase securities, the measure of damages for plaintiff broker, as to those securities not resold within a "commercially reasonable" time, was the difference between the market price at the time and place of tender and the unpaid contract price together with any incidental damages. Bache & Co., Inc. v. International Controls Corp., D.C.N.Y.1972, 339 F.Supp. 341.

Measure of seller's damages upon buyer's repudiation of contract for purchase of yarn after part of yarn had been manufactured, delivered, accepted, and paid for under contract

69

was difference between contract price and current market price at time and place of delivery. Jagger Bros., Inc. v. Technical Textile Co., 1M, 198 A. 2d 888, 202 Pa.Super. 639.

General rule that measure of damages in breach of sales contract action is the difference between contract price and market value is not a hard-and-fast rule, but may be varied as circumstances require it, and it will not be followed where a better method of measuring loss or damages is available under the circumstances. Sackett v. Spindler, 1967, 56 Cal. Rptr. 435, 248 C.A.2d 220.

Formula basing damages on difference between market price and contract price is without meaning in context of contract for specialty item which has no market value. Detroit

Power Screwdriver Co. v. Ladney, 1970, 181 N.W.2d 828, 384 Mich.App. 310. * * *

6. Loss of profits * * *

Where buyer breached contract of sale relating to specialized pumping equipment for use in a nuclear power plant, and where the equipment was not readily resalable and a market price therefor could not be ascertained, the seller's damages. were to be measured by the profit it would have made from full performance by the buyer, plus any incidental damages which the seller sustained as the result of the buyer's repudiation of the contract. Alter & Sons, Inc. v. United Engineers & Constructors, Inc., D.C.Ill.1973, 366 F.Supp. 959.

UNIFORM CONSUMER CREDIT CODE,[4] 1968

§ 2.104 Definition: "Consumer Credit Sale"

(1) Except as provided in subsection (2), "consumer credit sale" is a sale of goods, services, or an interest in land in which

(a) credit is granted by a person who regularly engages as a seller in credit transactions of the same kind,

(b) the buyer is a person other than an organization,

(c) the goods, services, or interest in land are purchased primarily for a personal, family, household, or agricultural purpose,

(d) either the debt is payable in instalments or a credit service charge is made, and

(e) with respect to a sale of goods or services, the amount financed does not exceed $25,000.

(2) Unless the sale is made subject to this Act by agreement (Section 2.601), "consumer credit sale" does not include

(a) a sale in which the seller allows the buyer to purchase goods or services pursuant to, a lender credit card or similar arrangement, or

---

4. Enacted in Colorado, Indiana, Oklahoma, South Carolina, Utah, Wisconsin, and Wyoming

(b) except as provided with respect to disclosure (Section 2.301) and debtors' remedies (Section 5.201), a sale of an interest in land if the credit service charge does, not exceed 10 per cent per year calculated according to the actuarial method on the unpaid balances of the amount financed on the assumption that the debt will be paid according to the agreed terms and will not be paid before the end of the agreed term.

(3) The amount of $25,000 in subsection (1) is subject to change pursuant to the provisions. on adjustment of dollar amounts (Section 1.106).

COMMENT

1. Since most of the operative provisions of this Act apply either to consumer credit sales, or to consumer loans, or to both, the definition of consumer credit sale is one of the key scope definitions of the Act. In defining a consumer credit sale as one made by a commercial seller to a buyer who is a natural person for an amount financed not exceeding $25,000 (except in the case of land sales) for a personal, family, household, or agricultural purpose, this Act applies to the same sales transactions as CCPA Sections 103(f) and (h), and 104(3) [15 U.S.C.A. §§ 1602(f), (h), 1603(3)]. This Act applies to credit jewelers or clothiers who sell on instalments but make no identifiable charge for credit. The requirement that a sale be either payable in instalments or subject to a finance charge to qualify as a consumer credit sale excludes a great mass of transactions, e.g., the 30–day retail charge account and the short-term credit furnished by professional men and artisans on a one-payment basis in connection with sales of their services for which no service charge is made. Sales by noncommercial creditors or sales for other than a consumer purpose are covered by this Act only to the extent of the limited provisions of Part 6 [Section 6.101 et seq.] on consumer related sales.

2. Drafts of the Uniform Consumer Credit Code prepared prior to enactment of the CCPA [15 U.S.C.A. § 1601 et seq.] completely excluded sales of interests in land where the rate of the credit service charge did not exceed 1091o from the definition of consumer credit sale and thus from coverage of the Act. The 10% cut-off was chosen as a convenient line of demarcation between two dissimilar transactions—L—the home mortgage and the high rate, "small loan" type of real estate loan. The exclusion of the home mortgage was made because the problems of home financing are sufficiently different to justify separate statutory treatment. On the other hand, the high rate second mortgage transaction has been a major source of consumer complaint and merits full coverage by the Act. Since the CCPA applies to all real estate credit without regard to the rate of finance charge, the Final Draft of this Act was changed to reflect this by making the 10% exclusion inapplicable to disclosure and related debtors' remedies.

§ 2.106 Definition: "Consumer Lease"

(1) "Consumer lease" means a lease of goods

(a) which a lessor regularly engaged in the business of leasing makes to a person, other than an organization, who takes under the lease primarily for a personal, family household, or agricultural purpose,

(b) in which the amount payable under the lease does not exceed $25,000, and

(c) which is for a term exceeding four months.

(2) "Consumer lease" does not include a lease made pursuant to a lender credit card or similar arrangement.

(3) The amount of $25,000 in subsection (1) is subject to change pursuant to the provisions on adjustment of dollar amounts (Section 1.106).

COMMENT

Leasing has become a popular means of distributing goods to alternative to credit sales as a consumers and merits inclusion in a comprehensive consumer credit code. The four month term requirement in subsection (1)(c) excludes from the Act the innumerable hourly, daily, or weekly rental or hire agreements typically involving automobiles, trailers, home repair tools., sick room equipment, and the like. If the transaction, though in form a lease, is in substance a sale within the meaning of Section 2.105(4), it is treated as a sale for all purposes in this Act and the provisions on consumer leases are inapplicable. The Act requires disclosure of the elements of the consumer lease transaction (Section 2.311); places limits on advertising respecting consumer leases (Section 2.313); contains a number of contract limitations applicable to consumer leases (Part 4 of Article 2, notably Section 2.406); makes provisions for remedies and penalties in consumer lease transactions (Article 5 [Section 5.101 et seq.]); and gives the Administrator powers over consumer lease transactions (Article 6 [Section 6.101 et seq.]). Since a credit service, charge is not made in the usual consumer lease transaction, the rate ceiling provisions of the Act are inapplicable.

§ 2.403 Certain Negotiable Instruments Prohibited

In a consumer credit sale or consumer lease, other than a sale or lease primarily for an agricultural purpose, the seller or lessor may not take a negotiable instrument other than a check as evidence of the obligation of the buyer or lessee. A holder is not in good faith if he takes a negotiable instrument with notice that it is issued in violation of this section. A holder in due course is not subject to the liabilities set forth in the provisions on the effect of violations on rights of parties (Section 5.202) and the provisions on civil actions by Administrator (Section 6.113).

COMMENT

Since the prohibition against certain negotiable instruments in consumer financing will be well known in the financial community after enactment of this Act, professional financiers buying consumer paper will normally not qualify as holders in due course with respect to instruments taken by dealers in violation of this section and negotiated to them. To qualify as a holder in due course all requirements of UCC Section 3–302 must be satisfied. However, it is possible that in rare cases second or third takers may not know of an instrument's consumer origin; in this unusual situation the policy favoring negotiability is upheld in order not to cast a cloud over negotiable instruments generally. A person who takes a negotiable instrument in violation of this section is subject to Sections 5.202 and 6.113. Compare Unico v. Owen, 50 N.J. 101, 232 A.2d 405 (1967).

Alternative A:

§ 2.404 Assignee Subject to Defenses

With respect to a consumer credit sale or consumer lease, other than a sale or lease primarily for an agricultural purpose, an assignee of the rights of the seller or lessor is subject to all claims and defenses of the buyer or lessee against the seller or lessor arising out of the sale or lease notwithstanding an agreement to the contrary, but the assignee's liability under this section may not exceed the amount owing to the assignee at the time the claim or defense is asserted against the assignee. Rights of the buyer or lessee under this section can only be asserted as a matter of defense to or set-off against a claim by the assignee.

COMMENT

This section codifies a growing body of decisions in connection with UCC Section 9–206. See, e.g., Quality Fin. Co. v. Hurley, 337 Mass. 150, 148 N.E.2d 385, 388–89 (1958); Unico v. Owen, 50 N.J. 101, 232 A.2d 405 (1967)

Alternative B:

§ 2.404 When Assignee Not Subject to Defenses

(1) With respect to a consumer credit sale or consumer lease, other than a sale or lease primarily for an agricultural purpose, an agreement by the buyer or lessee not to assert against an assignee a claim or defense arising out of the sale or lease is enforceable only by an assignee not related to the seller or lessor who acquires the buyer's or lessee's contract in good faith and for value, who gives the buyer or lessee notice of the assignment as provided in this section and who, within 3 months after the mailing of the notice of assignment, receives no written notice of the facts giving rise to the buyer's or lessee's claim or defense. This agreement is enforceable only with respect to claims or defenses which have arisen before the end of the 3–month period after notice was mailed. The notice of assignment shall be in writing and addressed to the buyer or lessee at his address as stated in the contract, identify the contract, describe the goods or services, state the names of the seller or lessor and buyer or lessee, the name and address of the assignee, the amount payable by the buyer or lessee and the number, amounts and due dates of the instalments, and contain a conspicuous notice to the buyer or lessee that he has 3 months within which to notify the assignee in writing of any complaints, claims or defenses he may have against the seller or lessor and that if written notification of the com-

plaints, claims or defenses is not received by the assignee within the 3–month period, the assignee will have the right to enforce the contract free of any claims or defenses the buyer or lessee may have against the seller or lessor which have arisen before the end of the 3–month period after notice was mailed.

(2) An assignee does not acquire a buyer's or lessee's contract in good faith within the meaning of subsection (1) if the assignee has knowledge or, from his course of dealing with the seller or lessor or his records, notice of substantial complaints by other buyers or lessees of the seller's or lessor's failure or refusal to perform his contracts with them and of the seller's or lessor's failure to remedy his defaults within a reasonable time after the assignee notifies him of the complaints.

(3) To the extent that under this section an assignee is subject to claims or defenses of the buyer or lessee against the seller or lessor, the assignee's liability under this section may not exceed the amount owing to the assignee at the time the claim or defense is asserted against the assignee and rights of the buyer or lessee under this section can only be asserted as a matter of defense to or set-off against a claim by the assignee.

COMMENT

This section follows statutes in a number of states but lengthens the period within which notice of claims or defenses may be given by the buyer.

Compliance with this section allows an assignee who acquires a contract in good faith to take free of claims or defenses that the buyer or lessee had against the assignor of which he fails to notify the assignee within 3 months after notice of the assignment is received. The basis of this section is that if the buyer or lessee wishes to maintain a claim or defense against the assignee he must give the assignee notice of the facts giving rise to it within the 3–month period. Since he cannot give this notice with respect to claims or defenses arising after the 3–month period, this section does not deprive the buyer or lessee of his right to raise these claims or defenses against the assignee. See Unico v. Owen, 50 N.J. 101, 232 A.2d 405 (1967).

§ 2.410 No Assignment of Earnings

A seller or lessor may not take an assignment of earnings of the buyer or lessee for payment or as security for payment of a debt arising out of a consumer credit sale or a consumer lease. An assignment of earnings in violation of this section is unenforceable by the assignee of the earnings and revocable by the buyer or lessee. This section does not prohibit an employee from authorizing deductions from his earnings if the authorization is revocable.

§ 3.104 Definition: "Consumer Loan"

(1) Except with respect to a loan primarily secured by an interest in land (Section 3.105), "consumer loan" is a loan made by a person regularly engaged in the business of making loans in which

(a) the debtor is a person other than an organization;

(b) the debt is incurred primarily for a personal, family, household, or agricultural purpose;

(c) either the debt is payable in instalments or a loan finance charge is made; and

(d) either the principal does not exceed $25,000 or the debt is secured by an interest in land.

(2) The amount of $25,000 in subsection (1) is subject to change pursuant to the provisions on adjustment of dollar amount (Section 1.106).

§ 3.403 No Assignment of Earnings

(1) A lender may not take an assignment of earnings of the debtor for payment or as security for payment of a debt arising out of a consumer loan. An assignment of earnings in violation of this section is unenforceable by the assignee of the earnings and revocable by the debtor. This section does not prohibit an employee from authorizing deductions from his earnings if the authorization is revocable.

(2) A sale of unpaid earnings made in consideration of the payment of money to or for the account of the seller of the earnings is deemed to be a loan to him secured by an assignment of earnings.

COMMENT

See Comment to Section 2.410. Subsection (2) makes clear that "salary buying" falls within the prohibition of subsection (1).

§ 5.104 No Garnishment Before Judgment

Prior to entry of judgment in an action against the debtor for debt arising from a consumer credit sale, a consumer lease, or a consumer loan, the creditor may not attach unpaid earnings of the debtor by garnishment or like proceedings.

§ 5.105 Limitation on Garnishment

(1) For the purposes of this Part

(a) "disposable earnings" means that part of the earnings of an, individual remaining after the deduction from those earnings of amounts required by law to be withheld; and

(b) "garnishment" means any legal or equitable procedure through which the earnings of an individual are required to be withheld for payment of a debt.

(2) The maximum part of the aggregate disposable earnings of an individual for any workweek which is subjected to garnishment to enforce payment of a judgment arising from a consumer credit sale, consumer lease, or consumer loan may not exceed the lesser of

(a) 25 per cent of his disposable earnings for that week, or

(b) the amount by which his disposable earnings for that week exceed forty times the Federal minimum hourly wage prescribed by Section 6(a)(1) of the Fair Labor Standards Act of 1938, U.S.C. tit. 29, § 206(a)(1), in effect at the time the earnings are payable.

(c) In the case of earnings for a pay period other than a week, the Administrator shall prescribe by rule a multiple of the Federal minimum hourly wage equivalent in effect to that set forth in paragraph (b).

(3) No court may make, execute, or enforce an order or process in violation of this section.

COMMENT

1. This section is derived from CCPA Sections 302 and 303 [15 U.S.C.A. §§ 1672, 1673]. The exemption has been increased from thirty times the minimum hourly wage to forty in the belief that the higher figure was justified in consumer transactions.

2. Section 5.104 prohibits all garnishment before judgment for collection of consumer debt. Section 5.105 limits the use of garnishment after judgment for collection of consumer debt. It complements rather than displaces local garnishment laws and applies only to garnishment and like proceedings directed toward one other than the consumer debtor, e.g., an employer. The consumer debtor's interests are adequately protected in proceedings supplementary to judgment in which the debtor is personally before the court and the court is therefore able to take his and his dependents' needs into consideration in granting an order against him for payment of a judgment on a consumer debt.

3. This section is designed to assure the consumer debtor that he will retain enough of his earnings to be able to support himself and his dependents by exempting a portion of his earnings from garnishment to enforce judgments for consumer debts. The exemption is based on the concept of "disposable earnings" rather than gross earnings. Disposable earnings are defined to include only those earnings which the debtor can spend after deductions required by law. If the law requires a portion of the debtor's wages to be withheld from him, the debtor has no power of disposition with respect to that portion, and that portion is therefore not included in disposable wages. Thus, amounts required to be withheld for social security or income taxes, amounts withheld pursuant to compulsory retirement, health insurance or similar plans imposed by law and amounts withheld because of a garnishment or levy by another creditor are excluded from "disposable earnings." However, if amounts are withheld from the debtor's earnings by the employer pursuant to a request by the employee or pursuant to a contract made by the employee or on his behalf by a labor union or similar organization, the amounts withheld are included in "disposable earnings" since the deduction is not required by law.

4. This section sets limits on the maximum amount of disposable earnings that a creditor in a consumer credit transaction may reach by garnishment. There is a double test. The creditor may not garnish more than (a) 25% of disposable earnings for any workweek or (b) the amount by which

disposable earnings exceed 40 times the Federal minimum hourly wage, whichever is less.

Example: An unmarried consumer debtor earns $3.10 an hour. Wages are paid on a weekly pay period running from Wednesday through Tuesday. During that period the debtor worked 38 hours. Gross wages were $117.80. The employer withholds Federal income taxes of $21.70, social security taxes of $5.18, union dues of $1.25 pursuant to a contract with the union, and $5 for a Christmas savings plan of which the employee is a member. Net wages paid to the employee are $84.67. "Disposable earnings" are $90,92; 25% of disposable earnings is $22.73; 40 X minimum hourly wage of $1.60 is $64; the excess of disposable earnings over $64.00 is $26.92.

Under Section 5.105 the creditor may garnish no more than $22.73, the lesser of $22.73 and $26.92.

5. This section is not meant to displace other provisions of state law which may provide additional protection to the debtor. For examples: (1) if state law provides that a debtor may defeat a garnishment by a showing that the wages subject to garnishment are necessary for the support of himself and his dependents, the debtor may take full advantage of that law; and (2) if state law exempts 90% of earnings, only $11.78 or 10% of earnings of $117.80 may be collected under the garnishment in the example above.

§ 5.106　No Discharge From Employment for Garnishment

No employer shall discharge an employee for the reason that a creditor of the employee has subjected or attempted to subject unpaid earnings of the employee to garnishment or like proceedings directed to the employer for the purpose of paying a judgment arising from a consumer credit sale, consumer lease, or consumer loan.

COMMENT

1. The penalty for violation of this section is found in Section 5.202(6).

2. This Section is derived from CCPA Section 304 [15 U.S.C.A. § 1674], but it prohibits an employer from discharging an employee by reason of any garnishment (whether one or more) under a judgment arising from a consumer credit sale, consumer lease, or consumer loan.

§ 5.202　Effect of Violations on Rights of Parties

(6) If an employer discharges an employee in violation of the provisions prohibiting discharge (Section 5.106), the employee may within [–] days bring a civil action for recovery of wages lost as a result of the violation and for an order requiring the reinstatement of the employee. Damages recoverable shall not exceed lost wages for six weeks.

(7) If the creditor establishes by a preponderance of evidence that a violation is unintentional or the result of a bona fide error, no liability is imposed under subsections (1), (2), and (4) and the validity of the transaction is not affected.

(8) In any case in which it is found that a creditor has violated this Act, the court may award reasonable attorney's fees, incurred by the debtor.

§ 6.111 Injunctions Against Unconscionable Agreements and Fraudulent or Unconscionable Conduct

(1) The Administrator may bring a civil action to restrain a creditor or a person acting in his behalf from engaging in a course of

(a) making or enforcing unconscionable terms or provisions of consumer credit sales, consumer leases, or consumer loans;

(b) fraudulent or unconscionable conduct in inducing debtors to enter into consumer credit sales, consumer leases, or consumer loans; or

(c) fraudulent or unconscionable conduct in the collection of-debts arising from consumer credit sales, consumer leases, or consumer loans.

(2) In an action brought pursuant to this section the court may grant relief only if it finds

(a) that the respondent has made unconscionable agreements or has engaged or is likely to engage in a course of fraudulent or unconscionable conduct;

(b) that the agreements or conduct of the respondent has caused or is likely to cause injury to consumers; and

(c) that the respondent has been able to cause or will be able to cause the injury primarily because the transactions involved are credit transactions.

(3) In applying this section, consideration shall be given to each of the following factors among others:

(a) belief by the creditor at the time consumer credit sales, consumer leases, or consumer loans are made that there was no reasonable probability of payment in full of the obligation by the debtor;

(b) in the case of consumer credit sales or consumer leases, knowledge by the seller or lessor at the time of the sale or lease of the inability of the buyer or lessee to receive substantial benefits from the property or services sold or leased;

(c) in the case of consumer credit sales or consumer leases, gross disparity between the price of the property or services sold or leased and the value of the property or services measured by the price at which similar property or service's are readily obtainable in credit transactions by like buyers or lessees;

(d) the fact that the creditor contracted for or received separate charges for insurance with respect to consumer credit sales or consumer loans with the effect of making the sales or loans, considered as a whole, unconscionable; and

(e) the fact that the respondent has knowingly taken advantage of the inability of the debtor reasonably to protect his interests by reason of physical or mental infirmities, ignorance, illiteracy or inability to understand the language of the agreement, or similar factors.

(4) In an action brought pursuant to this section, a charge or practice expressly, permitted by this Act is not in itself unconscionable.

COMMENT

1. Section 5.108 provides a private remedy for unconscionable consumer credit transactions. This section, in addition, permits the Administrator to bring suit to enjoin a person-subject to the provisions of this Act from engaging in a course of conduct Specified in subsection (1)(a), (b), or (c). These subsections cover three different areas of unconscionable conduct: (1) unconscionable contract terms, (2) fraudulent or unconscionable conduct in inducing consumers to enter into consumer credit transactions, and (3) fraudulent or unconscionable conduct in the collection of consumer credit debts.

2. One purpose of this section is to afford the Administrator a means of dealing with new patterns of fraudulent or unconscionable conduct unforeseen and, perhaps, unforeseeable at the writing of this Act. Another is to give him a more flexible remedy for halting reprehensible creditor practices that have been specifically and somewhat rigidly treated in previous consumer credit legislation. For instance, this Act has no specific prohibition against the creditor's allowing the debtor to sign a credit agreement containing blanks. In some situations there may be legitimate reasons for a contract to contain blanks at the time of signing. However, if the creditor deliberately leaves blanks to be filled in after the debtor's signature and without his consent, the Administrator may seek to restrain the practice as fraudulent or unconscionable conduct under this section.

3. Subsection (3) lists a number of specific factors to be considered on the issue of unconscionability. The following are illustrative of individual transactions which, if engaged in by or on behalf of a creditor as a course of conduct, would entitle the Administrator to injunctive relief under this section:

Under subsection (3)(a), a sale of goods to a low income consumer without expectation of payment but with the expectation of repossessing the goods sold and reselling them at a profit;

Under subsection (3)(b), a sale to a Spanish speaking laborer-bachelor of an English language encyclopedia set, or the sale of two expensive vacuum cleaners to two poor families sharing the same apartment and one rug;

Under subsection (3)(c), a home solicitation sale of a set of cookware or flatware to a housewife for $375 in an area where a set of comparable quality is readily available on credit in stores for $125 or less.

4. Subsection (4) prohibits a finding that a charge or practice expressly permitted by this Act is in itself unconscionable. However, even though a practice or charge is authorized by this Act, the totality of a particular creditor's conduct may show that the practice or charge is part of an unconscionable course of conduct. Therefore, in determining unconscionability, the creditor's total conduct, including that part of his conduct which is in accordance with the provisions of this Act, may be considered.

5. For cases illustrating the prior application of the doctrine of unconscionability in private actions, see Comment to Section 5.108. This doctrine was applied in an action by a

79

public official in State by Lefkowitz v.
ITM, Inc., 52 Misc.2d 39, 275
N.Y.S.2d 303 (Sup.Ct.1966).

———

UNIFORM CONSUMER CREDIT CODE, 1974[5]

§ 1.301   General Definitions

(12) "Consumer credit sale":

(a) Except as provided in paragraph (b), "consumer credit sale" means a sale of goods, services, or an interest in land in which:

(i) credit is granted either pursuant to a seller credit card or by a seller who regularly engages as a seller in credit transactions of the same kind;

(ii) the buyer is a person other than an organization;

(iii) the goods, services, or interest in land are purchased primarily for a personal, family, household, or agricultural purpose;

(iv) the debt is payable in instalments or a finance charge is made; and

(v) with respect to a sale of goods or services, the amount financed does not exceed $25,000.

(b) A "consumer credit sale" does not include:

(i) a sale in which the seller allows the buyer to purchase goods or services pursuant to a lender credit card, or

(ii) unless the sale is made subject to this Act by agreement (Section 1.109), a sale of an interest in land if the finance charge does not exceed 12 per cent per year calculated according to the actuarial method on the assumption that the debt will be paid according to the agreed term's and will not be paid before the end of the agreed term.

(c) The amount of $25,000 in paragraph (a)(v) is subject to change pursuant to the provisions of adjustment of dollar amounts (Section 1.106).

(13) "Consumer credit transaction" means a consumer credit sale or consumer loan or a refinancing or consolidation thereof, or a consumer lease.

(14) "Consumer lease":

(a) "Consumer lease" means a lease of goods:

(i) which a lessor regularly engaged in the business of leasing makes to a person, except an organization, who takes under the

———

5. Enacted in Colorado, Idaho, Iowa, Kansas, Maine.

lease primarily for a personal, family, household, or agricultural purpose;

(ii) in which the amount payable under the lease does not exceed $25,000;

(iii) which is for a term exceeding four months; and

(iv) which is not made pursuant to a lender credit card.

(b) The amount of $25,000 in paragraph (a)(ii) is subject to change pursuant to the provisions on adjustment of dollar amounts (Section 1.106).

(15) "Consumer loan":

(a) Except as provided in paragraph (b), "consumer loan" means a loan made by a creditor regularly engaged in the business of making loans in which:

(i) the debtor is a person other than an organization;

(ii) the debt is incurred primarily for a personal, family, household, or agricultural purpose;

(iii) the debt is payable in instalments or a finance charge is made; and

(iv) the amount financed does not exceed $25,000 or the debt, other than one incurred primarily for an agricultural purpose, is secured by an interest in land.

(b) A "consumer loan" does not include:

(i) a sale or lease in which the seller or lessor allows the buyer or lessee to purchase or lease pursuant to a seller credit card, or

(ii) unless the loan is made subject to this Act by agreement (Section 1.109), a loan secured by an interest in land if the security interest is bona fide and not for the purpose of circumvention or evasion of this Act and the finance charge does not exceed 12 per cent per year calculated according to the actuarial method on the assumption that the debt will be paid according to the agreed terms and will not be paid before the end of the agreed term.

(c) A loan that would be a consumer loan if the lender were regularly engaged in the business of making loans is a consumer loan if the loan is arranged for a commission or other compensation by a person regularly engaged in the business of arranging those loans and the lender is not regularly engaged in the business of making loans. The arranger is deemed to be the creditor making the loan.

(d) The amount of $25,000 in paragraph (a)(iv) is subject to change pursuant to the provisions on adjustment of dollar amounts (Section 1.106).

§ 3.305   No Assignment of Earnings

(1) A creditor may not take an assignment of earnings of the consumer for payment or as security for payment of a debt arising out of a consumer credit transaction. An assignment of earnings in violation of this section is unenforceable by the assignee of the earnings and revocable by the consumer. This section does not prohibit a consumer from authorizing deductions from his earnings in favor of his creditor if the authorization is revocable, the consumer is given a complete copy of the writing evidencing the authorization at the time he signs it, and the writing contains on its face a conspicuous notice of the consumer's right to revoke the authorization.

(2) A sale of unpaid earnings made in consideration of the payment of money to or for the account of the seller of the earnings is deemed to be a loan to him secured by an assignment of earnings.

COMMENT

This Act recognizes the potential for hardship for a consumer and his dependents which may result from a disruption of the steady flow of family income. Just as Section 5.104 prevents a creditor from attaching unpaid earnings of a consumer before he obtains judgment, this provision precludes a creditor from reaching the consumer's earnings pursuant to an irrevocable wage assignment obtained from the consumer. The purpose of both sections is to afford the consumer an opportunity to have his debt determined by a court before his unpaid earnings are taken against his will by a creditor. This provision prohibits a creditor from taking either an assignment of earnings as payment or as security for payment for a debt or a sale of earnings in payment of the price or rental. A revocable payroll deduction authorization in favor of a creditor is not forbidden by this section so long as the requisite notice is given to the consumer of his right to revoke.

§ 3.307   Certain Negotiable Instruments Prohibited

With respect to a consumer credit sale or consumer lease, [except a sale or lease primarily for an agricultural purpose,] the creditor may not take a negotiable instrument other than a check dated not later than ten days after its issuance as evidence of the obligation of the consumer.

COMMENT

This section, together with Sections 3.403, 3.404, and 3.405, states a major tenet of this Act: that the holder in due course doctrine should be abrogated in consumer cases. Whatever beneficial effects this doctrine may have in promoting the currency of paper is greatly outweighed by the harshness of its consequences in denying consumers the right to raise valid defenses arising out of credit transactions. The first step in abolition of the doctrine is the prohibition found in this section of the use of negotiable instruments in consumer credit sales and consumer leases. The presence of the bracketed language recognizes the strong tradition of the use of negotiable instruments in agricultural transactions in some States.

§ 3.404 Assignee Subject to Claims and Defenses

(1) With respect to a consumer credit sale or consumer lease [except one primarily for an agricultural purpose], an assignee of the rights of the seller or lessor is subject to all claims and defenses of the consumer against the seller or lessor arising from the sale or lease of property or services, notwithstanding that the assignee is a holder in due course of a negotiable instrument issued in violation of the provision s prohibiting certain negotiable instruments (Section 3.307).

(2) A claim or defense of a consumer specified in subsection (1) may be asserted against the assignee under this section only if the consumer has made a good faith attempt to obtain satisfaction from the seller or lessor with respect to the claim or defense and then only to the extent of the amount owing to the assignee with respect to the sale or lease of the property or services as to which the claim or defense arose at the time the assignee has notice of the claim or defense. Notice of the claim or defense may be given before the attempt specified in this subsection. Oral notice is effective unless the assignee requests written confirmation when or promptly after oral notice is given and the consumer fails to give the assignee written confirmation within the period of time, not less than 14 days, stated to the consumer when written confirmation is requested.

(3) For the purpose of determining the amount owing to the assignee with respect to the sale or lease:

(a) payments received by the assignee after the consolidation of two or more consumer credit sales, except pursuant to open-end credit, are deemed to have been applied first to the payment of the sales first made; if the sales consolidated arose from sales made on the same day, payments are deemed to have been applied first to the smallest sale; and

(b) payments received for an open-end credit account are deemed to have been applied first to the payment of finance charges in the order of their entry to the account and then to the payment of debts in the order in which the entries of the debts are made to the account.

(4) An agreement may not limit or waive the claims or defenses of a consumer under this section.

COMMENT

1. This section codifies a growing body of case law under UCC Section 9–206 to the effect that assignees take consumer paper subject to consumer claims and defenses. This section explicitly provides for preservation of consumer defenses even though the assignee is a holder in due course (subsection (1)) or the consumer has purported to waive his claims and defenses as against the assignee (subsection (4)). The policy justifications for the section are to protect the consumer from the harshness of the holder in due course doctrine as well as to encourage financial institutions taking assignments of consumer paper to use discretion in dealing with sellers and lessors whose transactions give rise to an unusual percentage of

83

consumer complaints. See Section 3.307.

2. The consumer, upon making a good faith attempt to obtain satisfaction from his seller or lessor, can assert his claim or defense against the assignee to the extent of the amount still owing to the assignee at the time the assignee learns of the claim or defense. If the assignee knows of the defense before any payments are made to him, the consumer can raise his claim or defense to the full amount of the assigned debt. Orderly procedures will necessitate some written record on the part of the assignee of the consumer's notification regarding his claim or defense, but the consumer ought to be able to rely on having given oral notification unless the assignee requests written confirmation. Hence, the assignee has the option of making his own written record upon receiving oral notice from the consumer or of requesting written notice from the consumer and allowing 14 days for the consumer to send his written confirmation. Subsection (3) uses the same tests for determining the amount owing on a debt as are used in Section 3.303.

§ 5.104   No Garnishment Before Judgment

Before entry of judgment in an action against a consumer for debt arising from a consumer credit transaction, the creditor may not attach unpaid earnings of the consumer by garnishment or like proceedings.

COMMENT

This section, within the scope date of the Supreme Court in the of this Act, carries out the mandate of the Supreme Court in the landmark decision of Sniadach v. Family Finance Corp., 89 S.Ct.1820, 395 U.S. 337, 23 L.Ed.2d 349 (1969) and further adopts the recommendation of the Report of the National Commission on Consumer Finance that prejudgment garnishment, even of nonresident consumers, should be abolished.

§ 5.1015   Limitation on Garnishment

(1) For purposes of this Part:

(a) "disposable earnings" means that part of the earnings of an individual remaining after the deduction from those earnings of amounts required by law to be withheld; and

(b) "garnishment" means any legal or equitable procedure through which earnings of an individual are required to be withheld for payment of a debt.

(2) The maximum part of the aggregate disposable earnings of an individual for any workweek which is subjected to garnishment to enforce payment of a judgment arising from a consumer credit transaction may not exceed the lesser of:

(a) 25 per cent of his disposable earnings for that week, or

(b) the amount by which his disposable earnings for that week exceed 40 times the Federal minimum hourly wage prescribed by Section 6(a)(1) of the Fair Labor Standards Act of 1938, U.S.C. tit. 29, § 206(a)(1), in effect at the time the earnings are payable.

In case of earnings for a pay period other than a week, the Administrator shall prescribe by rule a multiple of the Federal minimum hourly wage equivalent in effect to that set forth in paragraph (b).

(3) No court may make, execute, or enforce an order or process in violation of this section.

(4) At any time after entry of a judgment in favor of a creditor in an action against a consumer for debt arising from a consumer credit transaction, the consumer may file with the court his verified application for an order exempting from garnishment pursuant to that judgment, for an appropriate period of time, a greater portion or all of his aggregate disposable earnings for a workweek or other-applicable pay period than is provided for in subsection (2). He shall designate in the application the portion of his earnings not exempt from garnishment under this section and other law, the period of time for which the additional exemption is sought, describe the judgment with respect to which the application is made, and state that the designated portion as well as his earnings that are exempt by law are necessary for the maintenance of him or a family supported wholly or partly by the earnings. Upon filing a sufficient application under this subsection, the court may issue any temporary order necessary under the circumstances to stay enforcement of the judgment by garnishment, shall set a hearing on the application not less than [five] nor more than [ten] days after the date of filing of the application, and shall cause notice of the application and the hearing date to be served on the judgment creditor or his attorney of record. At the hearing, if it appears to the court that all or any portion of the earnings sought to be additionally exempt are necessary for the maintenance of the consumer or a family supported wholly or partly by the earnings of the consumer for all or any part of the time requested in the application, the court shall issue an order granting the application to that extent; otherwise it shall deny the application. The order is subject to modification or vacation upon further application of any party to it upon a showing of changed circumstances after a hearing upon notice to all interested parties.

COMMENT

1. This section is derived from the CCPA (15 U.S.C. § 1601 et seq., specifically §§ 1672, 1673). The exemption has been increased from thirty times the minimum hourly wage to forty in the belief that the higher figure is justified in consumer credit transactions, a belief substantiated by the recommendation of the Report of the National Commission on Consumer Finance.

2. Section 5.104 prohibits all garnishment before judgment for collection of consumer debt. This section limits the use of garnishment after judgment for collection of consumer debt. It complements rather than displaces local garnishment laws and applies only to garnishment and like proceedings directed toward one other than the consumer, e.g., an employer. The consumer's interests are adequately protected in proceedings supplementary to judgment in which the consumer is personally before the court and the court is therefore able

to take his and his dependents' needs into consideration in granting an order against him for payment of a judgment on a consumer debt.

3. Subsection (2) is designed to assure the consumer that under normal circumstances he will retain enough of his earnings to be able to support himself and his dependents by exempting a portion of his earnings from garnishment to enforce judgments for consumer debts. The exemption is based on the concept of "disposable earnings" rather than gross earnings. Disposable earnings are defined to include only those earnings which the consumer can spend after deductions required by law. If the law requires a portion of the consumer's wages to be withheld from him, the consumer has no power of disposition with respect to that portion, and that portion is therefore not included in disposable wages. Thus, amounts required to be withheld for social security or income taxes, amounts withheld pursuant to compulsory retirement, health insurance or similar plans imposed by law and amounts withheld because of a garnishment or levy by another creditor are excluded from "disposable earnings." However, if amounts are withheld from the consumer's earnings by the employer pursuant to a request by the employee or pursuant to a contract made by the employee or on his behalf by a labor union or similar organization, the amounts withheld are included in "disposable earnings" since the deduction is not required by law.

4. Subsection (2) sets limits on the maximum amount of disposable earnings that a creditor in a consumer credit transaction may reach by garnishment. There is a double test. The creditor may not garnish more than (a) 25 per cent of disposable earnings for any workweek or (b) the amount by which disposable earnings exceed 40 times the Federal minimum hourly wage, whichever is less.

Example: Assume that the Federal minimum hourly wage is $2.00. An unmarried consumer who has no dependents and therefore claims one withholding exemption earns $3.10 an. hour. Wages are paid for a weekly pay period. During that period the consumer worked 38 hours. His gross wages were $117.80. His employer withholds Federal income taxes of $16.60, social security taxes of $6.89, union dues of $1.25 pursuant to a contract with the union, and $5.00 for a Christmas savings plan of which the consumer is a member. Net wages paid to the employee are $88.06. "Disposable earnings" are $94.31; 25 per cent of disposable earnings is $23.57; 40 times the minimum hourly wage of $2.00 is $80.00; the excess of disposable earnings over $80.00 is $14.31. Under subsection (2), the creditor may garnish no more than $14.31, the lesser of $23.57 and $14.31.

5. Under unusual circumstances such as illness, an abnormally large number of dependents, or similar conditions, some or all of the amount of disposable earnings subject to garnishment by subsection (2) may be necessary for the support of the consumer or his family for a brief or an extended period of time. Subsection (4) affords the consumer in that instance an opportunity to be heard and introduce evidence, and in the event undue hardship is proved to the satisfaction of the court, the amount of the garnishment may be reduced or the garnishment removed. In this respect, subsection (4) follows a recommendation of the Report of the National Commission on Consumer Finance.

6. This section is not meant to displace other provisions of state law which may provide additional protec-

tion to the consumer. For example, if state law exempts 90 per cent of earnings, only $11.78 or 10 per cent of earnings of $117.80 may be collected under the garnishment in the example above.

7. There is no private right of action for monetary relief vested by this Act in the consumer for violation of this section; enforcement is expected to come primarily through the restriction imposed on the court in subsection (3) and appropriate action by the Administrator (Article 6, Part 1). However, this should not be construed as precluding an individual consumer from obtaining appropriate injunctive or other nonmonetary relief for violation of the section, or from obtaining monetary relief consistent with Section 1.103 against a creditor for wrongful seizure of exempt earnings. See, e.g., Albrecht v. Treitschke, 17 Neb. 205, 22 N.W. 418 (1885).

§ 5.106   No Discharge From Employment for Garnishment

An employer may not discharge an employee for the reason that a creditor of the employee has subjected or attempted to subject unpaid earnings of the employee to garnishment or like proceedings directed to the employer for the purpose of paying a judgment arising from a consumer credit transaction.

COMMENT

1. The employee's remedy for violation of this section is found in Section 5.201(5).

2. This section is derived from the CCPA (15 U.S.C. § 1601 et seq., specifically § 1674), but it prohibits an employer from discharging an employee by reason of any garnishment (whether one or more) under a judgment arising from a consumer credit transaction.

§ 6.111   Injunctions Against Unconscionable Agreements and Fraudulent or Unconscionable Conduct Including Debt Collection

(1) The Administrator may bring a civil action to restrain a person to whom this Part applies from engaging in a course of:

    (a) making or enforcing unconscionable terms or provisions of consumer credit transactions;

    (b) fraudulent or unconscionable conduct in inducing consumers to enter into consumer credit transactions;

    (c) conduct of any of the types specified in paragraph (a) or (b) with respect to transactions that give rise to or that lead persons to believe will give rise to consumer credit transactions; or

    (d) fraudulent or unconscionable conduct in the collection of debts arising from consumer credit transactions.

(2) In an action brought pursuant to this section the court may grant relief only if it finds:

    (a) that the respondent has made unconscionable agreements or has engaged or is likely to engage in a course of fraudulent or unconscionable conduct;

(b) that the respondent's agreements have caused or are likely to cause or the conduct of the respondent has caused or is likely to cause injury to consumers or debtors; and

(c) that the respondent has been able to cause or will be able to cause the injury, primarily because the transactions involved are credit transactions.

(3) In applying subsection (1)(a), (b), and (c), consideration shall be given to each of the factors specified in the provisions on unconscionability with respect to a transaction that is, gives rise to, or that a person leads the debtor to believe will give rise to, a consumer credit transaction (subsection (4) of Section 5.108), among others.

(4) In applying subsection (1)(d), consideration shall be given to each of the factors specified in the provisions on unconscionability with respect to. the collection of debts arising from consumer credit transactions (subsection (5) of Section 5.108), among others,

(5) In an action brought pursuant to this section, a charge or practice expressly permitted by this Act is not in itself unconscionable.

COMMENT

1. Section 5.108 provides a private remedy for unconscionable conduct. This section, in addition, permits the Administrator to bring suit to enjoin a person to whom this Part applies from engaging in a course of conduct specified in subsection (1)(a), (b), (c), or (d). These subsections cover three different areas of unconscionable conduct: (1) unconscionable contract terms, (2) fraudulent or unconscionable conduct in inducing persons to enter into transactions, and (3) fraudulent or unconscionable conduct in the collection of consumer credit debts.

2. One purpose of this section is to afford the Administrator a means of dealing with new patterns of fraudulent or unconscionable conduct unforeseen and, perhaps, unforeseeable at the writing of this Act. Another is to give. him a more flexible remedy for halting reprehensible creditor practices that have been specifically and somewhat rigidly treated in previous consume r credit legislation. For instance, this Act has no specific prohibition against the creditor's allowing the consumer to sign a credit agreement containing blanks. In some situations there may be legitimate reasons for a contract to contain blanks at the time of signing. However, if the creditor deliberately leaves blanks to be filled in after the consumer's signature and without his consent, the Administrator may seek to restrain the practice as fraudulent or unconscionable conduct under this section.

3. Subsections (3) and (4) refer to a number of specific factors to be considered on the issue of unconscionability which are listed in Section 5.108. The illustrative individual transactions described in the Comment to Section 5.108, if engaged in by a person to whom this Part applies as a course of conduct, would entitle the Administrator to injunctive relief under this section.

4. Subsection (5) prohibits a finding that a charge or practice expressly permitted by this Act is in itself unconscionable. However, even though a practice or charge is autho-

rized by this Act, the totality of a particular creditor's conduct may show that the practice or charge is part of an unconscionable course of conduct. Therefore, in determining unconscionability, the creditor's total conduct, including that part of his conduct which is in accordance with the provisions of this Act, may be considered.

5. For cases illustrating the prior application of the doctrine of unconscionability in private actions, see Comment to Section 5.108. This doctrine was applied in an action by a public official in State by Lefkowitz v. ITM, Inc., 52 Misc.2d 39, 275 N.Y.S.2d 308 (Sup.Ct.1966).

UNIFORM CONSUMER SALES PRACTICES ACT[6]

§ 1. Purposes, Rules of Construction

This Act shall be construed liberally to promote the following policies:

(1) to simplify, clarify, and modernize the law governing consumer sales practices;

(2) to protect consumers from suppliers who commit deceptive and unconscionable sales practices;

(3) to encourage the development of fair consumer sales practices;

(4) to make state regulation of consumer sales practices not inconsistent with the policies of the Federal Trade Commission Act relating to consumer protection; and

(5) to make uniform the law, including the administrative rules, with respect to the subject of this Act among those states which enact it.

§ 2. Definitions

As used in this, Act:

(1) "consumer transaction" means a sale, lease, assignment, award by chance, or other disposition of an item of goods, a service, or an intangible [except securities] to an individual for purposes that are primarily personal, family, or household, or that relate to a business opportunity that requires both his expenditure of money or property and his personal services on a continuing basis and in which he has not been previously engaged, or a solicitation by a supplier with respect to any of these dispositions;

(2) "Enforcing Authority" means [appropriate official or officials];

(3) "final judgment" means a judgment, including any supporting opinion, that determines the rights of the parties and concerning which appellate remedies have been exhausted or the time for appeal has expired;

(4) "person" means an individual, corporation, government, governmental subdivision or agency, business trust, estate, trust, partnership, association, cooperative, or any other legal entity;

6. Enacted in Kansas, Ohio, and Utah.

(5) "supplier" means a seller, lessor, assignor, or other person who regularly solicits, engages in, or enforces consumer transactions, whether or not he deals directly with the consumer.

§ 3. Deceptive Consumer Sales Practices

(a) A deceptive act or practice by a supplier in connection with a consumer transaction violates this Act whether it occurs before, during, or after the transaction.

(b) Without limiting the scope of subsection (a), the act or practice of a supplier. in indicating any of the following is deceptive:

(1) that the subject of a consumer transaction has sponsorship, approval, performance characteristics, accessories, uses, or benefits it does not have;

(2) that the subject of a consumer transaction is of a particular standard, quality, grade, style, or model, if it is not;

(3) that the subject of a consumer transaction is new, or unused, if it is not, or that, the subject of a consumer transaction has been used to an extent that is materially different from the fact;

(4) that the subject of a consumer transaction is. available to the consumer for a reason that does not exist;

(5) that the subject of a consumer transaction has been supplied in accordance with a previous representation, if it has not;

(6) that the subject of a consumer transaction will be supplied in greater quantity than the supplier intends;

(7) that replacement. or repair is needed, if it is not;

(8) that a specific price advantage exists, if it does not;

(9) that the supplier has a sponsorship, approval, or affiliation he does not have;

(10) that a consumer transaction involves or does not involve a warranty, a disclaimer of warranties, particular warranty terms, or other rights, remedies, or obligations if the indication is false; or

(11) that the consumer will receive a rebate, discount, or other benefit as an inducement for entering into a consumer transaction in return for giving the supplier the names of prospective consumers or otherwise helping the supplier to enter into other consumer transactions, if receipt of the benefit is contingent on an event occurring after the consumer enters into the transaction.

§ 4. Unconscionable Consumer Sales Practices

(a) An unconscionable act or practice by a supplier in connection with a consumer transaction violates this Act whether it occurs before, during, or after the transaction.

(b) The unconscionability of an act or practice is a question of law for the court. If it is claimed or appears to the court that an act or practice may be unconscionable, the parties shall be given a reasonable opportunity to present evidence as to its setting, purpose, and effect to aid the court in making its determination.

(c) In determining whether an act or practice is unconscionable, the court shall consider circumstances such as the following of which the supplier knew or had reason to know:

(1) that he took advantage of the inability of the consumer reasonably to protect his interests because of his physical infirmity, ignorance, illiteracy, inability to understand the language of an agreement, or similar factors;

(2) that when the consumer transaction was entered into the price grossly exceeded the. price at which similar property or services were readily obtainable in similar transaction by like consumers;

(3) that when the consumer transaction was entered into the consumer was unable to receive a substantial benefit from the subject of the transaction;

(4) that when the consumer transaction was entered into there was no reasonable probability of payment of the obligation in full by the consumer;

(5) that the transaction he induced the consumer to enter into was excessively one-sided in favor of the supplier; or,

(6) that he made a misleading statement of opinion on which the consumer was. likely to rely to his detriment.

§ 5. Duties of the Enforcing Authority

(a) The Enforcing Authority shall:

(1) enforce this Act throughout the State;

(2) cooperate with state and local officials, officials of other states, and officials of the Federal government in the administration of comparable statutes;

(3) inform consumers and suppliers on a continuing basis of the provisions of this Act and of acts or practices that violate this Act, including mailing information concerning final judgments to persons who request, it, for which he may charge a reasonable fee to cover the expense;

(4) receive and act on complaints;

(5) maintain a public file of (i) final judgments rendered under this Act that have been either reported officially or made available for public dissemination under Section 5(a)(3), (ii) final consent judgments, and (iii), to the extent the Enforcing Authority considers appropriate, assurances of voluntary compliance; and

(6) report [annually on or before January 1] to the (Governor and Legislature) on the operations of his office and on the acts or practices occurring in this State that violate this Act.

(b) The Enforcing Authority's report shall include a statement of the investigatory and enforcement procedures and policies of his office, of the number of investigations and enforcement proceedings instituted and of their disposition, and of the other activities of his office and of other persons to carry out the purposes of this Act.

(c) In carrying out his duties, the Enforcing Authority may not publicly disclose the identity of a person investigated unless his identity has become a matter of public record in an enforcement proceeding or he has consented to public disclosure.

§ 6. General Powers of the Enforcing Authority

(a) The Enforcing Authority may conduct research, hold public hearings, make inquiries, and publish studies relating to consumer sales acts or practices.

(b) The Enforcing Authority shall adopt substantive rules that prohibit with specificity acts or practices that violate Section 3 and appropriate procedural rules.

§ 9. Remedies of the Enforcing Authority

(a) The Enforcing Authority may bring an action:

(1) to obtain a declaratory judgment that an act or practice violates this Act; or

(2) to enjoin, in accordance with the principles of equity, a supplier who has violated, is violating, or is otherwise likely to violate this Act;

(3) to recover actual damages, or obtain relief under subsection (b)(2), on behalf of consumers who complained to the Enforcing Authority before he instituted enforcement proceedings under this Act.

(b)(1) The Enforcing Authority may bring a class action on behalf of consumers for the actual damages caused by an act or practice specified as violating this Act in a rule adopted by the Enforcing Authority under Section 6(b) before the consumer transactions on which the action is based, or declared to violate Section 3 or 4 by final judgment of [insert the appropriate court or courts of general jurisdiction and appellate courts] of this State that was either reported officially or made available for public dissemination under Section 5(a)(3) by the Enforcing Authority [10] days before the consumer transactions on which the action is based, or, with respect to a supplier who agreed to it, was prohibited specifically by the terms of a consent judgment that became final before the consumer transactions on which the action is based.

(2) On motion of the Enforcing Authority and without bond in an action under this subsection, the court may make appropriate orders, including appointment of a master or receiver or sequestration of assets, to reimburse consumers found to have been damaged, or to carry out a transaction in accordance with consumers' reasonable expectations, or to strike or limit the application of unconscionable clauses of contracts to avoid an unconscionable result, or to grant other appropriate relief. The court may assess the expenses of A master or receiver against a supplier.

(3) If a supplier shows by a preponderance of the evidence that a violation of this Act resulted from a bona fide error notwithstanding the maintenance of procedures reasonably adapted to avoid the error, recovery under Section 9(b) is limited to the amount, if any, by which the supplier was unjustly enriched by the violation.

(4) If an act or practice that violates this Act unjustly enriches a supplier and damages can be computed with reasonable certainty, damages recoverable on behalf of consumers who cannot be located with due diligence [shall escheat to the State] [shall be allocated under the Uniform Disposition of Unclaimed Property Act].

(5) No action may be brought by the Enforcing Authority under this subsection more than 2 years after the occurrence of a violation of this Act, or more than one year after the last payment in a consumer transaction involved in a violation of this Act, whichever is later.

(c) The Enforcing Authority may terminate an investigation or an action other than a class action upon acceptance of a supplier's written assurance of voluntary compliance with this Act. Acceptance of an assurance may be conditioned on a commitment to reimburse consumers or take other appropriate corrective action. An assurance is not evidence of a prior violation of this Act. However, unless an assurance has been rescinded by agreement of the parties or voided by a court for good cause, subsequent failure to comply with the terms of an assurance is prima facie evidence of a violation of this Act.

§ 11. Private Remedies

(a) Whether he seeks or is entitled to damages or has an adequate remedy at law, a consumer may bring an action to:

(1) obtain a declaratory judgment that an act or practice violates this Act; or

(2) enjoin, in accordance with the principles of equity, a supplier who has violated, is violating, or is otherwise likely to violate this Act.

(b) Except in a class action, a consumer who suffers loss as a result of a violation of this Act may recover actual damages or [$100], whichever is greater.

(c) Whether a consumer seeks or is entitled to recover damages or has an adequate remedy at law, he may bring a class action for declaratory judgment, an injunction, and appropriate ancillary relief, except damages, against an act or practice that violates this Act.

(d)(1) A consumer who suffers loss as a result of a violation of this Act may bring a class action for the actual damages caused by an act or practice (i) specified as violating this Act in a rule adopted by the Enforcing Authority under Section 6(b) before the consumer transactions on which the action is based, or (ii) declared to violate Section 3 or 4 by a final judgment of [insert the appropriate court or courts of general jurisdiction and appellate courts] of this State that was either reported officially or made available for public dissemination under Section 5(a)(3) by the Enforcing Authority 101 days before the consumer transaction on which the action is based, or (iii) with respect to a supplier who agreed to it, was prohibited specifically by the terms of a consent judgment which became final before the consumer transactions on which the action is based.

(2) If a supplier shows by a preponderance of the evidence that a violation of this Act resulted from a bona fide error notwithstanding the maintenance of procedures reasonably adapted it to avoid the error, recovery under this section is limited to the amount, if any, by which the supplier was unjustly enriched by the violation.

(3) If an act or practice that violates this Act unjustly enriches a supplier and the damages can be computed with reasonable certainty, damages recoverable on behalf of consumers who cannot be located with due diligence [shall escheat to the State] [shall be allocated under the Uniform Disposition of Unclaimed Property Act].

(e) Except for services performed by the Enforcing Authority, the court may award to the prevailing party a reasonable attorney's fee limited to the work reasonably performed if:

(1) the consumer complaining of the act or practice that violates this Act has brought or maintained an action he knew to be groundless; or a supplier has committed an act or practice that violates this Act; and

(2) an action under this section has been terminated by a judgment or required by the court to be settled under Section 13(a).

(f) Except for consent judgments entered before testimony is taken, a final judgment in favor of the Enforcing Authority under Section 9 is admissible as prima facie evidence of the facts on which it is based in later proceedings under this section against the same person or a person in privity with him.

(g) When a judgment under this section becomes final, the prevailing party shall mail a copy to the Enforcing Authority for inclusion in the public file maintained under Section 5(a)(5).

(h) An action under this section must be brought within 2 years after occurrence of a violation of this Act, within one year after the last payment in a consumer transaction involved in a violation of this Act, or within one year after the termination of proceedings by the Enforcing Authority with respect to a violation of this Act, whichever is later. However, when a supplier sues a consumer, he may assert as a counterclaim any claim under this Act arising out of the transaction on which suit is brought.

§ 12. Class Actions

(a) An action may be maintained as a class action under this Act only if:

(1) the class is so numerous that joinder of all members is impracticable;

(2) there are questions of law or fact common to the class;

(3) the claims or defenses of the representative parties are typical of the claims or defenses of the class;

(4) the representative parties will fairly and adequately protect the interests of the class; and

(5) either:

(A) the prosecution of separate actions by or against individual members of the class would create a risk of:

(i) inconsistent or varying adjudications with respect to individual members of the class which would establish incompatible standards of conduct for the party opposing the class; or

(ii) adjudications with respect to individual members of the class which would as a practical matter be dispositive of the interests of the other members not parties to the adjudications or substantially impair or impede their ability to protect their interests; or

(B) the party opposing the class has acted or refused to act on grounds generally applicable to the class, thereby making appropriate final injunctive relief or corresponding declaratory relief with respect to the class as a whole; or

(C) the court finds that the questions of law or fact common to the members of the class predominate over any questions affecting only individual members, and that a class action is superior to other available methods for the fair and efficient adjudication of the controversy.

(b) The matters pertinent to the findings under subsection (a)–(5)(C) include:

(1) the interest of members of the class in individually controlling the prosecution or defense of separate actions;

(2) the extent and nature of any, litigation concerning the controversy already commenced by or against members of the class;

(3) the desirability or undesirability of concentrating the litigation of the claims in the particular forum; and

(4) the difficulties likely to be encountered in the management of a class action.

(c) As soon as practicable after the commencement of an action brought as a class action, the court shall determine by order whether it is to be so maintained. An order under this subsection may be conditional, and may be amended before the decision on the merits.

(d) In a class action maintained under subsection (a)(5)(C) the court may direct to the members of the class the best notice practicable under the circumstances, including individual notice to all members who can be identified through reasonable effort. The notice shall advise each member that:

(1) the court will exclude him from the class, if he requests by a specified date;

(2) the judgment, whether favorable or not, will include all members who do not request exclusion; and

(3) any member who does not request exclusion may, if he desires, enter an appearance through his counsel.

(e) When appropriate, an action may be brought or maintained as a class action with respect to particular issues, or a class may be divided into subclasses and each subclass treated as a class.

(f) In the conduct of a class action the court may make appropriate orders:

(1) determining the course of proceedings or prescribing measures to prevent undue repetition or complication in the presentation of evidence or argument;

(2) requiring, for the protection of the members of the class or otherwise for the fair conduct of the action, that notice be given in the manner the court directs to some or all of the members or to the Enforcing Authority of any step in the action, or of the proposed extent of the judgment, or of the opportunity of members to signify whether they consider the representation fair and adequate, to intervene and present claims or defenses, or otherwise to come into the action;

(3) imposing conditions on the representative parties or on intervenors;

(4) requiring that the pleadings be amended to eliminate allegations as to representation of absent persons, and that the action proceed accordingly; or

(5) dealing with similar procedural matters.

(g) A class action shall not be dismissed or compromised without approval of the court. Notice of the proposed dismissal or compromise shall be given to all members of the class in such manner as the court directs.

(h) The judgment in an action maintained as a class action under subsection (a)(5)(A) or (B), whether or not favorable to the class, shall describe those whom the court finds to be members of the class. The judgment in a class action maintained under subsection (a)(5)(C), whether or not favorable to the class, shall specify or describe those to whom the notice provided in subsection (d) was directed, and who have not requested exclusion, and whom the court finds to be members of the class.

§ 13. Special Provisions Relating to Class Actions

(a)(1) A defendant in a class action may file a written offer of settlement. If it is not accepted within a reasonable time by a plaintiff class representative, the defendant may file an affidavit reciting the rejection. The court may determine that the offer has enough merit to present to the members of the class. If it so determines, it shall order a hearing to determine whether the offer should be approved. It shall give the best notice of the hearing that is practicable under the circumstances, including notice to each member who can be identified through reasonable effort. The notice shall specify the terms of the offer and a reasonable period within which members of the class who request it are entitled to be excluded from the class. The statute of limitations for those who are excluded pursuant to this subsection is tolled for the period the class action has been pending, plus an additional year.

(2) If a member who has previously lost an opportunity to be excluded from the class is excluded at his request in response to notice of the offer of settlement during the period specified under paragraph (1), he may not thereafter participate in a class action respecting the same consumer transaction, unless the court later disapproves the offer of settlement or approves a settlement materially different from that proposed in the original offer of settlement. After the expiration of the period specified under paragraph (1), a member of the class is not entitled to be excluded from it.

(3) If the court later approves the offer of settlement, including changes, if any, required by the court in the interest of a just settlement of the action, it shall enter a judgment, which is binding on all persons who are then members of the class. If the court disapproves the offer or approves a settlement materially different from that proposed in the original offer, notice shall be given to a person who was excluded from the action at his request in response to notice of the offer under paragraph (1) that he is entitled to rejoin the class, and, in the case of approval, participate in the settlement,

(b) On the commencement of a class action under Section 11, the class representative shall mail by certified mail with return receipt requested or personally serve a copy of the complaint on the Enforcing Authority. Within 30 days after the receipt of a copy of the complaint, but not thereafter, the Enforcing Authority may intervene in the class action.

§ 14. Application

(a) This Act does not apply to:

(1) an act or practice required or specifically permitted by or under Federal law, or by or under State law;

(2) a publisher, broadcaster, printer, or other person engaged in the dissemination of information or the reproduction of printed or pictorial matter insofar as the information or matter has been disseminated or reproduced on behalf of others without actual knowledge that it violated this Act;

(3) a claim for personal injury or death or a claim for damage to property other than the property that is the subject of the consumer transaction; or

(4) the credit terms of a transaction otherwise subject to this Act.

(b) A person alleged to have violated this Act has the burden of showing the applicability of this Section.

§ 15.   Effect on Other Remedies

The remedies of this Act are in addition to remedies otherwise available for the same conduct under state or local law, except that a class action relating to a transaction governed by this Act may be brought only as prescribed by this Act.

———

UNIFORM DECEPTIVE TRADE PRACTICES ACT[7]

1966 Revision

§ 2.   Deceptive Trade Practices

(a) A person engages in a deceptive trade practice when, in the course of his business, vocation, or occupation, he:

(9) advertises goods or services with intent not to sell them as advertised;

(10) advertises goods or services with intent not to supply reasonably expectable public demand, unless the advertisement discloses a limitation of quantity;

COMMENT

Subsections 2(a)(9) and 2(a)(10) deal with "bait advertising," a practice by which a seller seeks to attract customers through advertising at low prices products which he does not intend to sell in more than nominal amounts. When prospective buyers respond to the advertisement, sale of the "bait" is discouraged through various artifices including disparagement and exhaustion of a minuscule stock in order to induce purchase of unadvertised goods on which there is a greater mark-up. A bait advertising scheme which involved disparagement has been held enjoinable at common law by the manufacturer of the "bait." Electrolux Corp. v. ValWorth, Inc., 6 N.Y.2d 556, 161 N.E.2d 197, 190 N.Y.S.2d 977 (1959). A Connecticut statute similarly authorizes private parties to enjoin bait advertising. Conn. Gen.Stat.Ann. § 42–115(a) (Supp.1962). Odd lot or clearance sales in which bargains are offered in limited quantities will not run afoul of the proposed statute as long as disclosure is made of the limited stock. Cf. ibid.

(12) engages in any other conduct which similarly creates a likelihood of confusion or of misunderstanding.

(b) In order to prevail in an action under this Act, a complainant need not prove competition between the parties or actual confusion or misunderstanding.

---

7. Enacted in Colorado, Georgia, Hawaii, Minnesota, Nebraska, New Mexico, Ohio and Oregon.

(c) This section does not affect unfair trade practices otherwise actionable at common law or under other statutes of this state.

§ 3. Remedies

(a) A person likely to be damaged by a deceptive trade practice of another may be granted an injunction against it under the principles of equity and on terms that the court considers reasonable. Proof of monetary damage, loss of profits, or intent to deceive is not; required. Relief granted for the copying of an article shall be limited to the prevention of confusion or misunderstanding as to source.

(b) Costs shall be allowed to the prevailing party unless the court otherwise directs. The court [in its discretion] may award attorneys' fees to the prevailing party if (1) the party complaining of a deceptive trade practice has brought an action which he knew to be groundless or (2) the party charged with a deceptive trade practice has willfully engaged in the, trade practice knowing it to be deceptive.

(c) The relief provided in this section is, in addition to remedies otherwise available against the same conduct under the common law or other statutes of this state.

§ 4. Application

(a) This Act does not apply to:

(1) conduct in compliance with the orders or rules of, or a statute administered by, a federal, state, or local governmental agency;

(2) publishers, broadcasters, printers, or other persons engaged in the dissemination of information or reproduction of printed or pictorial matters who publish, broadcast, or reproduce material without knowledge of its deceptive character; or

(3) actions or appeals pending on the effective date of this Act.

(b) Subsections 2(a)(2) and 2(a)(3) do not apply to, the use of a service mark, trademark, certification mark, collective mark, trade name, or other trade identification that was used and not abandoned before the effective date of this Act, if the use was in good faith and is otherwise lawful except for this Act.

———

UNIFORM LAND TRANSACTIONS ACT[8]

ARTICLE 2

PART I
SHORT TITLE, GENERAL CONSTRUCTION, AND SUBJECT MATTER

§ 2–101. Short Title

This Article shall be known and may be cited as Uniform Land Transactions Act—Contracts and Conveyances.

COMMENT

This Article deals with contracts to sell and sales of real estate. It undertakes to bring uniformity and certainty to real estate transactions in the same way that the Uniform Sales Act in the early years of this century first brought uniformity and certainty to the law of the sale of goods. It also modernizes the law of real estate sales by, among other things, imposing implied warranties of quality and limiting the effectiveness of warranty disclaimers (particularly in consumer transactions).

The Article also simplifies the law by making the law applicable to sales of real estate conform to the law applicable to sales of goods except insofar as differences in the character of real estate justify a different law. In that regard, this Article follows the general organizational framework of the Uniform Commercial Code, Article 2–Sales. The rules or principles of the Uniform Commercial Code have been adopted unless good reason appeared not to do so.

§ 2–102. Scope

This Article applies to contracts to convey real estate other than conveyances of security interests (Article 3).

COMMENT

Under this Act, real estate includes rents and the interest of a landlord or tenant. See Section 1–201(16). Therefore, this Article applies to leases (of whatever duration) as well as to sales of freehold interests. It also applies to sales of all interests in land, such as mineral rights, easements, or restrictions.

This Article states the rules or principles applicable to the contract of

sale. The rules stated are primarily "gap-filling" rules. They state the applicable rules if the parties have not contracted with respect to a particular matter and are subject to contrary agreement by the parties. There are, however, some rules stated which are not subject to contrary agreement (e.g., Section 2–201 on the statute of frauds) and some sections which can be varied only according to rules stat-

8. As amended 1977. The ULTA is a large integrated act, similar to the UCC. The sections included here cannot be used in their proper context without examination of the remainder of the act, especially other sections

of Article 2 and Article 1. Answers to questions in the principal book relating to these sections can, therefore, be given only tentatively without checking a complete ULTA.

ed in this Article. (See Section 2–311 on disclaimer of warranties of quality, Section 2–516 on liquidated damages, and Section 2–517 on limitation or modification of remedy.)

The formal requisites necessary for an effective conveyance or for a recordable instrument of conveyance and the rights of either the buyer or the seller against third parties are not specified by this Article. (See, however, Sections 2–508 and 2–512 on Seller's and Buyer's Liens.)

This Article does not apply to gifts.

§ 2–103. Definitions

In this Article unless the context otherwise requires:

(1) "Contract to convey" includes a conveyance as well as an option or contract to convey real estate at a future time.

(2) "Seller" means a person who for value conveys or contracts to convey real estate. A broker or an agent acting for disclosed person and not for his own account is not a seller.

PART 4

§ 2–406. Risk of Loss, Casualty Loss, Real Estate Other than Leaseholds

(a) This section does not apply to transfers of leaseholds.

(b) Risk of loss or of taking by eminent domain and owner's liabilities remain on the seller until the occurrence of the events specified in subsection (c). In case of a casualty loss or taking by eminent domain while the risk is on the seller:

(1) if the loss or taking results in a substantial failure of the real estate to conform to the contract, the buyer may cancel the contract and recover any portion of the price he has paid, or accept the real estate with his choice of (i) a reduction of the contract price equal to the decrease in fair market value caused by the loss or taking, or (ii) the benefit of the seller's insurance coverage or the eminent domain payment for the loss or taking, but without further right against the seller; or

(2) if the real estate substantially conforms to the contract after the loss or taking, the buyer must accept the real estate, but is entitled to his choice of (i) a reduction of the contract price equal to the decrease in fair market value caused by the loss or taking or (ii) the benefit of the seller's insurance coverage or the eminent domain payment with respect to the loss or taking but without further right against the seller.

(c) Risk of loss or taking and owner's liabilities pass to the buyer:

(1) if sale is not to be consummated by means of an escrow, at the earlier of delivery of the instrument of conveyance or transfer of possession of the real estate to him; or

101

(2) if sale is to be consummated by means of an escrow, at the earlier of transfer of possession or fulfillment of the conditions of the escrow.

(d) Any loss or taking of the real estate after risk of loss or taking has passed to the buyer does not discharge him from his obligations under the contract of purchase.

(e) For the purposes of any provision of law imposing obligations or liabilities upon the holder of legal title, title does not pass to the buyer until he accepts the instrument of conveyance.

COMMENT

1. Subsection (c) adopts the position, first taken by the Uniform Vendor and Purchaser Risk Act, promulgated in 1935 by the National Conference of Commissioners on Uniform State Laws, that risk of loss or of taking by eminent domain does not pass to the buyer until he has possession or the instrument of conveyance has been delivered to him. This Act thus rejects the rule presently applied in many states that, because of the doctrine of equitable conversion, the risk of loss passes to the buyer immediately upon the making of the contract of purchase. In the case of a transaction handled by an escrow, the performance of the conditions of the escrow are treated as the equivalent of a delivery of the instrument of conveyance. If either party is at fault in causing a loss, the loss falls on him: this section applies only in the absence of fault.

2. Even though there is substantial damage to, or taking of, real estate while the risk is still on the seller, the buyer may, if he chooses, enforce the contract. If he enforces, he is entitled to a diminution of the purchase price for the loss or taking, or he may pay the fall purchase price and receive the benefit of seller's insurance proceeds or condemnation award. If the buyer chooses to enforce the contract with a diminution in price, he is entitled to a reduction based only on the decrease in value of the real estate. He is not entitled to any reduction based on any additional injury or harm caused to him by the destruction.

3. If, after a loss or taking the risk of which is on the seller, the real estate still substantially conforms to the contract, the buyer is obligated to accept the real estate, but with a diminution in price or the benefit of seller's insurance or condemnation payment.

4. This Act does not state risk of loss rules for leasehold estates: that law is left to further case law development.

PART 5

§ 2–505. Seller's Damages for Non–Acceptance or Repudiation

(a) Except as provided in subsection (b), if a buyer has not accepted real estate, the measure of damages for a buyer's wrongful rejection, other material breach, or repudiation of a substantial part of the contract (Section 2–502(a)), is the amount by which the unpaid contract price and any incidental and consequential damages (Section 2–507) exceeds the fair market value of the real estate at the time for conveyance under the contract, less expenses avoided because of the buyer's breach.

(b) If the measure of damages specified in subsection (a) i3 inadequate to put the seller in as good a position as performance would have, the measure of damages is the profit the seller would have made from full performance by the buyer, and any incidental and consequential damages (Section 2–507), less expenses avoided because of the buyer's breach.

COMMENT

A seller who, after the buyer's repudiation or refusal to accept, is not entitled, or does not elect to seek a recovery based on the difference between the contract price and the resale price under the previous section may recover damages under this section. (In limited situations he may be entitled to the price under the next section.) Under this section, the usual recovery will be the difference between the contract price and the fair market value of the real estate at the time for conveyance together with incidental and consequential damages, but less expenses saved because of buyer's breach. Having sold a unique piece of land that can only be sold once, seller is fully compensated if he receives the difference between the contract price and the market price. However, a seller may be able to establish that his total sales have diminished as a result of buyer's breach, and, in such a case, he should be able to recover lost profits. That is, there may be cases in which real estate, or at least a builder-seller's labor, is fungible for the purposes of damages theory. If the seller can establish that his total sales have been diminished by reason of buyer's breach, he may recover lost profits under subsection (b).

This section derives from UCC, Section 2–708.

§ 2–506. Seller's Action for the Price

(a) If a buyer fails to make a payment on the price of real estate accepted (Section 2–502(c)), the seller may recover the amount due on the price.

(b) A seller may also recover the unpaid contract price of real estate not accepted as provided in Section 2–502(a), but only if the seller is unable after a reasonable effort to resell it at a reasonable price or the circumstances reasonably indicate the effort will be unavailing.

(c) If the seller sues for the unpaid contract price of real estate the title to which he has retained, he must hold it for the buyer but may resell the real estate as a unit or in parcels at any time before collection of the judgment. Any resale after judgment is for the account of the buyer. Payment of the judgment entitles the buyer to a conveyance of the unsold real estate.

(d) A recovery under this section may include incidental and consequential damages (Section 2–507).

COMMENT

1. This section abandons the existing rule under which a seller of a freehold interest is automatically entitled to specific performance. An action for the price is, of course, the substantial equivalent of a seller's right to specific performance. Under this Act, if the real estate is resalable, a resale under Section 2–504 and recovery of the difference between the resale price and the contract price plus other damages will put the seller in substantially the position in which specific performance has put him under prior law. Therefore, this section gives the seller the right to the price of the real estate only where it is not resalable at a reasonable price with reasonable effort. The action for the price is not for specific performance and is not an action "in equity."

2. Even though a seller has instituted suit for the price, he may, if possible, resell the real estate. If he does so before judgment, he is, of course, not entitled to a judgment for the price, but may be entitled to recover under Section 2–504, if he has complied with the resale provisions of that section, or may recover damages under Section 2–505. A resale after judgment is for the account of the buyer. Therefore, the seller, in the after judgment sale, is a quasi-fiduciary in connection with the sale and has an obligation to the judgment-debtor to resell reasonably and in good faith. The price received in the after-judgment sale, after deduction of the expenses of sale, is to be credited to the judgment. If there is a surplus, it belongs to the buyer.

This section is similar to UCC, Section 2–709.

§ 2–507. Seller's Incidental and Consequential Damages

(a) Incidental damages to a seller include any reasonable out-of-pocket expenses or commissions incurred because of the buyer's breach.

(b) Consequential damages resulting from a buyer's breach include any loss the buyer at the time of contracting had reason to know would result from the breach and which reasonably could not be prevented.

COMMENT

1. A seller, whether he seeks the price (Section 2–506), the difference between the sales price and the resale price (Section 2–504), the difference between the sales price and the fair market value (Section 2–505(a)), or lost profit (Section 2–505(b)), is also entitled to recover incidental and consequential damages. This section states the elements of those damages.

2. Incidental damages are reasonable out-of-pocket expenses incurred because of the breach. There is no requirement of foresee ability as to incidental damages. The breaching buyer is protected from excessive incidental damage claims by the requirement that they be reasonable.

3. Consequential damages extend beyond out-of-pocket expenses to cover any foreseeable loss which the seller could not reasonably avoid. As to consequential damages, this section, therefore, continues the well-established contract rules relating to foresee ability and mitigation of damages.

4. This section, unlike UCC, Section 2–710, on which it is based, specifically allows a seller to recover consequential, as well as incidental,

damages. It may be that, in the usual case, a buyer reasonably could not foresee any consequential damages arising from his refusal to purchase. However, if such damages are foreseeable, there is no reason that the seller should not recover them.

§ 2–509. Buyer's Remedies

(a) Subject to the provisions on liquidated damages and modification of remedies (Sections 2–516 and 2–517), if a seller wrongfully fails to convey or repudiates with respect to a substantial part of the contract, or the buyer rightfully refuses to accept or rightfully revokes his acceptance, the buyer has a lien on the real estate for any part of the contract price already paid (Section 2–514), and may:

    (1) recover any part of the price already paid and damages for failure to perform or repudiation (Section 2–510); or

    (2) have specific performance of the contract (Section 2–511).

(b) If a seller breaches with respect to real estate accepted, the buyer may:

    (1) under the conditions stated in the provisions on revocation of acceptance (Section 2–402), revoke his acceptance and recover damages; or

    (2) recover damages for breach of contract (Section 2–513) or deduct his damages from the price still due (Section 2–515).

(c) If a seller's repudiation is not of a substantial part of the contract, the buyer may recover any damages sustained by him as a result of the repudiation and, if the repudiation impairs his expectation of securing substantial performance, demand assurances (Section 2–403).

COMMENT

1. This section is an index section which gathers together in one convenient place all of the various remedies open to a buyer for any breach by the seller. This Article rejects any doctrine of election of remedy as a fundamental policy and thus the remedies are essentially cumulative in nature and include all available remedies for breach. Whether the pursuit of one remedy bars another depends entirely on the facts of the individual case.

2. Subsection (a) catalogs remedies for substantial breach when the buyer fails to accept or revokes his acceptance; subsection (b) the remedies in case of accepted real estate; and subsection (c) the remedies for nonsubstantial repudiation. If a buyer has properly revoked acceptance (subsection (b)(2)) his remedies are those described in subsection (a).

3. No section of the Act specifies the buyer's damages for a non-substantial repudiation, but Section 1–106 provides that remedies provided by the Act are to be liberally construed to put the aggrieved party in as good a position as he would have been had the other party performed.

§ 2–510. Buyer's Damages for Seller's Failure to Convey

(a) Except as provided in subsection (b), the measure of damages for a seller's repudiation or wrongful failure to convey is the difference between the fair market value at the time for conveyance and the contract price and any incidental and consequential damages (Section 2–514), less expenses avoided because of the seller's breach.

(b) Unless the title defect is an encumbrance securing an obligation to pay money which could be discharged by application of all or a portion of the purchase price, if a seller is unable to convey because of a title defect of which the seller had no knowledge at the time of entering into the contract, the buyer is entitled only to restitution of any amounts paid on the contract price and incidental damages (Section 2–514).

COMMENT

1. Buyer's right to recover damages for seller's failure to convey under this section is alternative to his right to specific performance under the next section. Ordinarily, a buyer will have his choice of seeking recovery under this section or seeking specific performance. Except as provided in subsection (b) as to inability based on certain encumbrances, the measure of damages is the difference between the contract price and the fair market value at the time for conveyance plus incidental and consequential damages.

2. The difference between the contract price and fair market value is to be measured as of the time for conveyance, rather than the time of breach. The time for conveyance measure plus incidental and consequential damages is more likely to fairly compensate the buyer than damages based upon difference in contract and market price at the time of breach. The Act provides no special rule for cases in which the trial takes place prior to the time for conveyance, In such cases, it should be remembered that any difficulties or uncertainties as to damages have been caused by seller's breach and that, therefore, the buyer should riot be deprived of his remedy because of the difficulties of proof. In many cases it may be appropriate to allow the issue of damages to go to the finder of fact upon a showing of the difference between market value and contract price as of the time of trial.

3. If the seller is unable to perform because of a title defect of which he had no knowledge at the time of entering into the contract, buyer's remedy is limited to restitution of amounts paid and incidental damages. Under prior law, many courts allowed loss of bargain damages against a seller who was unable to perform because of an unknown title defect. At the same time, practically all jurisdictions limited a buyer to return of the purchase price if, after the conveyance, it was discovered that seller's title was defective. In pre-acceptance cases in which the seller is without knowledge of the title defect, this Act limits the buyer to the damages he would be entitled to after acceptance. See Section 2–513 as to damages after acceptance.

The question whether "warranty" analysis imposing loss of bargain liability on the seller or "mistake" analysis with only restitution liability should apply to unknown defects either of quality or of title is not an easy policy issue. In the case of unknown, title defects, this Act chooses "mistake" analysis as more consistent with general expectations given the difficulties of title examination, the small likelihood that a seller has reason to doubt his title, and the nearly universal practice of title examination prior to closing. For the rules under this Act as to seller's liability for breach of title warranties under a conveyance see Section 2–513(b) and the comments thereto.

4. Unless he has revoked his acceptance under Section 2–402, a lessee who has entered into possession and is thereafter dispossessed by a paramount title holder, or justifiably terminates the lease for other breach by the lessor, is not entitled to recover under this section. His remedy is under Section 2–513 on damages as to accepted real estate.

§ 2–511. Buyer's Right to Specific Performance

(a) Specific performance may be decreed against a seller. If the seller is unable to convey the full interest he contracted to convey because of a defect in title or otherwise, he may be compelled, except as provided in subsection (b) to convey the interest he has and to pay damages to the buyer (Section 2–513).

(b) If a seller is able to convey so small a part of the real estate he contracted to convey, in quantity, quality, or interest, as to make it inequitable specifically to enforce the contract and award damages for breach, the court may refuse specific performance or grant specific performance upon terms the court deems equitable.

COMMENT

This Act continues the existing law under which a buyer of real estate is entitled to specific performance. The existing equitable rules as to the right and limitations thereon are continued. A seller who secures, specific performance is also entitled to incidental and consequential damages.

Subsection (b) specifically recognizes a limitation on specific performance which has been applied by many courts.

§ 2–513. Buyer's Damages for Breach in Regard to Accepted Real Estate

If the buyer has accepted real estate he may recover:

(1) as damages for any breach of a warranty of quality, the difference at the time of acceptance between the value of the real estate and the value it would have had if it had been as warranted or, at his option, the cost of the repairs or improvements necessary to bring the real estate up to the quality warranted if the repair or improvement does not involve unreasonable economic waste, and, in either case, any incidental and consequential damages (Section 2–514).

(2) as damages for breach of warranty of title:

(i) the difference at the time of conveyance to the buyer between the value of the real estate and the value it would have had at that time if it had been as warranted, but if an encumbrance securing an obligation to pay money is involved the buyer may recover the cost incurred in good faith in discharging the encumbrance, but in either case the buyer may not recover more than the value of the consideration received by the particular seller for the real estate; and

(ii) any incidental damages (Section 2–514).

107

COMMENT

1. A buyer, including a lessee, has the option, under subsection (a), of charging the seller with the cost of repairs or improvements necessary to bring the real estate into compliance with the warranty terms of the contract unless that expenditure involves "unreasonable economic waste." While the unreasonable economic waste concept has been criticized, it is used in this Act as a desirable limitation on repair or improvement expense. As used in this Act, unreasonable economic waste is intended to be broader in concept than the sometimes stated case law limitation of destruction of an existing structure. For example, in the case of a lease the addition by the tenant of a partition promised by the landlord may not be justified where the cost of the partition is greatly out of proportion to the injury which its absence causes the tenant. In such a case, courts may, as they have in the past, take into account the good faith, or lack thereof, on the part of the landlord. In considering whether an improvement or repair on leased premises constitutes unreasonable economic waste, the value, or lack thereof, to the landlord at the end of the lease is a relevant consideration.

In case of a freehold estate, similarly, a repair or improvement to bring the real estate up to warranted quality may involve unreasonable economic waste even though no destruction of existing structures is involved. On the other hand, real estate buyers frequently contract for improvements or repairs which do not enhance the market value of the real, estate but rather advance esthetic or other notions of the buyer. Such buyers are entitled to get what they contracted for even though the expenditure does not, enhance the market value of the real estate, and, if the seller fails to perform his obligation, may be entitled to charge him with the cost of having another bring the real estate into compliance.

In addition to difference in value or cost of repair or improvements, a seller is entitled to incidental and consequential damages.

2. In the case of breaches of title warranties other than that involving a monetary encumbrance, the measure of damages is the difference in value, at the time of conveyance, between the real estate as is and as it would have been had it been as warranted but limited to the consideration received by the particular seller. If, for example, B purchased the real estate from A for $20,000, C purchased from B for $25,000 and C then loses the real estate to X who had title superior to that of A and B, C could recover $20,000 from A or $25,000 from B, plus, in either case, incidental damages. If C lost one half in value of the real estate to X, he could recover one-half the value of the real estate at the time he purchased from either A or B. If the purchase price and value were the same, C could recover $12,500, but, if he could show that the value was greater than the purchase price, he could recover one-half the value up to the consideration received by the defendant. That is, no matter who the defendant is, the damages are always measured by the difference in values, with and without the breach of warranty, at the time of the conveyance to the plaintiff, but remote defendants are never liable for more than the consideration they received.

The rule stated here is that followed in the great majority of states. See C. McCormick, Damages, sec. 185, 61 A.L.R. 11 (1929), 100 A.L.R. 1194 (1936). To the extent that real estate values increase after the sale, either because of increasing demand for real estate in the area, or because of improvements made by the buyer, the risk of title loss is on the buyer. While this result may seem harsh to the buyer there are sound reasons for the rule. Liability under title warranties is frequently imposed long after the sale. Under this Act all title warranties run to subsequent purchasers and as to some of the warranties, the statute of limitations does not begin running until the paramount title actually interferes with the buyer's possession. Therefore, in spite of adverse possession statutes, warranty claims may be made 15 or 20 years or more after the conveyance under which they arise. In that interval, land that was sold as relatively low priced farm or ranch land may have become extremely valuable residential, commercial, or industrial property. In such a case, the better policy probably continues to be that a seller has only to respond in damages based on values at the time of sale, rather than having to pay damages which may be ten or twenty or more times his contract price. Of course, it is true that loss of the real estate may cause heavy loss to the buyer. On the other hand, buyer can protect himself substantially by buying only after a title examination or, for even greater protection, purchasing title insurance. In the case of title insurance, the purchaser, at relatively small premium payments, can increase the insured amount under the title policy as the land becomes more valuable.

If the increase in value is the result of improvements made by the buyer, this Act, as already noted, denies a recovery under the title warranty for the value of the improvements. However, in practically all cases in which the improvements are lost to a paramount title holder, the paramount title holder, under the betterments statutes enacted in nearly all states, will either have to pay the buyer the value of the improvements or sell to him at a price which reflects the value of the land without the improvements. See J. Merryman, Improving the Lot of the Trespassing Improver, 11 Stan.L.Rev. 456 at 466, note 55, for a list of betterment statutes. Even in those few states which do not have betterment statutes, the same result may be reached on restitutionary principles. See Restatement of Restitution, Section 42.

It should be remembered that the damages rules of this section are subject to contract modification. If a buyer wishes to secure a greater obligation from a seller as to damages for title warranties, he may do so subject to the rules as to unconscionability and failure of essential purpose of remedies (see Section 2–517). A clause, for example, increasing liability by an inflation factor should be sustained.

In the case of a monetary encumbrance, costs incurred in good faith in discharging it are recoverable, but again not in excess of the contract price received by the particular defendant.

In addition to the recoveries discussed above, the buyer is also entitled to recover incidental damages which are described in Section 2–514. Those damages include the costs of defending the title, including attorney's fees.

§ 2–514. Buyer's Incidental and Consequential Damages

(a) Except as provided in subsection (b) as to mineral leases, incidental damages resulting from the seller's breach include out-of-pocket expenses reasonably incurred in inspection of the real estate, title examination, care and maintenance of the real. estate, defending the title, and any other reasonable out-of-pocket expense incident to the contract.

(b) In case of a mineral lease, incidental damages do not include expenses of defending the title, including attorney's fees; inspection of the real estate; title examination; or care and maintenance of the real estate other than expenses of protecting or maintaining the property imposed by the terms of the lease.

(c) Consequential damages resulting from the seller's breach include:

(1) any loss to the buyer which the seller at the time of contracting knew or had reason to know, would result from the seller's breach and which could not reasonably be avoided by the buyer; and

(2) injury to person or property proximately resulting from any breach of warranty.

(d) In the case of a mineral lease, the lessor's liability for consequential damages is limited to the return of any rentals or royalties received from the lessee.

COMMENT

1. A buyer, whether he seeks specific performance (Section 2–511), damages for failure to perform (Section 2–410), or damages with regard to accepted real estate (Section 2–513), also is entitled to recover incidental and consequential damages. This section states the elements of those damages.

2. Incidental damages are reasonable out-of-pocket expenses incurred because of the breach. There is no requirement of foreseeability as to incidental damages. The breaching seller is protected from excessive incidental damages claims by the requirement that they be reasonable.

3. Consequential damages extend beyond out-of-pocket loss to cover any foreseeable loss which the buyer could not reasonably avoid. As to consequential damages, therefore, this section continues the well-established contract rules relating to foreseeability and mitigation of damages.

However, in the case of physical injury to person or property, the test of liability is whether they "proximately resulted" from the breach, rather than whether they were foreseeable. * * *

UNIFORM VENDOR AND PURCHASER RISK ACT[9]

§ 1. Risk of Loss

Any contract hereafter made in this State for the purchase and sale of realty shall be interpreted as including an agreement that the parties shall

---

9. Since this act has been superseded as a Uniform Act by the Uniform Land Transac- tions Act, the Uniform Laws Annotated (Mas- ter Edition) no longer recognizes its exis-

have the following rights and duties, unless the contract expressly provides otherwise:

(a) If, when neither the legal title nor the possession of the subject matter of the contract has been transferred, all or a material part thereof is destroyed without fault of the purchaser or is taken by eminent domain, the vendor cannot enforce the contract, and the purchaser is entitled to recover any portion of the price that he has paid;

(b) If, when either the legal title or the possession of the-subject matter of the contract has been transferred, all or any part thereof is destroyed without fault of the vendor or is taken by eminent domain, the purchaser is not thereby relieved from a duty to pay the price, nor is he entitled to recover any portion thereof that he has paid. * * *

tence. As of 1967 it had been enacted in California, Hawaii, Illinois, Michigan, New York, North Carolina, Oklahoma, Oregon, South Dakota, Wisconsin. The New York version is a modification, see N.Y. Gen. Oblig. Law § 5–1311. None of these jurisdictions has enacted the ULTA.

PART III: STATE

ALABAMA CODE

Tit. 8

§ 8-1-1. Contracts Restraining Business Void; Exceptions

(a) Every contract by which anyone is restrained from exercising a lawful profession, trade or business of any kind otherwise than is provided by this section is to that extent void.

(b) One who sells the good will of a business may agree with the buyer and one who is employed as an agent, servant or employee may agree with his employer to refrain from carrying on or engaging in a similar business and from soliciting old customers of such employer within a specified county, city or part thereof so long as the buyer, or any person deriving title to the good will from him, or employer carries on a like business therein.

(c) Upon or in anticipation of a dissolution of the partnership, partners may agree that none of them will carry on a similar business within the same county, city or town, or within a specified. part thereof, where the partnership business has been transacted.

CALIFORNIA

AGRICULTURAL CODE[1]

§ 4201. Declaration of Facts

It is hereby declared that fluid milk and fluid cream are necessary articles of food for human consumption; that the production and maintenance of an adequate supply of healthful milk of proper chemical and physical content, free from contamination, is vital to the public health and welfare, and that the production, transportation, processing, storage, distribution or sale of fluid milk and fluid cream in the State of California is an industry affecting the public health and welfare; that unfair, unjust, destructive and demoralizing trade practices have been carried on and are now being carried on in the production, marketing, sale, processing or distribution of fluid milk and fluid cream, which constitute a constant menace to the health and welfare of the inhabitants of this State and tend to undermine sanitary regulations and standards of content and purity, however effectually such sanitary regulations may be enforced; that health regulations alone are insufficient to prevent disturbances in the milk industry which threaten to destroy and seriously impair the future supply of fluid milk; and to safeguard the consuming public from future inadequa-

1. This was the Code in effect prior to the 1967 Code.

cy of a supply of this necessary commodity; that it is the policy of this State to promote, foster and encourage the intelligent production and orderly marketing of commodities necessary to its citizens, including milk, and to eliminate speculation, waste, improper marketing, unfair and destructive trade practices, and improper accounting for milk purchased from producers.

§ 4280. Unfair Practices

Each stabilization and marketing plan shall contain provisions for prohibiting distributors and retail stores from engaging in the unfair practices hereinafter set forth:

(a) Rebates, discounts, etc. The payment, allowance or acceptance of secret rebates, secret refunds, or unearned discounts by any person, whether in the form of money or otherwise.

(b) Gifts. The giving of any milk, cream, dairy products, services or articles of any kind, except to bona fide charities, for the purpose of securing or retaining the fluid milk or fluid cream business of any customer. * * *

ARBITRATION ACT

CHAPTER 1.   GENERAL PROVISIONS

§ 1280.   Definitions

As used in this title:

(a) "Agreement" includes but is not limited to agreements providing for valuations, appraisals and similar proceedings and agreements between employers and employees or between their respective representatives.

(b) "Award" includes but is not limited to an award made pursuant to an agreement not in writing.

(c) "Controversy" means any question arising between parties to an agreement whether such question is one of law or of fact or both.

(d) "Neutral arbitrator" means an arbitrator who is (1) selected jointly by the parties or by the arbitrators selected by the parties or (2) appointed by the court when the parties or the arbitrators selected by the parties fail to select an arbitrator who was to be selected jointly by them.

(e) "Party to the arbitration" means a party to the arbitration agreement:

(1) Who seeks to arbitrate a controversy pursuant to the agreement;

(2) Against whom such arbitration is sought pursuant to the agreement; or

(3) Who is made a party to such arbitration by order of the neutral arbitrator upon such party's application, upon the application of any other party to the arbitration or upon the neutral arbitrator's own determination.

(f) "Written agreement" shall be deemed to include a written agreement which has been extended or renewed by an oral or implied agreement.

* * *

CHAPTER 2.   ENFORCEMENT OF ARBITRATION AGREEMENTS

§ 1281.   Validity, enforceability and irrevocability of agreements

A written agreement to submit to arbitration an existing controversy or a controversy thereafter arising is valid, enforceable and irrevocable, save upon such grounds as exist for the revocation of any contract.

§ 1281.1   Requests to arbitrate

For the purposes of this article, any request to arbitrate made pursuant to subdivision (a) of Section 1299.4 shall be considered as made pursuant to a written agreement to submit a controversy to arbitration.

§ 1281.2   Order to arbitrate controversy; petition; determination of court

On petition of a party to an arbitration agreement alleging the existence of a written agreement to arbitrate a controversy and that a party thereto refuses to arbitrate such controversy, the court shall order the petitioner and the respondent to arbitrate the controversy if it determines that an agreement to arbitrate the controversy exists, unless it determines that:

(a) The right to compel arbitration has been waived by the petitioner; or

(b) Grounds exist for the revocation of the agreement.

(c) A party to the arbitration agreement is also a party to a pending court action or special proceeding with a third party, arising out of the same transaction or series of related transactions and there is a possibility of conflicting rulings on a common issue of law or fact. For purposes of this section, a pending court action or special proceeding includes an action or proceeding initiated by the party refusing to arbitrate after the petition to compel arbitration has been filed, but on or before the date of the hearing on the petition. This subdivision shall not be applicable to an agreement to arbitrate disputes as to the professional negligence of a health care provider made pursuant to Section 1295.

If the court determines that a written agreement to arbitrate a controversy exists, an order to arbitrate such controversy may not be refused on the ground that the petitioner's contentions lack substantive merit.

If the court determines that there are other issues between the petitioner and the respondent which are not subject to arbitration and which are the subject of a pending action or special proceeding between the petitioner and the respondent and that a determination of such issues may make the arbitration unnecessary, the court may delay its order to arbitrate until the determination of such other issues or until such earlier time as the court specifies.

If the court determines that a party to the arbitration is also a party to litigation in a pending court action or special proceeding with a third party as set forth under subdivision (c) herein, the court (1) may refuse to enforce the arbitration agreement and may order intervention or joinder of all parties in a, single action or special proceeding; (2) may order intervention or joinder as to all or only certain issues; (3) may order arbitration among the parties who have agreed to arbitration and stay the pending court action or special proceeding pending the outcome of the arbitration proceeding; or (4) may stay arbitration pending the outcome of the court action or special proceeding.

§ 1281.3   Consolidation of separate arbitration proceedings; petition; grounds; procedure

A party to an arbitration agreement may petition the court to consolidate separate arbitration proceedings, and the court may order consolidation of separate arbitration proceedings when:

(1) Separate arbitration agreements or proceedings exist between the same parties; or one party is a party to a separate arbitration agreement or proceeding third party; and

(2) The disputes arise from the same transactions or series of related transactions; and

(3) There is common issue or issues of law or fact creating the possibility of conflicting rulings by more than one arbitrator or panel of arbitrators.

If all of the applicable arbitration agreements name the same arbitrator, arbitration panel, or arbitration tribunal, the court, if it orders consolidation, shall order all matters to be heard before the arbitrator, panel, or tribunal agreed to by the parties. If the applicable arbitration agreements name separate arbitrators, panels, or tribunals, the court, if it orders consolidation, shall, in the absence of an agreed method of selection by all parties to the consolidated arbitration, appoint an arbitrator in accord with the procedures set forth in Section 1281.6.

In the event that the arbitration agreements in consolidated proceedings contain inconsistent provisions, the court shall resolve such conflicts and determine the rights and duties of the various parties to achieve substantial justice under all the circumstances.

The court may exercise its discretion under this section to deny consolidation of separate arbitration proceedings or to consolidate separate arbitration proceedings only as to certain issues, leaving other issues to be resolved in separate proceedings This section shall not be applicable to an agreement to arbitrate disputes as to the professional negligence of a health care provider made pursuant to Section 1295.

§ 1281.4   Stay of pending actions or proceedings

If a court of competent jurisdiction, whether in this State or not, has ordered arbitration of a controversy which is an issue involved in an action or proceeding pending before a court of this State, the court in which such action or proceeding is pending shall, upon motion of a party to such action or proceeding, stay the action or proceeding until an arbitration is had in accordance with the order to arbitrate or until such earlier time as the court specifies.

If an application has been made to a court of competent jurisdiction, whether in this State or not, for an order to arbitrate a controversy which is an issue involved in an action or proceeding pending before a court of this State and such application is undetermined, the court in which such action or proceeding is pending shall, upon motion of a party to such action or proceeding, stay the action or proceeding until the application for an order to arbitrate is determined and, if arbitration of such controversy is ordered, until an arbitration is had in accordance with the order to arbitrate or until such earlier time as the court specifies.

If the issue which is the controversy subject to arbitration is severable, the stay may be with respect to that issue only.

§ 1281.5   Waiver of right of arbitration; actions to enforce liens on works of improvement

(a) Any person who proceeds to record and enforce a claim of lien by commencement of an action pursuant to Title 15 (commencing with Section 3082) of Part 4 of Division 3 of the Civil Code, shall not thereby waive any right of arbitration which that person may have pursuant to a written agreement to arbitrate, if, in filing an Action to enforce the claim of lien, the claimant at the same time presents to the court an application that the action be stayed pending the arbitration of any issue, question, or dispute which is claimed to be arbitrable under the agreement and which is relevant to the action to enforce the claim of lien. In a county in which there is a municipal court, the applicant may join with the application for the stay, pending arbitration, a claim of lien otherwise within the jurisdiction of the municipal court.

(b) The failure of a defendant to file a petition pursuant to Section 1281.2 at or before the time he or she answers the complaint filed pursuant to subdivision (a) shall constitute a waiver of that party's right to compel arbitration.

§ 1281.6   Appointment of arbitrator

If the arbitration agreement provides a method of appointing an arbitrator, that method shall be followed. If the arbitration agreement does not provide a method for appointing an arbitrator, the parties to the agreement who seek arbitration and against whom arbitration is sought may agree on a method of appointing an arbitrator and that method shall be followed. In the absence of an agreed method, or if the agreed method fails or for any reason cannot be followed, or when an arbitrator appointed fails to act and his or her successor has not been appointed, the court, on petition of a party to the arbitration agreement, shall appoint the arbitrator.

When a petition is made to the court to appoint a neutral arbitrator, the court shall nominate five persons from lists of persons supplied jointly by the parties to the arbitration or obtained from a governmental agency concerned with arbitration or private disinterested association concerned with arbitration. The parties to the agreement who seek arbitration and against whom arbitration is sought may within five days of receipt of notice of the nominees from the court jointly select the arbitrator whether or not the arbitrator is among the nominees. If the parties fail to select an arbitrator within the five-day period, the court shall appoint the arbitrator from the nominees.

All neutral arbitrators shall comply with the requirements of subdivision (a) of Section 1297.121, which requirements shall apply to every agreement to arbitrate pursuant to this title.

§ 1281.7   Petition in lieu of answer

A petition pursuant to Section 1281.2 may be filed in lieu of filing an answer to a complaint. The petitioning defendant shall have 15 days after any denial of the petition to plead to the complaint.

§ 1281.8   Provisional remedies; attachment, temporary protective or restraining order, writ of possession, preliminary injunction, or receiver

(a) As used in this section, "provisional remedy" includes the following:

(1) Attachments and temporary protective orders issued pursuant to Title 6.5 (commencing with Section 481.010) of Part 2.

(2) Writs of possession issued pursuant to Article 2 (commencing with Section 512.010) of Chapter 2 of Title 7 of Part 2.

(3) Preliminary injunctions and temporary restraining orders issued pursuant to Section 527.

(4) Receivers appointed pursuant to Section 564.

(b) A party to an arbitration agreement may file in the court in the county in which an arbitration proceeding is pending, or if an arbitration proceeding has not commenced, in any proper court, an application for a provisional remedy in connection with an arbitrable controversy, but only upon the ground that the award to which the applicant may be entitled may be rendered ineffectual without provisional relief. The application shall be accompanied by a complaint or by copies of the demand for arbitration and any response thereto. If accompanied by a complaint, the application shall also be accompanied by a statement stating whether the party is or is not reserving the party's right to arbitration.

(c) A claim by the party opposing issuance of a provisional remedy, that the controversy is not subject to arbitration, shall not be grounds for denial of any provisional remedy.

(d) An application for a provisional remedy under subdivision (b) shall not operate to waive any right of arbitration which the applicant may have pursuant to a written agreement to arbitrate, if, at the same time as the application for a provisional remedy is presented, the applicant also presents to the court an application that all other proceedings in the action be stayed pending the arbitration of any issue, question, or dispute which is claimed to be arbitrable under the agreement and which is relevant to the action pursuant to which the provisional remedy is sought.

§ 1281.9 Neutral arbitrators; disclosure of information; disqualification; waiver

(a) In any arbitration pursuant to an arbitration agreement, when a person is to serve as a neutral arbitrator, subject only to the disclosure requirements of law, the proposed neutral arbitrator shall disclose in writing within 10 calendar days of service of notice of the proposed nomination or appointment, to all parties, all of the following:

(1) The names of the parties to all prior or pending noncollective bargaining cases in which the proposed neutral arbitrator served or is serving as a party arbitrator for any party to the arbitration proceeding or for a lawyer for a party and the results of each case arbitrated to conclusion, including the date of the arbitration award, identification of the prevailing party, the names of the parties' attorneys and the amount of monetary damages awarded, if any. In order to preserve confidentiality, it shall be sufficient to give the name of any party who is not a party to the pending arbitration as "claimant" or "respondent" if the party is an individual and not a business or corporate entity.

(2) The names of the parties to all prior or pending noncollective bargaining cases involving any party to the arbitration or lawyer for a party for which the proposed neutral arbitrator served or is serving as neutral arbitrator, and the results of each case arbitrated to conclusion, including the date of the arbitration award, identification of the prevailing party, the names of the parties' attorneys and the amount of monetary damages awarded, if any. In order to preserve confidentiality, it shall be sufficient to give the name of any party not a party to the pending arbitration as "claimant" or"respondent" if the party is an individual and not a business or corporate entity.

(3) Any attorney-client relationship the proposed neutral arbitrator has or had with any party or lawyer for a party to the arbitration proceeding.

(4) Any professional or significant personal relationship the proposed neutral arbitrator or his or her spouse or minor child living in the

household has or has had with any party to the arbitration proceeding or lawyer for a party.

(b) A proposed neutral arbitrator shall be disqualified if he or she fails to comply with subdivision (a) and any party entitled to receive the disclosure serves a notice of disqualification within 15 calendar days after the proposed nominee or appointee fails to comply with subdivision (a). A proposed neutral arbitrator shall be deemed to have complied with subdivision (a) with respect to any arbitration commenced prior to January 1, 1995, if the person declares in writing that he or she has disclosed all required information pertaining to those arbitrations within his or her knowledge or possession and has made a good faith effort to obtain the required information from any arbitration service administering those prior cases.

(c)(1) If the proposed neutral arbitrator complies with subdivision (a), the proposed neutral arbitrator shall be disqualified on the basis of the disclosure statement after any party entitled to receive the disclosure serves a notice of disqualification, within 15 calendar days after service of the disclosure statement.

(2) A party shall have the right to disqualify one court-appointed arbitrator without cause in any one arbitration, and may petition the court to disqualify a subsequent appointee only upon a showing of cause.

(d) The right of a party to disqualify a proposed neutral arbitrator pursuant to this section shall be waived if the party fails to serve the notice pursuant to the times set forth in this section, unless the proposed nominee or appointee makes a material omission or material misrepresentation in his or her disclosure. In no event may a notice of disqualification be given after a hearing of any contested issue of fact relating to the merits of the claim or after any ruling by the arbitrator regarding any contested matter. Nothing in this subdivision shall limit the right of a party to vacate an award pursuant to Section 1286.2, or to disqualify an arbitrator pursuant to any other law or statute.

(e) An arbitrator shall disclose to all parties the existence of any grounds specified in Section 170.1 for disqualification of a judge; and, if any such ground exists, shall disqualify himself or herself upon demand of any party made before the conclusion of the arbitration proceeding. However, this subdivision does not apply to arbitration proceedings conducted under a collective bargaining agreement between employers and employees or their respective representatives.

(f) For purposes of this section, "lawyer for a party" includes any lawyer or law firm currently associated in the practice of law with the lawyer hired to represent a party.

(g) For purposes of this section, "prior cases" means noncollective bargaining cases in which an arbitration award was rendered within one. of the following time periods:

(1) Three years prior to the date of the proposed nomination or appointment if the proposed nomination or appointment occurs on or between January 1, 1995, and December 31, 1995.

(2) Four years prior to the date of the proposed nomination or appointment if the proposed nomination or appointment occurs on or between January 1, 1996, and December 31, 1996.

(3) Five years prior to the date of the proposed nomination or appointment if the proposed nomination or appointment occurs on or after January 1, 1997.

(h) For purposes of this section, "any arbitration" does not include an arbitration conducted pursuant to the terms of a public or private sector collective bargaining agreement

§ 1281.95   Residential construction or improvements; arbitrator disclosures; disqualification

(a) In a binding arbitration of any claim for more than three thousand dollars ($3,000) pursuant to a contract for the construction or improvement of residential property consisting of one to four units, the arbitrator shall, within 10 days following his or her appointment, provide to each party a written declaration under penalty of perjury. This declaration shall disclose (1) whether the arbitrator or his or her employer or arbitration service had or has a personal or professional affiliation with either party, and (2) whether the arbitrator or his or her employer or arbitration service has been selected or designated as an arbitrator by either party in another transaction.

(b) If the arbitrator discloses an affiliation with either party, discloses that the arbitrator has been selected or designated as an arbitrator by either party in another arbitration, or fails to comply with this section, he or she may be disqualified from the arbitration by either party.

(c) A notice of disqualification shall be served within 15 days after the arbitrator makes the required disclosures or fails to comply. The right of a party to disqualify an arbitrator shall be waived if the party fails to serve the notice of disqualification pursuant to this subdivision unless the arbitration makes a material omission or material misrepresentation in his or her disclosure. Nothing in this section shall limit the right of a party to vacate an award or to disqualify an arbitrator pursuant to subdivision (e) of Section 1282, Section 1286.2, or any other law or statute.

CHAPTER 3.   CONDUCT OF ARBITRATION PROCEEDINGS

§ 1282.   Exercise of powers and duties of neutral arbitrator

Unless the arbitration agreement otherwise provides, or unless the parties to the arbitration otherwise provide by an agreement which is not contrary to the arbitration agreement as made or as modified by all of the parties thereto:

120

(a) The arbitration shall be by a single neutral arbitrator.

(b) If there is more than one arbitrator, the powers and duties of the arbitrators, other than the powers and duties of a neutral arbitrator, may be exercised by a majority of them if reasonable notice of all proceedings has been given to all arbitrators.

(c) If there is more than one neutral arbitrator:

(1) The powers and duties of a neutral arbitrator may be exercised by a majority of the neutral arbitrators.

(2) By unanimous agreement of the neutral arbitrators, the powers and duties may be delegated to one of their number but the power to make or correct the award may not be so delegated.

(d) If there is no neutral arbitrator, the powers and duties of a neutral arbitrator may be exercised by a majority of the arbitrators.

§ 1282.2 Hearing; time and place; witness lists; adjournment or postponement; conduct; evidence; procedure

Unless the arbitration agreement otherwise provides, or unless the parties to the arbitration otherwise provide by an agreement which is not contrary to the arbitration agreement as made or as modified by all the parties thereto:

(a)(1) The neutral arbitrator shall appoint a time and place for the hearing and cause notice thereof to be served personally or by registered or certified mail on the parties to the arbitration and on the other arbitrators not less than seven days before the hearing. Appearance at the hearing waives the right to notice.

(2) With the exception of matters arising out of collective-bargaining agreements, those described in Section 1283.05, actions involving personal injury or death, or as provided in the parties' agreement to arbitrate, in the event the aggregate amount in controversy exceeds fifty thousand dollars ($50,000) and the arbitrator is informed thereof by any party in writing by personal service, registered or certified mail, prior to designating a time and place of hearing pursuant to paragraph (1), the neutral arbitrator by the means prescribed in paragraph (1) shall appoint a time and place for hearing not less than 60 days before the hearing, and the following provisions shall apply:

(A) Either party shall within 15 days of receipt of the notice of hearing have the right to demand in writing, served personally or by registered or certified mail, that the other party provide a list of witnesses it intends to call designating which witnesses will be called as expert witnesses and a list of documents it intends to introduce at the hearing provided that the demanding party provides such lists at the time of its demand. A copy of such demand and the demanding party's lists shall be served on the arbitrator.

(B) Such lists shall be served personally or by registered or certified mail on the requesting party 15 days thereafter. Copies thereof shall be served on the arbitrator.

(C) Listed documents shall be made available for inspection and copying at reasonable times prior to the hearing.

(D) Time limits provided herein may be waived by mutual agreement of the parties if approved by the arbitrator.

(E) The failure to list a witness or a document shall not bar the testimony of an unlisted witness or the introduction of an undesignated document at the hearing, provided that good cause for omission from the requirements of subparagraph (A) is shown, as determined by the arbitrator.

(F) The authority of the arbitrator to administer and enforce this paragraph shall be as provided in subdivisions (b) to (e), inclusive, of Section 1283.05.

(b) The neutral arbitrator may adjourn the hearing from time to time as necessary. On request of a party to the arbitration for good cause, or upon his own determination, the neutral arbitrator may postpone the hearing to a time not later than the date fixed by the agreement for making the award, or to a later date if the parties to the arbitration consent thereto.

(c) The neutral arbitrator shall preside at the hearing, shall rule on the admission and exclusion of evidence and on questions of hearing procedure and shall exercise all powers relating to the conduct of the hearing.

(d) The parties to the arbitration are entitled to be heard, to present evidence and to cross-examine witnesses appearing at the hearing, but rules of evidence and rules of judicial procedure need not be observed. On request of any party to the arbitration, the testimony of witnesses shall be given under oath.

(e) If a court has ordered a person to arbitrate a controversy, the arbitrators may hear and determine the controversy upon the evidence produced notwithstanding the failure of a party ordered to arbitrate, who has been duly notified, to appear.

(f) If an arbitrator, who has been duly notified, for any reason fails to participate in the arbitration, the arbitration shall continue but only the remaining neutral arbitrator or neutral arbitrators may make the award.

(g) If a neutral arbitrator intends to base an award upon information not obtained at the hearing, he shall disclose the information to all parties to the arbitration and give the parties an opportunity to meet it.

§ 1282.4   Representation by counsel

Text of section operative until Jan. 1, 2006.

(a) A party to the arbitration has the right to be represented by an attorney at any proceeding or hearing in arbitration under this title. A waiver of this right may be revoked; but if a party revokes such waiver, the other party is entitled to a reasonable continuance for the purpose of procuring an attorney.

(b) Notwithstanding any other provision of law, including Section 6125 of the Business and Professions Code, an attorney admitted to the bar of any other state may represent the parties in the course of, or in connection with, an arbitration proceeding in this state, provided that the attorney, if not admitted to the State Bar of California, timely files the certificate described in subdivision (c) and the attorney's appearance is approved by the arbitrator, the arbitrators, or the arbitral forum.

(c) Prior to the first scheduled hearing in an arbitration, the attorney described in subdivision (b) shall serve a certificate on the arbitrator or arbitrators, the State Bar of California, and all other parties and counsel in the arbitration whose addresses are known to the attorney. In the event that the attorney is retained after the first hearing has commenced, then the certificate shall be served prior to the first hearing at which the attorney appears. The certificate shall state all of the following:

(1) The attorney's residence and office address.

(2) The courts before which the attorney has been admitted to practice and the dates of admission.

(3) That the attorney is currently a member in good standing of, and eligible to practice law before, the bar of those courts.

(4) That the attorney is not currently on suspension or disbarred from the practice of law before the bar of any court.

(5) That the attorney is not a resident of the State of California.

(6) That the attorney is not regularly employed in the State of California.

(7) That the attorney is not regularly engaged in substantial business, professional, or other activities in the State of California.

(8) That the attorney agrees to be subject to the jurisdiction of the courts of this state with respect to the law of this state governing the conduct of. attorneys to the same extent as a member of the State Bar of California.

(9) The title of the court and the cause in which the attorney has filed an application to appear as counsel pro hac vice in this state or filed a certificate pursuant to this section in the preceding two years, the date of each application, and whether or not it was granted.

(10) The name, address, and telephone number of the active member of the State Bar of California who is the attorney of record.

(d) Failure to timely, file the certificate described in subdivision (c) or, absent special circumstances, repeated appearances shall be grounds for disqualification from serving as the attorney of record in the arbitration in which the certificate, was filed.

(e) An attorney who files a certificate containing false information or who otherwise fails to comply with the standards of professional conduct required of members of the State Bar of California shall be subject to the disciplinary jurisdiction. of the State Bar with respect to any of his, or her acts occurring in the course of the arbitration.

(f) Notwithstanding any other provision of law, including Section 6125 of the Business and Professions Code, an attorney who is a member in good standing of the bar of any state may represent the parties in connection with rendering legal services in this state in the course of and in connection with an arbitration pending in another state.

(g) Notwithstanding any other provision of law, including Section 6125 of the Business and Professions Code, any party to an arbitration arising under collective bargaining agreements in industries and provisions subject to either state or federal law may be represented in the course of, and in connection with, those proceedings by any person, regardless of whether that person is licensed to practice law in. this state.

(h) Nothing in this section shall apply to Division 4 (commencing with Section 3201) of the Labor Code.

(i)(1) In enacting the amendments to this section made by Assembly Bill 2086 of the 1997–98 Regular Session, it is the intent of the Legislature to respond to the holding in Birbrower v. Superior Court (1998) 17 Cal.4th 117, as modified at 17 Cal.4th 643a (hereafter Birbrower), to provide a procedure for nonresident attorneys who are not licensed in this state to appear in California arbitration proceedings.

(2) In enacting subdivision (g), it is the intent of the Legislature to make clear that any party to an arbitration arising under a collective bargaining agreement governed by the laws of this state may be represented in the course of and in connection with those proceedings by any person regardless of whether that person is licensed to practice law in this state.

(3) Except as otherwise specifically provided in this section, in enacting the amendments to this section made by Assembly Bill 2086 of the 1997–98 Regular Session, it is the Legislature's intent that nothing in this section is intended to expand or restrict the ability of a party prior to the decision in Birbrower to elect to be represented by any person in a nonjudicial arbitration proceeding, to the extent those rights or abilities existed prior to that decision. To the extent that Birbrower is interpreted to expand or restrict that right or ability pursuant to the laws of this state, it is hereby abrogated except as specifically provided in this section.

(4) In enacting subdivision (h), it is the intent of the Legislature to make clear that nothing in this section shall affect those provisions of law governing the right of injured workers to elect to be represented by any person, regardless of whether that person is licensed to practice law in this state, as set forth in Division 4 (commencing with Section 3200) of the Labor Code.

(j) This section shall be operative until January 1, 2006, and on that date shall be repealed.

§ 1282.4   Representation by counsel

Text of section operative Jan. 1, 2006.

(a) A party to the arbitration has the right to be represented by an attorney at any proceeding or hearing in arbitration under this title. A waiver of this right may be revoked; but if a party revokes the waiver, the other party is entitled to a reasonable continuance for the purpose of procuring an attorney.

(b) This section shall become operative on January 1, 2006.

§ 1282.6   Issuance of subpoenas

(a) A subpoena requiring the attendance of witnesses, and a subpoena duces tecum for the production of books, records, documents and other evidence, at an arbitration proceeding or a deposition under Section 1283, and if Section 1283.05 is applicable, for the purposes of discovery, shall be issued as provided in this section. In addition, the neutral arbitrator upon his own determination may issue subpoenas for the attendance of witnesses and subpoenas duces tecum for the production of books, records, documents and other evidence.

(b) Subpoenas shall be issued, as of course, signed but otherwise in blank, to the party requesting them, by a neutral association, organization, governmental agency, or office if the arbitration agreement provides for administration of the arbitration proceedings by, or under the rules of, a neutral association, organization, governmental agency or office or by the neutral arbitrator.

(c) The party serving the subpoena shall fill it in before service. Subpoenas shall be served and enforced in accordance with Chapter 2 (commencing with Section 1985) of Title 3 of Part 4 of this code.

§ 1282.8   Administration of oaths

The neutral arbitrator may administer oaths.

§ 1283.   Depositions

On application of a party to the arbitration the neutral arbitrator may order the deposition of a witness to be taken for use as evidence and not for discovery if the witness cannot be compelled to attend the hearing or if such exceptional circumstances exist as to make it desirable, in the interest of justice and with due regard to the importance of presenting the testimony of witnesses orally at the hearing, to allow the deposition to be taken. The deposition shall be taken in the manner prescribed by law for the taking of depositions in civil actions. If the neutral arbitrator orders the taking of the deposition of a witness who resides outside the state, the party who applied for the taking of the deposition shall obtain a commission therefor from the superior court in accordance with Sections 2024 to 2028, inclusive, of this code.

§ 1283.05   Manner of taking deposition

To the extent provided in Section 1283.1 depositions may be taken and discovery obtained in arbitration proceedings as follows:

(a) After the appointment of the arbitrator or arbitrators, the parties to the arbitration shall have the right to take depositions and to obtain discovery regarding the subject matter of the arbitration, and, to that end, to use and exercise all of the same rights, remedies, and procedures, and be subject to all of the same duties, liabilities, and obligations in the arbitration with respect to the subject matter thereof, as provided in Chapter 2 (commencing with Section 1985) of, and Article 3 (commencing with Section 2016) of Chapter 3 of Title 3 of Part 4 of this code, as if the subject matter of the arbitration were pending before a superior court of this state in a civil action other than a limited civil case, subject to the limitations as to depositions set forth in subdivision (e) of this section.

(b) The arbitrator or arbitrators themselves shall have power, in addition to the power of determining the merits of the arbitration, to enforce the rights, remedies, procedures, duties, liabilities, and obligations of discovery by the imposition of the same terms, conditions, consequences, liabilities, sanctions, and penalties. as can be or may be imposed in like circumstances in a civil action by a superior court of this state under the provisions of this code, except the power to order the arrest or imprisonment of a person.

(c) The arbitrator or arbitrators may consider, determine, and make such orders imposing such terms, conditions, consequences, liabilities, sanctions, and penalties, whenever necessary or appropriate at any time or stage in the course of the arbitration, and such orders shall be as conclusive, final, and enforceable as an arbitration award on the merits, if the making of any such order that is equivalent to an award or correction of an award is subject to the same conditions, if any, as are applicable to the making of an award or correction of an award.

(d) For the purpose of enforcing the duty to make discovery, to produce evidence or information, including books and records, and to produce persons to testify at a deposition or at a hearing, and to impose terms, conditions, consequences, liabilities, sanctions, and penalties upon a party for violation of any such duty, such party shall be deemed to include every affiliate of such party as defined in this section. For such purpose:

(1) The personnel of every such affiliate shall be deemed to be the officers, directors, managing agents, agents, and employees of such party to the same degree as each of them, respectively, bears such status to such affiliate; and

(2) The files, books, and records of every such affiliate shall be deemed to be in the possession and control of, and capable of production by, such party. As used in this section, "affiliate" of the party to the arbitration means and includes any party or person for whose immediate benefit the action or proceeding is prosecuted or defended, or an officer, director,

superintendent, member, agent, employee, or managing agent of such party or person.

(e) Depositions for discovery shall not be taken unless leave to do so is first granted by the arbitrator or arbitrators.

§ 1283.1 Incorporation of § 1283.05 in arbitration agreements

(a) All of the provisions of Section 1283.05 shall be conclusively deemed to be incorporated into, made a part of, and shall be applicable to, every agreement to arbitrate any dispute, controversy, or issue arising out of or resulting from any injury to, or death of, a person caused by the wrongful act or neglect of another.

(b) Only if the parties by their agreement so provide, may the provisions of Section 1283.05 be incorporated into, made a part of, or made applicable to, any other arbitration agreement.

§ 1283.2 Witnesses; fees and mileage; payment

Except for the parties to the arbitration and their agents, officers and employees, all witnesses appearing pursuant to subpoena are entitled to receive fees and mileage in the same amount and under the same circumstances as prescribed by law for witnesses in civil actions in the superior court. The fee and mileage of a witness subpoenaed upon the application of a party to the arbitration shall be paid by such party. The fee and mileage of a witness subpoenaed solely upon the determination of the neutral arbitrator shall be paid in the manner provided for the payment of the neutral arbitrator's expenses.

§ 1283.4 Form and contents of award

The award shall be in writing and signed by the arbitrators concurring therein. It shall include a determination of all the questions submitted to the arbitrators the decision of which is necessary in order to determine the controversy.

§ 1283.6 Service of award

The neutral arbitrator shall serve a signed copy of the award on each party to the arbitration personally or by registered or certified mail or as provided in the agreement.

§ 1283.8 Time for making award

The award shall be made within the time fixed therefor by the agreement or, if not so fixed, within such time as the court orders on petition of a party to the arbitration. The parties to the arbitration may extend the time either before or after the expiration thereof. A party to the arbitration waives the objection that an award was not made within the time required unless he gives the arbitrators written notice of his objection prior to the service of a signed copy of the award on him.

127

§ 1284. Correction of award; application; objections; action by arbitrators; service of copy of denial or correction

The arbitrators, upon written application of a party to the arbitration, may correct the award upon any of the grounds set forth in subdivisions (a) and (c) of Section 1286.6 not later than 30 days after service of a signed copy of the award on the applicant.

Application for such correction shall be made not later than 10 days after service of a signed copy of the award on the applicant. Upon or before making such application, the applicant shall deliver or mail a copy of the application to all of the other parties to the arbitration.

Any party to the arbitration may make written objection to such application. The objection shall be made not later than 10 days after the application is delivered or mailed to the objector. Upon or before making such objection, the objector shall deliver or mail a copy of the objection to the applicant and all the other parties to the arbitration.

The arbitrators shall either deny the application or correct the award. The denial of the application or the correction of the award shall be in writing and signed by the arbitrators concurring therein, and the neutral arbitrator shall serve a signed copy of such denial or correction on each party to the arbitration personally or by registered or certified mail or as provided in the agreement. If no denial of the application or correction of the award is served within the 30–day period provided in this section, the application for correction shall be deemed denied on the last day thereof.

§ 1284.2 Payment of expenses

Unless the arbitration agreement otherwise provides or the parties to the arbitration otherwise agree, each party to the arbitration shall pay his pro rata share of the expenses and fees of the neutral arbitrator, together with other expenses of the arbitration incurred or approved by the neutral arbitrator, not including counsel fees or witness fees or other expenses incurred by a party for his own benefit.

CHAPTER 4. ENFORCEMENT OF THE AWARD

ARTICLE 1. CONFIRMATION, CORRECTION OR VACATION OF THE AWARD

§ 1285. Petition; parties

Any party to an arbitration in which an award has been made may petition the court to confirm, correct or vacate the award. The petition shall name as respondents all parties to the arbitration and may name as respondents any other persons bound by the arbitration award.

§ 1285.2 Response to petition

A response to a petition under this chapter may request the court to dismiss the petition or to confirm, correct or vacate the award.

§ 1285.4   Contents of petition

A petition under this chapter shall:

(a) Set forth the substance of or have attached a copy of the agreement to arbitrate unless the petitioner denies the existence of such an agreement.

(b) Set forth the names of the arbitrators.

(c) Set forth or have attached a copy of the award and the written opinion of the arbitrators, if any.

§ 1285.6   Contents of response to petition

Unless a copy thereof is set forth in or attached to the petition, a response to a petition under this chapter shall:

(a) Set forth the substance of or have attached a copy of the agreement to arbitrate unless the respondent denies the existence of such an agreement.

(b) Set forth the names of the arbitrators.

(c) Set forth or have attached a copy of the award and the written opinion of the arbitrators, if any.

§ 1285.8   Grounds for relief

A petition to correct or vacate an award, or a response requesting such relief, shall set forth the grounds on which the request for such relief is based.

§ 1286.   Powers of court

If a petition or response under this chapter is duly served and filed, the court shall confirm the award as made, whether rendered in this state or another state, unless in accordance with this chapter it corrects the award and confirms it as corrected, vacates the award or dismisses the proceeding.

§ 1286.2   Grounds for vacation of award

Subject to Section 1286.4, the court shall vacate the award if the court determines any of the following:

(a) The award was procured by corruption, fraud or other undue means.

(b) There was corruption in any of the arbitrators.

(c) The rights of the party were substantially prejudiced by misconduct of a neutral arbitrator.

(d) The arbitrators exceeded their powers and the award cannot be corrected without affecting the merits of the decision upon the controversy submitted.

(e) The rights of the party were substantially prejudiced by the refusal of the arbitrators to postpone the hearing upon sufficient cause being shown therefor or by the refusal of the arbitrators to hear evidence material to the controversy or by other conduct of the arbitrators contrary to the provisions of this title.

(f) An arbitrator making the award was subject to disqualification upon grounds specified in Section 1281.9, but failed upon receipt of timely demand to disqualify himself or herself as required by that provision. However, this subdivision does not apply to arbitration proceedings conducted under a collective bargaining agreement between employers and employees or between their respective representatives.

§ 1286.4   Conditions to vacation of award

The court may not vacate an award unless:

(a) A petition or response requesting that the award be vacated has been duly served and filed; or

(b) A petition or response requesting that the award be corrected has been duly served and filed and:

(1) All petitioners and respondents are before the court; or

(2) All petitioners and respondents have been given reasonable notice that the court will be requested at the hearing to vacate the award or that the court on its own motion has determined to vacate the award and all petitioners and respondents have been given an opportunity to show why the award should not be vacated.

§ 1286.6   Grounds for correction of award

Subject to Section 1286.8, the court, unless it vacates the award pursuant to Section 1286.2, shall correct the award and confirm it as corrected if the court determines that:

(a) There was an evident miscalculation of figures or an evident mistake in the description of any person, thing or property referred to in the award;

(b) The arbitrators exceeded their powers but the award may be corrected without affecting the merits of the decision upon the controversy submitted; or

(c) The award is imperfect in a matter of form, not affecting the merits of the controversy.

§ 1286.8   Conditions to correction of award

The court may not correct an award unless:

(a) A petition or response requesting that the award be corrected has been duly served and filed; or

(b) A petition or response requesting that the award be vacated has been duly served and filed and;

(1) All petitioners and respondents are before the court; or

(2) All petitioners and respondents have been given reasonable notice that the court will be requested at the hearing to correct the award or that

the court on its own motion has determined to correct the award and all petitioners and respondents have been given an opportunity to show why the award should not be corrected.

§ 1287. Rehearing

If the award is vacated, the court may order a rehearing before new arbitrators. If the award is vacated on the grounds set forth in subdivision (d) or (e) of Section 1286.2, the court with the consent of the parties to the court proceeding may order a rehearing before the original arbitrators.

If the arbitration agreement requires that the award be made within a specified period of time, the rehearing may nevertheless be held and the award made within an equal period of time beginning with the date of the order for rehearing but only if the court determines that the purpose of the, time limit agreed upon by the parties to the arbitration agreement will not be frustrated by the application of this provision.

§ 1287.2 Dismissal of proceeding as to person not bound by award and not party to arbitration

The court shall dismiss the proceeding under this chapter as to any person named as a respondent if the court determines that such person was not bound by the arbitration award and was not a party to the arbitration.

§ 1287.4 Entry of judgment on confirmation of award; force and effect; enforcement

If an award is confirmed, judgment shall be entered in conformity therewith. The judgment so entered has the same force and effect as, and is subject to all the provisions, of law relating to, a judgment in a civil action of the same jurisdictional classification; and it may be enforced like any other judgment of the court in which it is entered, in an action of the same jurisdictional classification.

§ 1287.6 Force and effect of unconfirmed or vacated award

An award that has not been confirmed or vacated has the same force and effect as a contract in writing between the parties to the arbitration.

ARTICLE 2.   LIMITATIONS OF TIME

§ 1288. Petition; time for service and filing

A petition to confirm an award shall be served and filed not later than four years after the date of service of a signed copy of the award on the petitioner. A petition to vacate an award or to correct an award shall be served and filed not later than 100 days after the date of the service of a signed copy of the award on the petitioner.

§ 1288.2 Response; time for service and filing

A response requesting that an award be vacated or that an award be corrected shall be served and filed not later than 100 days after the date of service of a signed copy of the award upon:

(a) The respondent if he was a party to the arbitration; or

(b) The respondent's representative if the respondent was not a party to the arbitration.

§ 1288.4 Petition; service and filing at least ten days after service of copy of award

No petition may be served and filed under this chapter until at least 10 days after service of the signed copy of the award upon the petitioner.

§ 1288.6 Application for correction of award; service and filing of petition after determination by arbitrators

If an application is made to the arbitrators for correction of the award, a petition may not be served and filed under this chapter until the determination of that application.

§ 1288.8 Application for correction of award; date of service of award

If an application is made to the arbitrators for correction of the award, the date of the service of the award for the purposes of this article shall be deemed to be whichever of the following dates is the earlier:

(a) The date of service upon the petitioner of a signed copy of the correction of the award or of the denial of the application.

(b) The date that such application is deemed to be denied under Section 1284.

CHAPTER 5. GENERAL PROVISIONS RELATING
TO JUDICIAL PROCEEDINGS

ARTICLE 1. PETITIONS AND RESPONSES

§ 1290. Commencement of proceedings by filing petition; response; allegations

A proceeding under this title in the courts of this State is commenced by filing a petition. Any person named as a respondent in a petition may file a response thereto. The allegations of a petition are deemed to be admitted by a respondent duly served therewith unless a response is duly served and filed. The allegations of a response are deemed controverted or avoided.

§ 1290.2 Summary hearing; notice

A petition under this title shall be heard in a summary way in the manner and upon the notice provided by law for the making and hearing of motions, except that not less than 10 days' notice of the date set for the hearing on the petition shall be given.

§ 1290.4 Service of copy of petition and notice of hearing

(a) A copy of the petition and a written notice of the time and place of the hearing thereof and any other papers upon which the petition is based shall be served in the manner provided in the arbitration agreement for the service of such petition and notice.

(b) If the arbitration agreement does not provide the manner in which such service shall be made and the person upon whom service is to be made has not previously appeared in the proceeding and has not previously been served in accordance with this subdivision:

(1) Service within this State shall be made in the manner provided by law for the service of summons in an action.

(2) Service outside this State shall be made by mailing the copy of the petition and notice and other papers by registered or certified mail. Personal service is the equivalent of such service by mail. Proof of service by mail shall be made by affidavit showing such mailing together with the return receipt of the United States Post Office bearing the signature of the person on whom service was made. Notwithstanding any other provision of this title, if service is made in the manner provided in this paragraph, the petition may not be heard until at least 30 days after the date of such service.

(c) If the arbitration agreement does not provide the manner in which such service shall be made and the person on whom service is to be made has previously appeared in the proceeding or has previously been served in accordance with subdivision (b) of this section, service shall be made in the manner provided in Chapter 5 (commencing with Section 1010) of Title 14 of Part 2 of this code.

§ 1290.6   Time for service and filing of response; extension

A response shall be served and filed within 10 days after service of the petition except that if the petition is served in the manner provided in paragraph (2) of subdivision (b) of Section 1290.4, the response shall be served and filed within 30 days after service of the petition. The time provided in this section for serving and filing a response may be extended by an agreement in writing between the parties to the court proceeding or, for good cause, by order of the court.

§ 1290.8   Manner of serving response

A response shall be served as provided in Chapter 5 (commencing with Section 1010) of Title 14 of Part 2 of this code.

§ 1291.   Statement of decision

A statement of decision shall be made by the court, if requested pursuant to Section 632, whenever an order or judgment, except a special order after final judgment, is made that is appealable under this title.

§ 1291.2   Setting for hearing; hearing; preference

In all proceedings brought under the provisions of this title, all courts wherein such proceedings are pending shall give such proceedings preference over all other civil actions or proceedings, except older matters of the same character and matters to which special precedence may be given by law, in the matter of setting the same for hearing and in hearing the same to the end that all such proceedings shall be quickly heard and determined.

ARTICLE 2.   VENUE, JURISDICTION AND COSTS

§ 1292.   Petition made prior to commencement of arbitration; place of filing

Except as otherwise provided in this article, any petition made prior to the commencement of arbitration shall be filed in a court having jurisdiction in:

(a) The county where the agreement is to be performed or was made.

(b) If the agreement does not specify a county where the agreement is to be performed and the agreement was not made in any county in this state, the county where any party to the court proceeding resides or has a place of business.

(c) In any case not covered by subdivision (a) or (b) of this section, in any county in this state.

§ 1292.2   Petition made after commencement or completion of arbitration; place of filing

Except as otherwise provided in this article, any petition made after the commencement or completion of arbitration shall be filed in a court having jurisdiction in the county where the arbitration is being or has been held, or, if not held exclusively in any one county of this state, or if held outside of this state, then the petition shall be filed as provided in Section 1292.

§ 1292.4   Order to arbitrate; filing in pending action or proceeding

If a controversy referable to arbitration under an alleged agreement is involved in an action or proceeding pending in a superior court, a petition for an order to arbitrate shall be filed in such action or proceeding.

§ 1292.6   Continuing jurisdiction

After a petition has been filed under this title, the court in which such petition was filed retains jurisdiction to determine any subsequent petition involving the same agreement to arbitrate and the same controversy, and any such subsequent petition shall be filed in the same proceeding.

§ 1292.8   Motion for stay of action

A motion for a stay of an action on the ground that an issue therein is subject to arbitration shall be made in the court where the action is pending.

§ 1293.   Making of agreement as consent to jurisdiction of state courts

The making of an agreement in this State providing for arbitration to be had within this State shall be deemed a consent of the parties thereto to the jurisdiction of the courts of this State to enforce such agreement by the making of any orders provided for in this title and by entering of judgment on an award under the agreement.

§ 1293.2   Costs

The court shall award costs upon any judicial proceeding under this title as provided in Chapter 6 (commencing with Section 1021) of Title 14 of Part 2 of this code.

ARTICLE 3.   APPEALS

§ 1294.   Appealable orders

An aggrieved party may appeal from:

(a) An order dismissing or denying a petition to compel arbitration.

(b) An order dismissing a petition to confirm, correct or vacate an award.

(c) An order vacating an award unless a rehearing in arbitration is ordered.

(d) A judgment entered pursuant to this title.

(e) A special order after final judgment.

§ 1294.2   Manner of taking appeal; scope of review

The appeal shall be taken in the same manner as an appeal from an order or judgment in a civil action. Upon an appeal from any order or judgment under this title, the court may review the decision and any intermediate ruling, proceeding, order or decision which involves the merits or necessarily affects the order or judgment appealed from, or which substantially affects the rights of a party. The court may also on such appeal review any order on motion for a new trial. The respondent on the appeal, or party in whose favor the judgment or order was given may, without appealing from such judgment, request the court to and it may review any of the foregoing matters for the purpose of determining whether or not the appellant was prejudiced by the error or errors upon which he relies for reversal or modification of the judgment or order from which the appeal is taken. The provisions of this section do not authorize the court to review any decision or order from which an appeal might have been taken.

CALIFORNIA CIVIL CODE

§ 1623.   Statute of Frauds; Enforcement of Contract Oral by Reason of Fraud

CONTRACT NOT IN WRITING THROUGH FRAUD, MAY BE ENFORCED AGAINST FRAUDULENT PARTY. Where a contract, which is required by law to be in writing, is prevented from being put into writing by the fraud of a party thereto, any other party who is by such fraud led to believe that it is in writing, and acts upon such belief to his prejudice, may enforce it against the fraudulent party.

§ 1624.   Statute of Frauds

(a) The following contracts are invalid, unless they, or some note or memorandum thereof, are in writing and subscribed by the party to be charged or by the party's agent:

(1) An agreement that by its terms is not to be performed within a year from the making thereof.

(2) A special promise to answer for the debt, default, or miscarriage of another, except in the cases provided for in Section 2794.

(3) An agreement for the leasing for a longer period than one year, or for the sale of real property, or of an interest therein; such an agreement, if made by an agent of the party sought to be charged, is invalid, unless the authority of the agent is in writing, subscribed by the party sought to be charged.

(4) An agreement authorizing or employing an agent, broker, or any other person to purchase or sell real estate, or to lease real estate for a longer period than one year, or to procure, introduce, or find a purchaser or seller of real estate or a lessee or lessor of real estate where the lease is for a longer period than one year, for compensation or a commission.

(5) An agreement that by its terms is not to be performed during the lifetime of the promisor.

(6) An agreement by a purchaser of real property to pay an indebtedness secured by a mortgage or deed of trust upon the property purchased, unless assumption of the indebtedness by the purchaser is specifically provided for in the conveyance of the property.

(7) A contract, promise, undertaking, or commitment to loan money or to grant or extend credit, in an amount greater than one hundred thousand dollars ($100,000), not primarily for personal, family, or household purposes, made by a person engaged in the business of lending or arranging for the lending of money or extending credit. For purposes of this section, a contract, promise, undertaking or commitment to loan money secured solely by residential property consisting of one to four dwelling units shall be deemed to be for personal, family, or household purposes.

(b) Notwithstanding paragraph (1) of subdivision (a):

(1) An agreement or contract that is valid in other respects and is otherwise enforceable is not invalid for lack of a note, memorandum or other writing and is enforceable by way of action or defense, provided that the agreement or contract is a qualified contract as defined in paragraph (2) and (A) there is, as provided in paragraph (3), sufficient evidence to indicate that a contract has been made or (B) the parties thereto by means of a prior or subsequent written contract have agreed to be bound by the

terms of the qualified financial contract from the time they reached agreement (by telephone, by exchange of electronic messages, or otherwise) on these terms.

(2) For purposes of this subdivision, a "qualified financial contract" means an agreement as to which each party thereto is other than a natural person and that is any of the following:

(A) For the purchase and sale of foreign exchange, foreign currency, bullion, coin or precious metals on a forward, spot, next-day value or other basis.

(B) A contract (other than a contract for the purchase of a commodity for future delivery on, or subject to the rules of, a contract, market or board of trade) for the purchase, sale, or transfer of any commodity or any similar good, article, service, right, or interest, that is presently or in the future becomes the subject of a dealing in the forward contract trade, or any product or byproduct thereof, with a maturity date more than two days after the date the contract is entered into.

(C) For the purchase and sale of currency, or interbank deposits denominated in United States dollars.

(D) For a currency option, currency swap, or cross-currency rate swap.

(E) For a commodity swap or a commodity option (other than an option contract traded on, or subject to the rules of a contract market or board of trade).

(F) For a rate swap, basis swap, forward rate transaction, or an interest rate option.

(G) For a security-index swap or option, or a security or securities price swap or option.

(H) An agreement that involves any other similar transaction, relating to a price or index (including, without limitation, any transaction or agreement involving any combination of the foregoing, any cap, floor, collar, or similar transaction with respect to a rate, commodity price, commodity index, security or securities price, security index, other price index, or loan price).

(I) An option with respect to any of the foregoing.

(3) There is sufficient evidence that a contract has been made in any of the following circumstances:

(A) There is evidence of an electronic communication (including, without limitation the recording of a telephone call or the tangible written text produced by computer retrieval), admissible in evidence under the laws of this state, sufficient to indicate that in the communication a contract was made between the parties.

(B) A confirmation in writing sufficient to indicate that a contract has been made between the parties and sufficient against the sender is received by the party against whom enforcement is sought no later than the fifth business day after the contract is made (or any other period of time that the parties may agree in writing) and the sender does not receive, on or before the third business day after receipt (or the other period of time that the parties may agree in writing), written objection to a material term of the confirmation. For purposes of this subparagraph, a confirmation or an objection thereto is received at the time there has been an actual receipt by an individual responsible for the transaction or, if earlier, at the time there has been constructive receipt, which is the time actual receipt by that individual would have occurred if the receiving party, as an organization, had exercised reasonable diligence. For the purposes of this subparagraph, a "business day" is a day on which both parties are open and transacting business of the kind involved in that qualified financial contract that is the subject of confirmation.

(C) The party against whom enforcement is sought admits in its pleading, testimony, or otherwise in court that a contract was made.

(D) There is a note, memorandum, or other writing sufficient to indicate that a contract has been made, signed by the party against whom in enforcement is sought or by its authorized agent or broker.

For purposes of this paragraph, evidence of an electronic communication indicating the making in that communication of a contract, or a confirmation, admission, note, memorandum, or writing is not insufficient because it omits or incorrectly states one or more material terms agreed upon, as long as the evidence provides a reasonable basis for concluding that a contract was made.

(4) For purposes of this subdivision, the tangible written text produced by telefacsimile, computer retrieval, or other process by which electronic signals are transmitted by telephone or otherwise shall constitute a writing, and any symbol executed or adopted by a party with the present intention to authenticate a writing shall constitute a signing. The confirmation and notice of objection referred to in subparagraph (B) of paragraph (3) may be communicated by means of telex, telefacsimile, computer, or other similar process by which electronic signals are transmitted by telephone or otherwise provided that a party claiming to have communicated in that manner shall, unless the parties have otherwise agreed in writing, have the burden of establishing actual or constructive receipt by the other party as set forth in subparagraph (B) of paragraph (3).

(c) This section does not apply to leases subject to Division 10 (commencing with Section 10101) of the Commercial Code.

§ 1668. Contracts Contrary to Policy of Law

CERTAIN CONTRACTS UNLAWFUL. All contracts which have for their object, directly or indirectly, to exempt any one from responsibility for his own fraud, or willful injury to the person or property of another, or violation of law, whether willful or negligent, are against the policy of the law.

LIQUIDATED DAMAGES

§ 1671. Validity; standards for determination; applicability of section

(a) This section does not apply in any case where another statute expressly applicable to the contract prescribes the rules or standard for determining the validity of a provision in the contract liquidating the damages for the breach of the contract.

(b) Except as provided in subdivision (c), a provision in a contract liquidating the damages for the breach of the contract is valid unless the party seeking to invalidate the provision establishes that the provision was unreasonable under the circumstances existing at the time the contract was made.

(c) The validity of a liquidated damages provision shall be determined under subdivision (d) and not under subdivision (b) where the liquidated damages are sought to be recovered from either:

(1) A party to a contract for the retail purchase, or rental, by such party of personal property or services, primarily for the party's personal, family or household purposes; or

(2) A party to a lease of real property for use as a dwelling by the party or those dependent upon the party for support.

(d) In the cases described in subdivision (c), a provision in a contract liquidating damages for the breach of the contract is void except that the parties to such a contract may agree therein upon an amount which shall be presumed to be the amount of damage sustained by a breach thereof, when, from the nature of the case, it would be impracticable or extremely difficult to fix the actual damage.

§ 1698. Written Contract

A contract in writing may be altered by a contract in writing, or by an executed oral agreement and not otherwise. (In effect until 1976 amendment, see next item.)

§ 1698. Written Contract; Oral Agreement; Rules of Law (1976)

(a) A contract in writing may be modified by a contract writing.

(b) A contract in writing may be modified by an oral agreement to the extent that the oral agreement is executed by the parties.

(c) Unless the contract otherwise expressly provides, a contract in writing may be modified by an oral agreement supported by new consideration. The statute of frauds (Section 1624) is required to be satisfied if the contract as modified is within its provisions.

(d) Nothing in this section precludes in an appropriate case the application of rules of law concerning estoppel, oral novation and substitution of a new agreement, rescission of a written contract by an oral agreement, waiver of a provision of a written contract, or oral independent collateral contracts.

§ 1916–1. Legal Rate of Interest; Contract Rate[2]

The rate of interest upon the loan or forbearance of any money, goods or things in action or on accounts after demand or judgments rendered in any court of this state, shall be seven dollars upon the one hundred dollars for one year and at that rate for a greater or less sum or for a longer or a shorter time; but it shall be competent for parties to contract for the payment and receipt of a rate of interest not exceeding twelve dollars on the one hundred dollars for one year and not exceeding that rate for a greater or less sum or for a longer or shorter time, in which case such rate exceeding seven dollars on one hundred dollars shall be clearly expressed in writing.

§ 1916–3. Civil and Criminal Liability for Violations

Every person, company, association or corporation, who for any loan or forbearance of money, goods or things in action shall have paid or delivered any greater sum or value than is allowed to be received under the preceding sections, one and two, may either in person or his or its personal representative, recover in an action at law against the person, company, association or corporation who shall have taken or received the same, or his or its personal representative, treble the amount of the money so paid or value delivered in violation of said sections, providing such action shall be brought within one year after such payment or delivery. * * *

§ 2778. Rules of interpretation

RULES FOR INTERPRETING AGREEMENT OF INDEMNITY. In the interpretation of a contract of indemnity, the following rules are to be applied, unless a contrary intention appears:

1. Upon an indemnity against liability, expressly, or in other equivalent terms, the person indemnified is entitled to recover upon becoming liable;

2. Upon an indemnity against claims, or demands, or damages, or costs, expressly, or in other equivalent terms, the person indemnified is not entitled to recover without payment thereof;

3. An indemnity against claims, or demands, or liability, expressly, or in other equivalent terms, embraces the costs of defense against such claims, demands, or liability incurred in good faith, and in the exercise of a reasonable discretion;

4. The person indemnifying is bound, on request of the person indemnified, to defend actions or proceedings brought against the latter in respect to the matters embraced by the indemnity, but the person indemnified has the right to conduct such defenses, if he chooses to do so;

---

2. Cal.Const. Art. 15, § 1, now regulates interest rates.

5. If, after request, the person indemnifying neglects to defend the person indemnified, a recovery against the latter suffered by him in good faith, is conclusive in his favor against the former;

6. If the person indemnifying, whether he is a principal or a surety in the agreement, has not reasonable notice of the action or proceeding against the person indemnified, or is not allowed to control its defense, judgment against the latter is only presumptive evidence against the former;

7. A stipulation that a judgment against the person indemnified shall be conclusive upon the person indemnifying, is inapplicable if he had a good defense upon the merits, which by want of ordinary care he failed to establish in the action.

§ 2782. Construction Contracts; Invalidity of Provisions to Indemnify Promisee Against Liability; Exceptions

All provisions, clauses, covenants, or agreements contained in, collateral to, or affecting any construction contract and which purport to indemnify the promisee against liability for damages for (a) death or bodily injury to persons, (b) injury to property, (c) design defects or (d) any other loss, damage or expense arising under either (a), (b), or (c) from the sole negligence or willful misconduct of the promisee or the promisee's agents, servants or independent contractors who are directly responsible to such promisee, are against public policy and are void and unenforceable; provided, however, that this provision shall not affect the validity of any insurance contract, workmen's compensation or agreement issued by an admitted insurer as defined by the Insurance Code.

§ 2783. "Construction Contract" Defined

As used in Sections 2782 and 2782.5, "construction contract" is defined as any agreement or understanding, written or oral, respecting the construction, surveying, design, specifications, alteration, repair, improvement, maintenance, removal of or demolition of any building, highway, road, parking facility, bridge, railroad, airport, pier or dock, excavation or other structure, development or other improvement to real or personal property, or an agreement to perform any portion thereof or any act collateral thereto, or to perform any service reasonable related thereto, including, but not limited to, the erection of all structures or performance of work in connection therewith, the rental of all equipment, all incidental transportation, crane and rigging service and other goods and services furnished in connection therewith.

§ 3423. Injunction; Circumstances Requiring Denial

An injunction cannot be granted:

Fifth—To prevent the breach of a contract, other than a contract in writing for the rendition or furnishing of personal services from one to another where the minimum compensation for such service is at the rate of not less than six thousand dollars per annum. and where the promised service is of a special, unique, unusual, extraordinary or intellectual character, which gives it peculiar value the loss of which cannot be reasonably or adequately compensated in damages in an action at law, the performance of which would not be specifically enforced; provided, however, that an injunction may be granted to prevent the breach of a contract entered into between any nonprofit cooperative corporation or association and a member or stockholder thereof in respect to any provision regarding the sale or delivery to the corporation or association of the products produced or acquired by such member or stockholder.

CALIFORNIA CODE OF CIVIL PROCEDURE

§ 526. Cases in Which [Injunction] Authorized; Restrictions on Grant

An injunction may be granted in the following cases:

1. When it appears by the complaint that the plaintiff is entitled to the relief demanded, and such relief, or any part thereof, consists in restraining the commission or continuance of the act complained of, either for a limited period or perpetually;

2. When it appears by the complaint or affidavits that the commission or continuance of some act during the litigation would produce waste, or great or irreparable injury, to a party to the action;

3. When it appears, during the litigation, that a party to the action is doing, or threatens, or is about to do, or is procuring or suffering to be done, some act in violation of the rights of another party to the action respecting the subject of the action, and tending to render the judgment ineffectual;

4. When pecuniary compensation would not afford adequate relief;

5. Where it would be extremely difficult to ascertain the amount of compensation which would afford adequate relief; * * *

An injunction cannot be granted:

5. To prevent the breach of a contract (other than a contract in writing for the rendition or furnishing of personal service from one to another where the minimum compensation for such service is at the rate of not less than six thousand dollars per annum, and where the promised service is of a special, unique, unusual, extraordinary or intellectual character which gives it peculiar value the loss of which cannot be reasonably or adequately compensated in damages in an action at law) the performance of which would not be specifically enforced; provided, however, that an injunction may be granted to prevent the breach of a contract entered into between any nonprofit cooperative or association and a member or stockholder thereof, in respect to any provision regarding the sale or delivery to

the corporation or association of the products produced or acquired by such member or stockholder. * * *

§ 580b. Purchase Money Mortgages, etc.; No Deficiency Judgment

No deficiency judgment shall lie in any event after any sale of real property for failure of the purchaser to complete his contract of sale, or under a deed of trust, or mortgage, given to the vendor to secure payment of the balance of the purchase price of real property, or under a deed of trust, or mortgage, on a dwelling for not more than four families given to A lender to secure repayment of a loan which was in fact used to pay all or part of the purchase price of such dwelling occupied, entirely or in part, by the purchaser.

Where both a chattel mortgage and a deed of trust or mortgage have been given to secure payment of the balance of the combined purchase price of both real and personal property, no deficiency judgment shall lie at any time under any one thereof if no deficiency judgment would lie under the deed of trust or mortgage on real property.

CALIFORNIA GOVERNMENT CODE

§ 4107. Substitution of Subcontractors; Consent; Assignment of Subcontract; Subcontracting After Award

No prime contractor whose bid is accepted shall:

(a) Substitute any person as subcontractor in place of the subcontractor listed in the original bid, except that the awarding authority, or its duly authorized officer, may, except as otherwise provided in Section 4107.5, consent to the substitution of another person as a subcontractor:

(1) When the subcontractor listed in the bid after having had a reasonable opportunity to do so fails or refuses to execute a written contract, when such written contract, based upon the general terms, conditions, plans and specifications for the project involved or the terms of such subcontractor's written bid, is presented to him by the prime contractor.

(2) When the listed subcontractor becomes bankrupt or insolvent, or

(3) When the listed subcontractor fails or refuses to perform his subcontract, or

(4) When the listed subcontractor fails or refuses to meet the bond requirements of the prime contractor as set forth in Section 4108, or

(5) When the prime contractor demonstrates to the awarding authority, or its duly authorized officer, subject to the further provisions set forth in Section 4107.5, that the name of the subcontractor was listed as the result of an inadvertent clerical error, or

(6) When the listed subcontractor is not licensed pursuant to the Contractors License Law, or

143

(7) When the awarding authority, or its duly authorized officer, determines that the work performed by the listed subcontractor is substantially unsatisfactory and not in substantial accordance with the plans and specifications, or that the subcontractor is substantially delaying or disrupting the progress of the work.

Prior to approval of the prime contractor's request for such substitution the awarding authority, or its duly authorized officer, shall give notice in writing to the listed subcontractor of the prime contractor's request to substitute and of the reasons for such request. Such notice shall be served by certified or registered mail to the last known address of such subcontractor. The listed subcontractor who has been so notified shall have five working days within which to submit written objections to the substitution to the awarding authority. Failure to file such written objections shall constitute the listed subcontractor's consent to the substitution.

If written objections are filed, the awarding authority shall give notice in writing of at least five working days to the listed subcontractor of a hearing by the awarding authority on the prime contractor's request for substitution.

(b) Permit any such subcontract to be voluntarily assigned or transferred or allow it to be performed by anyone other than the original subcontractor listed in the original bid, without the consent of the awarding authority, or its duly authorized officer.

(c) Other than in the performance of "change orders" causing changes or deviations from the original contract, sublet or subcontract any portion of the work in excess of one-half of 1 percent of the prime contractor's total bid as to which his original bid did not designate a subcontractor.

§ 4107.5 Clerical Error in Listing Subcontractor; Objections by Listed Subcontractor; Substitution of Intended Subcontractor

The prime contractor as a condition to assert a claim of inadvertent clerical error in the listing of a subcontractor shall within two working days after the time of the prime bid opening by the awarding authority give written notice to the awarding authority and copies of such notice to both the subcontractor he claims to have listed in error and the intended subcontractor who had bid to the prime contractor prior to bid opening.

Any listed subcontractor who has been notified by the prime contractor in accordance with the provisions of this section as to an inadvertent clerical error shall be allowed six working days from the time of the prime bid opening within which to submit to the awarding authority and to the prime contractor written objection to the prime contractor's claim of inadvertent clerical error. Failure of such listed subcontractor to file such written notice within the six working days shall be primary evidence of his agreement that an inadvertent clerical error was made.

The awarding authority shall, after a public hearing as provided in Section 4107 and in the absence of compelling reasons to the contrary, consent to the substitution of the intended subcontractor:

(a) If (1) the prime contractor, (2) the subcontractor listed in error and (3) the intended subcontractor each submit an affidavit to the awarding authority along with such additional evidence as the parties may wish to submit that an inadvertent clerical error was in fact made, provided that the affidavits from each of the three parties are filed within eight working days from the time of the prime bid opening, or

(b) If such affidavits are filed by both the prime contractor and the intended subcontractor within such specified time but the subcontractor whom the prime contractor claims to have listed in error does not submit within six working days, to the awarding authority and to the prime contractor, written objection to the prime contractor's claim of inadvertent clerical error as, provided in this. section.

If such affidavits are filed by both the prime contractor and the intended subcontractor but the listed subcontractor has, within six working days from the time of the prime bid opening, submitted to the awarding authority and to the prime contractor written objection to the prime contractor's claim of inadvertent clerical error, the awarding authority shall investigate the claims of the parties and shall hold a public hearing as provided in Section 4107 to determine the validity of such claims. Any determination made shall be based on the facts contained in the declarations submitted under penalty of perjury by all three parties and supported by testimony under oath and subject to cross-examination. The awarding authority may, on its own motion or that of any other party, admit testimony of other contractors, any bid registries or depositories, or any other party in possession of facts which may have a bearing on the decision of the awarding authority.

§ 4110. Violation of Chapter as Contract Violation; Hearing; Cancellation; Penalty

A prime contractor violating any of the provisions of this chapter violates his contract. and the awarding authority may exercise the option, in its own discretion, of (1) cancelling his contract or (2) assessing the prime contractor a penalty in an amount of not more than 10 percent of the amount of the sub-contract involved, and this penalty shall be deposited in the fund out of which the prime contract is awarded. In any proceedings under this section the prime contractor shall be entitled to a public hearing and to five days' notice of the time and place thereof.

––––––

CALIFORNIA INSURANCE CODE

§ 533. Wilful Act of Insured; Negligence

An insurer is not liable for a loss caused by the wilful act of the insured; but he is not exonerated by the negligence of the insured, or of the insured's agents or others.

––––––

LABOR CODE

§ 2922. Termination at will upon notice; employment for a specified term

An employment, having no specified term, may be terminated at the will of either party on notice to the other. Employment for a specified term means an employment for a period greater than one month.

MAINE
REVISED STATUTES, 1903

Chapter 75

§ 14. There can be no trust concerning lands, except trusts arising or resulting by implication of law, unless created or declared by some writing signed by the party or his attorney.

MICHIGAN
STATUTES ANNOTATED

§ 27A.1405 Rights of Third Party Beneficiaries in Contracts

Any person for whose benefit a promise is made by way of contract, as hereinafter defined, has the same right to enforce said promise that he would have had if the said promise had been made directly to him as the promisee.

(1) A promise shall be construed to have been made for the benefit of a person whenever the promisor of said promise has undertaken to give or to do or refrain from doing something directly to or for said person.

(2)(a) The rights of a person for whose benefit a promise has been made, as defined in (1), shall be deemed to have become vested, subject always to such express or implied conditions, limitations, or infirmities of the contract to which the rights of the promisee or the promise are subject, without any act or knowledge on his part, the moment the promise becomes legally binding on the promisor, unless there is some stipulation, agreement or understanding in the contract to the contrary.

(b) If such person is not in being or ascertainable at the time the promise becomes legally binding on the promisor then his rights shall become vested the moment he comes into being or becomes ascertainable if the promise has not been discharged by agreement between the promisor and the promisee in the meantime.

(c) If the promisee is indebted or otherwise obligated to the person for whose benefit the promise was made and the promise in question is intended when performed to discharge that debt or obligation, then the promisor and the promisee may, by mutual agreement, divest said person of his rights, if this is done without intent to hinder, delay or defraud said person in the collection or enforcement of the said debt or other obligation which the promisee owes him and before he has taken any legal steps to enforce said promise made for his benefit.

(3) Nothing herein contained shall be held to abridge, impair or destroy the rights which the promisee of a promise made for the benefit of another person would otherwise have as a result of such promise.

(4) The provisions of this section shall be construed to be applicable to contracts made prior to its enactment as well as to those made subsequent thereto, unless such construction is held to be unconstitutional, in which case they shall be held to be applicable only to contracts made subsequent to its enactment.

MISSOURI
REVISED STATUTES

§ 379.140   Company Not to Deny Value—Full Amount Of Policy to be Paid

In all suits brought upon policies of insurance against loss or damage by fire hereafter issued or renewed, the defendant shall not be permitted to deny that the property insured thereby was worth at the time of the issuing of the policy the full amount insured therein on said property; and in case of total loss of the property insured, the measure of damage shall be the amount for which the same was insured, less whatever depreciation in value, below the amount for which the property is insured, the property may have sustained between the time of issuing the policy and the time of the loss, and the burden of proving such depreciation shall be upon the defendant; and in case of partial loss, the measure of damage shall be that portion of the value of the whole property insured, ascertained in the manner prescribed in this chapter, which the part injured or destroyed bears to the whole property insured.

MONTANA CODE ANNOTATED
TITLE 39

Part 9
Wrongful Discharge From Employment

39–2–901. Short title. This part maybe cited as the "Wrongful Discharge From Employment Act".

39–2–902. Purpose. This part sets forth certain rights and remedies with respect to wrongful discharge. Except as limited in this part, employment having no specified term may be terminated at the will of either the employer or the employee on notice to the other for any reason considered sufficient by the terminating party. Except as provided in 39–2–912, this part provides the exclusive remedy for a wrongful discharge from employment.

39–2–903. Definitions. In this part, the following definitions apply:

(1) "Constructive discharge" means the voluntary termination of employment by an employee because of a situation created by an act or omission of the employer which an objective, reasonable person would find so intolerable that voluntary termination is the only reasonable alternative. Constructive discharge does not mean voluntary termination because of an employer's refusal to promote the employee or improve wages, responsibilities, or other terms and conditions of employment.

(2) "Discharge" includes a constructive discharge as defined in subsection (1) and any other termination of employment, including resignation, elimination of the job, layoff for lack of work, failure to recall or rehire, and any other cutback in the number of employees for a legitimate business reason.

(3) "Employee" means a person who works for another for hire. The term does not include a person who is an independent contractor.

(4) "Fringe benefits" means the value of any employer-paid vacation leave, sick leave, medical insurance plan, disability insurance plan, life insurance plan, and pension benefit plan in force on the date of the termination.

(5) "Good cause" means reasonable job-related grounds for dismissal based on a failure to satisfactorily perform job duties, disruption of the employer's operation, or other legitimate business reason. The legal use of a lawful product by an individual off the employer's premises during nonworking hours is not a legitimate business reason, unless the employer acts within the provisions of 39–2–313(3) or (4).

(6) "Lost wages" means the gross amount of wages that would have been reported to the internal revenue service as gross income on Form W–2 and includes additional compensation deferred at the option of the employee.

(7) "Public policy" means a policy in effect at the time of the discharge concerning the public, health, safety, or welfare established by constitutional provision, statute, or administrative rule.

39–2–904. Elements of wrongful discharge. A discharge is wrongful only if:

(1) it was in retaliation for the employee's refusal to violate public policy or for reporting a violation of public policy;

(2) the discharge was not for good cause and the employee had completed the employer's probationary period of employment; or

(3) the employer violated the express provisions of its own written personnel policy.

39–2–905. Remedies.

(1) If an employer has committed a wrongful discharge, the employee may be awarded lost wages and fringe benefits for a period not to exceed 4 years from the date of discharge, together with interest thereon. Interim earnings, including amounts the employee could have earned with reasonable diligence, must be deducted from the amount awarded for lost wages. Before interim earnings are deducted from lost wages, there must be deducted from the interim earnings any reasonable amounts expended by the employee in searching for, obtaining, or relocating to new employment.

(2) The employee may recover punitive damages otherwise allowed by law if it is established by clear and convincing evidence that the employer engaged in actual fraud or actual malice in the discharge of the employee in violation of 39–2–904(1).

(3) There is no right under any legal theory to damages for wrongful discharge under this part for pain and suffering, emotional distress, compensatory damages, punitive damages, or any other form of damages, except as provided for in subsections (1) and (2).

39–2–911. Limitation of actions. (1) An action under this part must be filed within 1 year after the date of discharge.

(2) If an employer maintains written internal procedures, other than those specified in 39–2–912, under which an employee may appeal a discharge within the organizational structure of the employer, the employee shall first exhaust those procedures prior to filing an action under this part. The employee's failure to initiate or exhaust available internal procedures is a defense to an action brought under this part. If the employer's internal procedures are not completed within 90 days from the date the employee initiates the internal procedures, the employee may file an action under this part and for purposes of this subsection the employer's internal procedures are considered exhausted. The limitation period in subsection (1) is tolled until the procedures are exhausted. In no case may the provisions of the employer's internal procedures extend the limitation period in subsection (1) more than 120 days.

(3) If the employer maintains written internal procedures under which an employee may appeal a discharge within the organizational structure of the employer, the employer shall within 7 days of the date of the discharge notify the discharged employee of the existence of such procedures and

shall supply the discharged employee with a copy of them. If the employer fails to comply with this subsection, the discharged employee need not comply with subsection (2).

39-2-912.   Exemptions. This part does not apply to a discharge:

(1) that is subject to any other state or federal statute that provides a procedure or remedy for contesting the dispute. The statutes include those that prohibit discharge for filing complaints, charges, or claims with administrative bodies or that prohibit unlawful discrimination based on race, national origin, sex, age, disability, creed, religion, political belief, color, marital status, and other similar grounds.

(2) of an employee covered by a written collective bargaining agreement or a written contract of employment for a specific term.

39-2-913.   Preemption of common-law remedies. Except as provided in this part, no claim for discharge may arise from tort or express or implied contract.

39-2-914.   Arbitration. (1) A party may make a written offer to arbitrate a dispute that otherwise could be adjudicated under this part.

(2) An offer to arbitrate must be in writing and contain the following provisions:

(a) A neutral arbitrator must be selected by mutual agreement or, in the absence of agreement, as provided in 27-5-211.

(b) The arbitration must be governed by the Uniform Arbitration Act, Title 27, chapter 5. If there is a conflict between the Uniform Arbitration Act and this part, this part applies.

(c) The arbitrator is bound by this part.

(3) If a complaint is filed under this part, the offer to arbitrate must be made within 60 days after service of the complaint and must be accepted in writing within 30 days after the date the offer is made.

(4) A discharged employee who makes a valid offer to arbitrate that is accepted by the employer and who prevails in such arbitration is entitled to have the arbitrator's fee and all costs of arbitration paid by the employer.

(5) If a valid offer to arbitrate is made and accepted, arbitration is the exclusive remedy for the wrongful discharge dispute and there is no right to bring or continue a lawsuit under this part. The arbitrator's award is final and binding, subject to review of the arbitrator's decision under the provisions of the Uniform Arbitration Act.

39-2-915.   Effect of rejection of offer to arbitrate. A party who makes a valid offer to arbitrate that is not accepted by the other party and who prevails in an action under this part is entitled as an element of costs to reasonable attorney fees incurred subsequent to the date of the offer.

NEW JERSEY STATUTES ANNOTATED

TITLE 34

CHAPTER 19
EMPLOYMENT PROTECTION

34:19–1. Short title

This act shall be known and may be cited as the "Conscientious Employee Protection Act."

34:19–2. Definitions

As used in this act:

a. "Employer" means any individual, partnership, association, corporation or any person or group of persons acting directly or indirectly on behalf of or in the interest of an employer with the employer's consent and shall include all branches of State Government, or the several counties and municipalities thereof, or any other political subdivision of the State, or a school district, or any special district or any authority, commission, or board or any other agency or instrumentality thereof.

b. "Employee" means any individual who performs services for and under the control and direction of an employer for wages or other remuneration.

c. "Public body" means:

(1) the United States Congress, and State legislature, or any popularly-elected local governmental body, or any member or employee thereof;

(2) any federal, State, or local judiciary, or any member or employee thereof, or any grand or petit jury;

(3) any federal, State, or local regulatory, administrative, or public agency or authority, or instrumentality thereof;

(4) any federal State, or local law enforcement agency, prosecutorial office, or police or peace officer;

(5) any federal, State, or local department of an executive branch of government; or

(6) any division, board, bureau, office, committee or commission of any of the public bodies described in the above paragraphs of this subsection.

d. "Supervisor" means any individual with an employer's organization who has the authority to direct and control the work performance of the affected employee, who has authority to take corrective action regarding the violation of the law, rule or regulation of which the employee complains, or who has been designated by the employer on the notice required under section 7 of this act.

e. "Retaliatory action" means the discharge, suspension or demotion of an employee, or other adverse employment action taken against an employee in the terms and conditions of employment.

151

f. "Improper quality of patient care" means, with respect to patient care, any practice, procedure, action or failure to act of an employer that is a health care provider which violates any law or any rule, regulation or declaratory ruling adopted pursuant to law, or any professional code of ethics.

34:19–3. Employer retaliatory action; protected employee actions

An employer shall not take any retaliatory action against an employee because the employee does any of the following:

a. Discloses, or threatens to disclose to a supervisor or to a public body an activity, policy or practice of the employer or another employer, with whom there is a business relationship, that the employee reasonably believes is in violation of a law, or a rule or regulation promulgated pursuant to law, or, in the case of an employee who is a licensed or certified health care professional, reasonably believes constitutes improper quality of patient care;

b. Provides information to, or testifies before, any public body conducting an investigation, hearing or inquiry into any violation of law, or a rule or regulation promulgated pursuant to law by the employer or another employer, with whom there is a business relationship, or, in the case of an employee who is a licensed or certified health care professional, provides information to, or testifies before any public body conducting an investigation, hearing or inquiry into the quality of patient care or

c. Objects to, or refuses to participate in any activity, policy or practice which the employee reasonably believes:

(1) is in violation of a law, or a rule or regulation promulgated pursuant to law or, if the employee is a licensed or certified health care professional, constitutes improper quality of patient care;

(2) is fraudulent or criminal; or

(3) is incompatible with a clear mandate of public policy concerning the public health, safety or welfare or protection of the environment.

34:19–4. Disclosure to public body; requirement of notice and opportunity to correct

The protection against retaliatory action provided by this act pertaining to disclosure to a public body shall not apply to an employee who makes a disclosure to a public body unless the employee has brought the activity, policy or practice in violation of a law, or a rule or regulation promulgated pursuant to law to the attention of a supervisor of the employee by written notice and has afforded the employer a reasonable opportunity to correct the activity, policy or practice. Disclosure shall not be required where the employee is reasonably certain that the activity, policy or practice is known to one or more supervisors of the employer or where the employee reasonably fears physical harm as a result of the disclosure provided, however, that the situation is emergency in nature.

34:19–5. Violations; civil action

Upon a violation of any of the provisions of this act, an employee or former employee may, within one year, institute a civil action in a court of competent jurisdiction. Upon the application of any party, a jury trial shall be directed to try the validity of the claim under this act specified in the suit. All remedies available in common law tort actions shall be available to prevailing plaintiffs. These remedies are in addition to any legal or equitable relief provided by this act or any other statute. The court may also order:

a. An injunction to restrain continued violation of this act;

b. The reinstatement of the employee to the same position held before the retaliatory action, or to an equivalent position;

c. The reinstatement of full fringe benefits and seniority rights;

d. The compensation for lost wages, benefits and other remuneration;

e. The payment by the employer of reasonable costs, and attorney's fees;

f. Punitive damages; or

g. An assessment of a civil fine of not more than $1,000.00 for the first violation of the act and not more than $5,000.00 for each subsequent violation, which shall be paid to the State Treasurer for deposit in the General Fund.

34:19–6. Award of attorney's fees and costs to employer; action without basis in law or fact

A court, upon notice of motion in accordance with the Rules Governing the Courts of the State of New Jersey, may also order that reasonable attorneys' fees and court costs be awarded to an employer if the court determines that an action brought by an employee under this act was without basis in law or in fact. However, an employee shall not be assessed attorneys' fees under this section if, after exercising reasonable and diligent efforts after filing a suit, the employee files a voluntary dismissal concerning the employer, within a reasonable time after determining that the employer would not be found to be liable for damages.

34:19–7. Informing employees of protections and obligation under act; name of person designated to receive notices

An employer shall conspicuously display notices of its employees' protections and obligations under this act, and use other appropriate means to keep its employees so informed. Each notice posted pursuant to this section shall include the name of the person or persons the employer has designated to receive written notifications pursuant to section 4 of this act.

34:19–8. Effect of act on rights, privileges, or remedies of employees under other laws, regulations, or agreements

Nothing in this act shall be deemed to diminish the rights, privileges, or remedies of any employee under any other federal or State law or regulation, or under any collective bargaining agreement. or employment contract; except that the institution of an action in accordance with this act shall be deemed a waiver of the rights and remedies available under any other contract, collective bargaining agreement, State law, rule or regulation or under the common law.

NEW YORK

CIVIL PRACTICE LAW AND RULES

§ 3005.   Relief Against Mistake of Law

When relief against a mistake is sought in an action or by way of defense or counterclaim, relief shall not be denied merely because the mistake is one of law rather than one of fact.

NEW YORK GENERAL OBLIGATIONS LAW

§ 5–701.   Agreements Required to Be in Writing

a.   Every agreement, promise or undertaking is void, unless it or some note or memorandum thereof be in writing, and subscribed by the party to be charged therewith, or by his lawful agent, if such agreement, promise or undertaking:

1.   By its terms is not to be performed within one year from the making thereof or the performance of which is not to be completed before the end of a lifetime;

2.   Is a special promise to answer for the debt, default or miscarriage of another person;

3.   Is made in consideration of marriage, except mutual promises to marry;

4.   Is a subsequent or new promise to pay a debt discharged in bankruptcy;

5.   Notwithstanding section 2–201 of the Uniform Commercial Code, if the goods be sold at public auction, and the auctioneer at the time of the sale, enters in a sale book, a memorandum specifying the nature and price of the property sold, the terms of the sale, the name of the purchaser, and the name of the person on whose account the sale was made, such memorandum is equivalent in effect to a note of the contract or sale, subscribed by the party to be charged therewith;

6.   Is a contract to assign or an assignment, with or without consideration to the promisor, of a life or health or accident insurance policy, or a promise, with or without consideration to the promisor, to name a benefi-

ciary of any such policy. This provision shall not apply to a policy of industrial life or health or accident insurance.

7. Is a contract to pay compensation for services rendered in negotiating a loan, or in negotiating the purchase, sale, exchange, renting or leasing of any real estate or interest therein, or of a business opportunity, business, its good will, inventory, fixtures or an interest therein, including a majority of the voting stock interest in a corporation and including the creating of a partnership interest. ''Negotiating'' includes procuring an introduction to a party to the transaction or assisting in the negotiation or consummation of the transaction. This provision shall apply to a contract implied in fact or in law to pay reasonable compensation but shall not apply to a contract to pay compensation to an auctioneer, an attorney at law, or a duly licensed real estate broker or real estate salesman.

b. Every written agreement entered into after June first, nineteen hundred seventy-eight, for the lease of space to be occupied for residential purposes, or to which a consumer is a party wherein the money, property or service which is the subject of the transaction is primarily for personal, family or household purposes must be:

1. Written in non-technical language and in a clear and coherent manner using words with common and every day meanings;

2. Appropriately divided and captioned by its various sections.

Any creditor, seller or lessor who fails to comply with the foregoing provisions of this subdivision shall be liable to a consumer who is a party to a written agreement governed by the provisions thereof in an amount equal to the sum of any actual damages sustained plus fifty dollars. The total class action penalty against any such creditor, seller or lessor shall not exceed ten thousand dollars. These penalties may be enforced only in a court of competent jurisdiction, but not after both parties to the agreement have fully performed their obligation under such agreement, nor against any creditor, seller or lessor who attempts in good faith to comply with this section. This subdivision shall not apply to agreements involving amounts in excess of fifty thousand dollars.

c. A violation of the provisions of subdivision b of this section shall not render any such agreement void or voidable nor shall it constitute:

1. A defense to any action or proceeding to enforce such agreement; or

2. A defense to any action or proceeding for breach of such agreement.

§ 5–1103. Written Agreement for Modification or Discharge

An agreement, promise or undertaking to change or modify, or to discharge in whole or in part, any contract, obligation, or lease, or any mortgage or other security interest in personal or real property shall not be invalid because of the absence of consideration, provided that the agreement, promise or undertaking changing, modifying, or discharging such contract, obligation, lease, mortgage or security interest, shall be in writing and signed by the party against whom it is sought to enforce the change, modification or discharge, or by his agent.

§ 5–1105. Written Promise Expressing Past Consideration

A promise in writing and signed by the promisor or by his agent shall not be denied effect as a valid contractual obligation on the ground that consideration for the promise is past or executed, if the consideration is expressed in the writing and is proved to have been given or performed and would be a valid consideration but for the time when it was given or performed.

§ 5–1109. Written Irrevocable Offer

Except as otherwise provided in section 2–205 of the Uniform Commercial Code with respect to an offer by a merchant to buy or sell goods, when an offer to enter into a contract is made in a writing signed by the offeror, or by his agent, which states that the offer is irrevocable during a period set forth or until a time fixed, the offer shall not be revocable during such period or until such time because of the absence of consideration for the assurance of irrevocability. When such a writing states that the offer is irrevocable but does not state any period or time of irrevocability, it shall be construed to state that the offer is irrevocable for a reasonable time.

§ 15–301. When Written Agreement or Other Instrument Cannot be Changed by Oral Executory Agreement, or Discharged or Terminated by Oral Executory Agreement or Oral Consent or by Oral Notice

1. A written agreement or other written instrument which contains a provision to the effect that it cannot be changed orally, cannot be changed by an executory agreement unless such executory agreement is in writing and signed by the party against whom enforcement of the change is sought or by his agent.

2. A written agreement or other written instrument which contains a provision to the effect that it cannot be terminated orally, cannot be discharged by an executory agreement unless such executory agreement is in writing and signed by the party against whom enforcement of the discharge is sought, or by his agent, and cannot be terminated by mutual consent unless such termination is effected by an executed accord and satisfaction other than the substitution of one executory contract for another, or is evidenced by a writing signed by the party against whom it is sought to enforce the termination, or by his agent.

3. a. A discharge or partial discharge of obligations under a written agreement or other written instrument is a change of the agreement or instrument for the purpose of subdivision one of this section and is not a discharge or termination for the purpose of subdivision two, unless all executory obligations under the agreement or instrument are discharged or terminated.

b. A discharge or termination of all executory obligations under a written agreement or other written instrument is a discharge or termination for the purpose of subdivision two even though accrued obligations remaining unperformed at the date of the discharge or termination are not affected by it.

c. If a written agreement or other written instrument containing a provision that it cannot be terminated orally also provides for termination or discharge on notice by one or either party, both subdivision two and subdivision four of this section apply whether or not the agreement or other instrument states specifically that the notice must be in writing.

4. If a written agreement or other written instrument contains a provision for termination or discharge on written notice by one or either party, the requirement that such notice be in writing cannot be waived except by a writing signed by the party against whom enforcement of the waiver is sought or by his agent.

5. If executed by an agent, any agreement; evidence of termination, notice of termination or waiver, required by this section to be in writing, which affects or relates to real property or an interest therein as defined in section 5–101 in any manner stated in subdivisions one or two of section 5–703 of this chapter shall be void unless such agent was thereunto authorized in writing.

6. As used in this section the term "agreement" includes promise and undertaking.

§ 15–303. Release in Writing Without Consideration or Seal

A written instrument which purports to be a total or partial release of all claims, debts, demands or obligations, or a total or partial release of any particular claim, debt, demand or obligation, or a release or discharge in whole or in part of a mortgage, lien, security interest or charge upon personal or real property, shall not be invalid because of the absence of consideration or of a seal.

§ 15–501. Executory Accord

1. Executory accord as used in this section means an agreement embodying a promise express or implied to accept at some future time a stipulated performance in satisfaction or discharge in whole or in part of any present claim, cause of action, contract, obligation, or lease, or any mortgage or other security interest in personal or real property, and a promise express or implied to render such performance in satisfaction or in discharge of such claim, cause of action, contract, obligation, lease, mortgage or security interest.

2. An executory accord shall not be denied effect as a defense or as the basis of an action or counterclaim by reason of' the fact that the satisfaction or discharge of the claim, cause of action, contract, obligation, lease, mortgage or other security interest which is the subject of the accord was to occur at a time after the making of the accord, provided the promise

of the party against whom it is sought to enforce the accord is in writing and signed by such party or by his agent. If executed by an agent, any promise required by this section to be in writing which affects or relates to real property or an interest therein as defined in section 5–101 in any manner stated in subdivisions one or two of section 5–703 of this chapter shall be void unless such agent was thereunto authorized in writing.

3.   If an executory accord is not performed according to its terms by one party, the other party shall be entitled either to assert his rights under the claim, cause of action, contract, obligation, lease, mortgage or other security interest which is the subject of the accord, or to assert his right under the accord.

§ 15–503.   Offer of Accord Followed by Tender

1.   An offer in writing, signed by the offeror or by his agent, to accept a performance therein designated in satisfaction or discharge in whole or in part of any claim, cause of action, contract, obligation, or lease, or any mortgage or other security interest in personal or real property, followed by tender of such performance by the offeree or by his agent before revocation of the offer, shall not be denied effect as a defense or as the basis of an action or counterclaim by reason of the fact that such tender was not accepted by the offeror or by his agent.

2.   If executed by an agent, any offer required by this section to be in writing which affects or relates to real property or an interest therein as defined in section 5–101 in any manner stated in subdivisions one or two of section 5–703 of this chapter shall be void unless such agent was thereunto authorized in writing.

———

NEW YORK JUDICIARY LAW[3]

§ 753.   Power of Courts to Punish for Civil Contempts

A.   A court of record has power to punish, by fine and imprisonment, or either, a neglect or violation of duty, or other misconduct, by which a right or remedy of a party to a civil action or special proceeding, pending in the court may be defeated, impaired, impeded, or prejudiced, in any of the following cases:

3.   A party to the action or special proceeding, an attorney, counselor, or other person, for the non-payment of a sum of money, ordered or adjudged by the court to be paid, in a case where by law execution can not be awarded for the collection of such sum except as otherwise specifically provided by the civil practice law and rules; or for any other disobedience to a lawful mandate of the court.

3.   Prior to 1977 Amendments.

§ 754. Special Proceeding to Punish for Contempt Punishable Civilly

Sections seven hundred and fifty, seven hundred and fifty-one, and seven hundred and fifty-two, do not extend to a special proceeding to punish a person in a case specified in section seven hundred and fifty-three. In a case specified in section seven hundred and fifty-three, or in any other case where it is specially prescribed by law, that a court of record, or a judge thereof, or a referee appointed by the court, has power to, punish, by fine and imprisonment, or either, or generally as a contempt, a neglect or violation of duty, or other misconduct; and a right or remedy of a party to a civil action or special proceeding pending in the court, or before the judge or the referee, may be defeated, impaired, impeded, or prejudiced thereby, the offense must be punished as prescribed in the following sections of this article.

§ 761. Order to Show Cause Defined; Service

An order to show cause is equivalent to a notice of motion; and. the subsequent proceedings thereupon are taken in the action or special proceeding, as upon a motion made therein. In a civil contempt proceeding such order to show cause shall be served upon the accused, unless service upon the attorney for the accused be ordered by the court or judge.

§ 770. Final Order Directing Punishment; Exception

If it is determined that the accused has committed the offense charged; and that it was calculated to, or actually did, defeat, impair, impede, or prejudice the rights or remedies of a party to an action or special proceeding, brought in the court, or before the judge or referee; the court, judge, or referee must make a final order directing that he be punished by fine or imprisonment, or both, as the nature of the case requires. A warrant of commitment must issue accordingly, except where an application is made under this article and in pursuance of section two hundred forty-five of the domestic relations law or any other section of law for a final order directing punishment for failure to pay alimony and/or counsel fees pursuant to an order of the court or judge in an action for divorce or separation and the husband appear and satisfy the court or a judge before whom the application may be pending that he has no means or property or income to comply with the terms of the order at the time, the court or judge may in its or his discretion deny the application to punish the husband, without prejudice to the wife's rights and without prejudice to a renewal of the application by the wife upon notice and after proof that the financial condition of the husband is changed.

§ 772. Punishment Upon Return of Order to Show Cause

Upon the return of an order to show cause, the questions which arise must be determined, as upon any other motion; and, if the determination is to the effect specified in section seven hundred and seventy, the order thereupon must be to the same effect as the final *order therein prescribed.

159

Upon a certified copy of the order so made, the offender may be committed, without further process.

§ 773. Amount of Fine

If an actual loss or injury has been produced to a party to an action or special proceeding, by reason of the misconduct proved against the offender, and the case is not one where it is specially prescribed by law, that an action may be maintained to recover damages for the loss or injury, a fine, sufficient to indemnify the aggrieved party, must be imposed upon the offender, and collected, and paid over to the aggrieved party, under the direction of the court. The payment and acceptance of such a fine constitute a bar to an action by the aggrieved party, to recover damages for the loss or injury. Where it is not shown that such an actual loss or injury has been produced, a fine must be imposed, not exceeding the amount of the complainant's costs and expenses, and two hundred and fifty dollars in addition thereto, and must be collected and paid, in like manner. A corporation may be fined as prescribed in this section.

NEW YORK PERSONAL PROPERTY LAW

§ 302. Requirements as to Retail Instalment Contracts

1. A retail instalment contract shall be in writing, shall contain all the agreements of the parties and shall be signed by the buyer and the seller.

2. The printed portion of the contract shall be in at least eight point type. The contract shall contain printed or written in a size equal to, at least ten-point bold type:

(a) Both at the top of the contract and directly above the space reserved for the signature of the buyer, the words "RETAIL INSTALMENT CONTRACT";

(b) A specific statement that liability insurance coverage for bodily injury and property damage caused to others is not included, if that is the case; and

(c) One of the following notices: "NOTICE TO THE BUYER: 1. Do not sign this contract before you read it or if it contains any blank space. 2. You are entitled to a completely filled in copy of this contract when you sign it. 3. Under the law, you have the following rights, among others: (a) To pay off in advance the full amount due and to obtain a partial refund of the credit service charge; (b) To redeem the property if repossessed for a default; (c) To require, under certain conditions, a resale of the property if repossessed. 4. According to law you have the privilege of purchasing the insurance on the motor vehicle provided for in this contract from an agent or broker of your own selection," or "NOTICE TO THE BUYER: 1. Do not sign this agreement before you read it or if it contains any blank space. 2.

You are entitled to a completely filled in copy of this agreement. 3. Under the law, you have the right to pay off in advance the full amount due and under certain conditions to obtain a partial refund of the credit service charge. 4. According to law you have the privilege of purchasing the insurance on the motor vehicle provided for in this contract from an agent or broker of your own selection". * * *

VEHICLE AND TRAFFIC LAW

ARTICLE 17–A
FRANCHISED MOTOR VEHICLE DEALER ACT

§ 460. Legislative findings

The legislature finds and declares that the distribution and sale of motor vehicles within this state vitally affects the general economy of the state and the public interest and the public welfare, and that in order to promote the public interest and the public welfare and in the exercise of its police power, it is necessary to regulate motor vehicle manufacturers, distributors and factory or distributor representatives and to regulate dealers of motor vehicles doing business in this state in order to prevent frauds, impositions and other abuses upon its citizens and to protect and preserve the investments and properties of the citizens of this state.

§ 461. Short title

This article shall be known and may be cited as the "franchised motor vehicle dealer act".

§ 462. Definitions

Whenever used in this article:

1. "Distributor" means any person who primarily offers, sells or distributes new motor vehicles to franchised motor vehicle dealers or maintains distributor representatives within the state.

2. "Distributor branch" means a branch office maintained by a distributor which offers, sells or distributes new motor vehicles to franchised motor vehicle dealer's in this state.

3. "Distributor representative" means a representative employed by a distributor branch or distributor.

4. "Factory branch" means a branch office maintained for directing and supervising the representatives of the manufacturer or which office is maintained for the sale of motor vehicles.

5. "Factory representative" means a representative employed by a factory branch for the purpose of making or promoting the sale of motor vehicles or for supervising, servicing, instructing or contacting franchised motor vehicle dealers or prospective motor vehicle dealers.

6. "Franchise" means a written arrangement for a definite or indefinite period in which a manufacturer or distributor grants to a franchised motor vehicle dealer a license to use a trade name, service mark or related characteristic, and in which there is a community of interest in the marketing of motor vehicles or services related thereto at wholesale, retail, by lease or otherwise and/or pursuant to which a franchised motor vehicle dealer purchases and resells or offers (as agent, principal, or otherwise) products associated with the name or mark or related components of the franchise.

7. "Franchised motor vehicle dealer" means any person required to be registered pursuant to section four hundred fifteen of this chapter and who has been granted a "franchise" as defined herein.

8. "Franchisor" means any manufacturer, distributor, distributor branch or factory branch, importer or other person, partnership, corporation, association, or entity, whether resident or non-resident, which enters into or is presently a party to a franchise with a franchised motor vehicle dealer.

9. "Manufacturer" means any person, partnership, corporation, association, factory branch or other entity engaged in the business of manufacturing or assembling new and unused motor vehicles for sale in this state.

10. "Motor vehicle" means any motor vehicle as defined in section one hundred twenty-five of this chapter provided the commissioner shall have authority to except by regulation vehicles other than passenger automobiles, trucks and motorcycles from such definition.

11. "New motor vehicle" means a vehicle sold or transferred by a manufacturer, distributor or dealer, which has not been placed in consumer use or used as a demonstrator.

§ 463. Unfair business practices by franchisors

1. It shall be unlawful for any franchisor to directly or indirectly coerce or attempt to coerce any franchised motor vehicle dealer:

(a) To order or accept delivery of any motor vehicle or vehicles; appliances, tools, machinery, equipment, parts or accessories therefor or any other commodity or commodities which shall not have been voluntarily ordered by said franchised motor vehicle dealer except any such items required by a recall campaign.

(b) To order or accept delivery of any motor vehicle with special features, appliances, accessories or equipment not included in the list price of said motor vehicle as publicly advertised by the franchisor.

(c) To contribute or pay money or anything of value into any cooperative or other advertising program or fund unless such program or fund shall be controlled by a dealer or group of dealers.

2. It shall be unlawful for any franchisor:

(a) To refuse to deliver in reasonable quantity and within a reasonable time after receipt of a dealer's order to any franchised motor vehicle dealer any vehicle covered by such franchise which is publicly advertised by such franchisor to be available for immediate delivery. *Provided*, however, the failure to deliver any motor vehicle shall not be considered a violation of this article if such failure be due to acts of God, work stoppages or delays due to strikes or labor difficulties, freight embargoes, shortage of materials, a lack of manufacturing capacity or other causes over which the franchisor shall have no control.

(b) To directly or indirectly coerce or attempt to coerce any franchised motor vehicle dealer to enter into any agreement with such franchisor or officer, agent or other representative thereof, or to do any other act prejudicial to the monetary interests or property rights of said dealer by threatening to cancel any unexpired contractual agreement existing between such franchisor and said dealer. *Provided*, however, that good faith notice to any franchised motor vehicle dealer of said dealer's violation of any terms or provisions of such franchise shall not constitute a violation of this article.

(c) To condition the renewal or extension of a franchise on a franchised motor vehicle dealer's substantial renovation of the dealer's place of business or on the construction, purchase, acquisition or rental of a new place of business by the franchised motor vehicle dealer unless the franchisor has advised the franchised motor vehicle dealer in writing of its intent to impose such a condition within a reasonable time prior to the effective date of the proposed date of renewal or extension (but in no case less than one hundred eighty days) and provided the franchisor demonstrates the need for such change in the place of business and the reasonableness of such demand in view of the need to service the public and the economic conditions existing in the automobile industry at the time such action would be required of the franchised motor vehicle dealer. As part of any such condition the franchisor shall agree, in writing, to supply the dealer with an adequate supply of automobiles to meet the sales levels necessary to support the increased overhead incurred by the dealer by reason of such renovation, construction, purchase or rental of a new place of business.

(d)(1) To terminate, cancel or refuse to renew the franchise of any franchised motor vehicle dealer except for due cause, regardless of the terms of the franchise. A franchisor shall notify a franchised motor vehicle dealer, in writing, of its intention to terminate, cancel or refuse to renew the franchise of such dealer at least ninety days before the effective date thereof, stating the specific grounds for such termination, cancellation or refusal to renew. In no event shall the term of any such franchise expire without the written consent of the franchised motor vehicle dealer involved prior to the expiration of at least ninety days following such written notice except as hereinafter provided.

(2) The provisions of subparagraph one of this paragraph notwithstanding, a franchisor may terminate its franchise with a franchised motor vehicle dealer upon at least fifteen days written notice upon the occurrence of any of the following: (i) conviction of a franchised motor vehicle dealer, or one of its principal owners, of a felony or a crime punishable by

imprisonment which substantially adversely affects the business of the franchisor, or (ii) the failure of the franchised motor vehicle dealer to conduct its customary sales and service operations for a continuous period of seven business days, except for acts of God or circumstances beyond the direct control of the franchised motor vehicle dealer or when any license required by the franchised motor vehicle dealer is suspended for a period of thirty days or less, or (iii) insolvency of the franchised motor vehicle dealer, or filing of any petition by or against the franchised motor vehicle dealer under any bankruptcy or receivership law.

(e) Any franchised motor vehicle dealer who receives a written notice of termination, cancellation or refusal to renew a franchise or a written notice of a franchisor's demand that the dealer substantially renovate an existing place of business or buy, construct or rent a new place of business as a condition of franchise renewal or extension may, within one hundred twenty days of receipt of such notice, have a review of the demand to change the place of business or the threatened termination, cancellation or nonrenewal by instituting an action in a court of competent jurisdiction as provided in section four hundred sixty-nine of this article.

(f) To intentionally resort to or use any false or misleading advertisements.

(g) To sell or offer to sell any new motor vehicle to any franchised motor vehicle dealer at a lower actual price therefor than the actual price offered to any other franchised motor vehicle dealer for the same model vehicle similarly equipped or to utilize any device including, but not limited to, sales promotion plans or programs which result in such lesser actual price. *Provided*, however, the provisions of this paragraph shall not apply to sales to a franchised motor vehicle dealer for: (i) resale to any unit of government, or (ii) donation or use by said dealer in a driver education program. This paragraph shall not be construed to prevent the offering of incentive programs or other discounts if such discounts are available to all franchised motor vehicle dealers in this state on a proportionately equal basis.

(h) To sell or offer to sell any new motor vehicle to any person, except a distributor; at a lower actual price therefor than the actual price offered and charged to a franchised motor vehicle dealer for the same model vehicle similarly equipped or to utilize any device which results in such lesser actual price.

(i) To sell or offer to sell parts and/or accessories to any franchised motor vehicle dealer at a lower actual price therefor than the actual price offered to any other franchised motor vehicle dealer for similar parts and/or accessories for use in his own business. *Provided*, however, that nothing herein contained shall be construed to prevent a manufacturer or distributor, or any agent thereof, from selling to a franchised motor vehicle dealer, who operates and serves as a wholesaler of parts and accessories, such parts and accessories as may be ordered by such franchised motor vehicle dealer for resale to retail outlets at a lower actual price than the actual price offered a franchised motor vehicle dealer who does not operate or serve as a wholesaler of parts and accessories. This paragraph shall not be construed to prevent the offering of incentive programs or other discounts available to all franchised motor vehicle dealers in the state on a proportionately equal basis.

(j) To prevent or attempt to prevent, by contract or otherwise, any franchised motor vehicle dealer from changing the capital structure of its dealership or the means by or through which it finances the operation of its dealership, provided the dealer at all times meets any capital standards agreed to between the dealer and the franchisor and as applied by the franchisor to all other comparable franchised motor vehicle dealers of the franchisor located within the state.

(k) To unreasonably withhold consent to the sale or transfer of an interest, in whole or in part, to any other person or party by any franchised motor vehicle dealer or any partner or stockholder of any franchised motor vehicle dealer. If such consent to sale or transfer shall be withheld by the franchisor, the franchisor shall provide specific reasons for its withholding of consent within sixty days of receipt of the request for such consent provided such request is accompanied by proper documentation as may reasonably be required by the franchisor. Upon receipt of notice and reasons for the franchisor's withholding of consent, the franchised motor vehicle dealer may within one hundred twenty days have a review of the manufacturer's decision as provided in section four hundred sixty-nine of this article.

(*l*) To require a franchised motor vehicle dealer to assent to a release, assignment, novation, waiver or estoppel which would relieve any person from liability imposed under this article, provided that this paragraph shall not be construed to prevent a franchised motor vehicle dealer from entering into a valid release or settlement agreement with a franchisor.

(m)(1) To deny to the surviving spouse or heirs of an individual franchised motor vehicle dealer or of a partner of an unincorporated franchised motor vehicle dealer or of a stockholder of a corporate franchised motor vehicle dealer the right to succeed to the interest of the decedent in such franchised motor vehicle dealership enterprise or directly or indirectly to interfere with, hinder or prevent the continuance of the business of the franchised motor vehicle dealer by reason of such succession to the interest of the decedent. *Provided*, however, that the continuation of the business of the franchised motor vehicle dealer shall be conducted under competent management acceptable to the franchisor, whose acceptance shall not be unreasonably withheld.

(2) Notwithstanding the foregoing, in the event the franchised motor vehicle dealer and franchisor have duly executed an agreement concerning succession rights prior to the individual dealer's, partner's or stockholder's death and if such agreement has not been revoked by the franchised motor vehicle dealer, such agreement shall be observed, even if it designates an individual other than the surviving spouse or heirs of the decedent.

(n) To fail to indemnify and hold harmless its franchised motor vehicle dealers against any losses or damages including, but not limited to, court costs and attorneys' fees arising out of actions, claims or proceedings including, but not limited to, those based upon strict liability, negligence, misrepresentation, warranty (expressed or implied) or revocation as described in section 2–608 of the uniform commercial code, where the action, claim or proceeding directly relates to the manufacture, assembly or design of new motor vehicles, parts or accessories or other functions of the franchisor including, without limitation, the selection by the franchisor of parts or components for the vehicle or any damages to merchandise or vehicles occurring in transit where the carrier is designated by the franchisor, notwithstanding the terms of any franchise. If the action, claim or proceeding includes independent allegations against the franchised motor vehicle dealer, the franchisor shall bear only that portion of the cost, fees and judgment which is directly related to the manufacture, assembly or design of the vehicle, parts or accessories, or other function of the franchisor beyond the control of the franchised motor vehicle dealer.

(o)(1) Upon a termination, cancellation or nonrenewal of a franchise by a franchisor or franchised motor vehicle dealer under this article, to refuse to accept a return of new and unused current model motor vehicle inventory which has been acquired from the franchisor, new and unused noncurrent model motor vehicle inventory which has been acquired from the franchisor within one hundred twenty days of the effective date of the termination, cancellation or nonrenewal; supplies, parts, equipment and furnishings purchased from the franchisor or its approved sources and special tools. The obligation of the franchisor shall be limited to the repurchase of the above property which is unaltered and undamaged, in good and useable condition, and, in the. case of supplies, parts and equipment to those items which are currently listed in the franchisor's supplies and parts list. Furthermore, the obligation of the franchisor to repurchase supplies upon a termination, cancellation or nonrenewal by a franchised motor vehicle dealer shall be limited to supplies mandated by the franchisor. Parts eligible for repurchase shall include parts which have been renumbered in the current parts list but which are identical in design and material to the currently numbered part. The return rights afforded the franchised motor vehicle dealer under the provisions of the paragraph shall be in addition to those, if any, provided in the franchise.

(2) The franchisor shall pay fair and reasonable compensation for the above described property upon repurchase. In the case of new motor vehicle inventory, accessories and parts, fair and reasonable compensation shall in no instance be less than the net acquisition price paid by the franchised motor vehicle dealer to the franchisor or its approved sources. Upon a termination, cancellation or nonrenewal of a franchise by a franchisor, within thirty days of such termination, cancellation or nonrenewal, the franchisor shall send to the franchised motor vehicle dealer instructions on the methodology by which the franchised motor vehicle dealer must ship the above described property to the franchisor, the franchisor shall then

remit payment for such property to the franchised motor vehicle dealer within sixty days after receipt of such property.

(3) Upon a termination, cancellation or nonrenewal of a franchise by a franchised motor vehicle dealer where the franchise consists primarily of the distribution and sale of house coaches, the franchisor's repurchase obligations set forth in this paragraph shall not apply.

(p) To refuse to repurchase for cost, including transportation charges, a new vehicle which has been substantially damaged by the franchisor or its agent, or to sell or transfer to a franchised motor vehicle dealer a new motor vehicle which has been subjected to repairs with a retail value in excess of five percent of the lesser of the manufacturer's or distributor's suggested retail price where such repairs are performed after shipment from the franchisor including damage to the vehicle while in transit without so notifying the franchised motor vehicle dealer to whom such new motor vehicle so repaired is sold or transferred. Such notice shall be in writing, advise of such repairs, and be provided prior to the receipt of any payment for such motor vehicle. If the franchisor shall fail to provide such notice, any franchised motor vehicle dealer suffering a loss by reason of such failure shall be entitled to reimbursement from the franchisor who failed to provide such notice.

(q) To grant to any person the right to perform warranty service on any new motor vehicle line other than a house coach line but deny to said person the right to purchase the motor vehicles of that line for resale to consumers in this state as new motor vehicles provided, however, that this paragraph shall not prohibit a franchisor from:

(1) authorizing warranty service by employees of a fleet operator or governmental entity on owned vehicles; or

(2) authorizing such other persons to perform warranty service as the franchisor deems necessary to protect its interests as they may be affected by section one hundred ninety-eight-a of the general business law; or

(3) establishing and maintaining diagnostic centers or other types of service arrangements to improve the quality, convenience or availability of customer service.

A "fleet operator" shall be required to own for its own use or for the use of others the minimum number of vehicles of the current or preceding model year manufactured or sold by the same franchisor as determined by the standards of such franchisor applied on a general and consistent basis to substantially all fleet operators. Notwithstanding the preceding, a franchisor which withdraws from the United States market shall continue to allow its former franchised motor vehicle dealers to continue servicing and supplying parts, including service and parts supplied under the franchisor's warranty to vehicle owners, for a period of at least five years after such withdrawal from the United States market.

(r) To establish or attempt to establish the actual resale price for any new motor vehicle, part or accessory charged by a franchised motor vehicle dealer in the state, provided, however, nothing contained herein shall prohibit publication of recommended resale prices or historical information by a franchisor.

(s) To grant a commission to any person other than a franchised motor vehicle dealer within the state involved in the sale of a new motor vehicle by such franchised motor vehicle dealer without said franchised motor vehicle dealer's written consent. This prohibition shall not apply to sales incentive programs for employees of franchised motor vehicle dealers as long as the payments are made by the franchisor to such employees and not charged to the dealer.

(t) To require or attempt to require by the terms of the franchise that any dispute arising out of or in connection with the interpretation, performance or nonperformance of the parties to the franchise or in any way related to the franchise be determined through the application of any other state's laws or in a federal court sitting in a state other than New York or in a state court of a state other than the state of New York; provided, however, that the provisions of this paragraph shall not apply to:

(1) any new franchise agreement entered into between a franchisor and any individual or entity which has not previously been granted a franchise by such franchisor and which franchise provides for the operation of the business pursuant to such franchise at a location or dealership point not then being used in the operation of such business; or

(2) any renewal of an existing franchise between a franchised motor vehicle dealer and a franchisor which contains a preexisting venue clause, or

(3) a franchise between a franchised motor vehicle dealer or its assignee and a franchisor which franchise grants to such franchised motor vehicle dealer or its assignee rights related solely to a new line and make of automobile manufactured or distributed by such franchisor.

(u) To use any subsidiary corporation, affiliated corporation, or any other controlled corporation, partnership, association or person to accomplish what would otherwise be unlawful conduct under this article on the part of the franchisor.

3.   In any action or proceeding instituted pursuant to the provisions of this section, there shall be available to the franchisor all of the defenses provided for under section thirteen-b of title fifteen, United States code, known as the Robinson–Patman Act.

§ 464.   Obligations of dealers prior to delivery to retail buyers

Every franchisor shall specify in writing the delivery and preparation obligations of its franchised motor vehicle dealers prior to delivery of new motor vehicles to retail buyers.

§ 466.   Unreasonable restrictions

1.   It shall be unlawful for a franchisor directly or indirectly to impose unreasonable restrictions on the franchised motor vehicle dealer relative to transfer, sale, right to renew or termination of a franchise, discipline,

noncompetition covenants, site-control (whether by sublease, collateral pledge of lease or otherwise), right of first refusal to purchase, option to purchase, compliance with subjective standards and assertion of legal or equitable rights with respect to its franchise or dealership.

2. It shall be deemed an unreasonable restriction upon the sale or transfer of a dealership for a franchisor directly or indirectly to prevent or attempt to prevent a franchised motor vehicle dealer from obtaining the fair value of the franchise or the fair value of the dealership business as a going concern.

§ 467. Dealership facilities assistance upon termination, cancellation or nonrenewal

Upon a permitted termination, cancellation or nonrenewal by the franchisor, unless such termination, cancellation or nonrenewal is for a reason or reasons set forth in subparagraph two of paragraph (d) of subdivision two of section four hundred sixty-three of this article, the franchisor shall assume the obligations for any lease of the dealership facilities or arrange for a new lease of the dealership facilities or pay the dealer the lease payments for one year, whatever is less, or negotiate a lease termination for the dealership facilities at the franchisor's expense. If the facilities are owned by the franchised motor vehicle dealer, the franchisor shall pay such dealer a sum equivalent to the reasonable rental value of the dealership facility for one year, provided the franchised motor vehicle dealer shall mitigate damages in the case of an owned facility.

§ 468. Preservation of consumer protection statutes

Nothing contained herein shall in any way be construed or interpreted to modify, limit or affect the full powers and duties heretofore or hereafter granted to consumer protection agencies created by statute or regulation enacted by state, city, county or local municipalities and the rights of consumers to make complaints thereto, it being the intent of this article to provide for the settlement and/or determination of disputes under the franchised motor vehicle dealer act as between franchisors and franchised motor vehicle dealers as defined herein.

§ 469. Private actions

A franchised motor vehicle dealer who is or may be aggrieved by a violation of this article shall be entitled to sue for, and have, injunctive relief and damages in any court of the state having jurisdiction over the parties. In any such action or proceeding, the court may award necessary costs and disbursements plus a reasonable attorney's fee to any party.

§ 471. Notice requirement

1. A dealer shall not display for sale, exchange or sell any new motor vehicle, or any used motor vehicle, that was originally sold by a manufacturer for distribution outside the United States without prominently displaying a label on the vehicle stating that "This vehicle was not sold by the

manufacturer for distribution within the United States. It may not have the same standard features, emissions equipment, safety equipment, optional equipment, specifications and warranty, or otherwise be identical to the other motor vehicles which are sold by the manufacturer for distribution in the United States".

2. Any person who violates this section and any person who knowingly aids and abets any such violation of this section shall be liable to any person aggrieved to the extent of any additional margin obtained or obtainable on such purchase and resale.

§ 472. Separability

If any part or provision of this article or the application thereof to any person or circumstance be adjudged invalid by any court of competent jurisdiction, such judgment shall be confined in its operation to the part, provision or application directly involved in the controversy in which such judgment shall have been rendered and shall not affect or impair the validity of the remainder of this article or the application thereof to other persons or circumstances.

OKLAHOMA STATUTES ANNOTATED

Tit. 15

§ 216. Resort to Courts, Provisions Restricting—Limiting Time Therefor

Every stipulation or condition in a contract, by which any party thereto is restricted from enforcing his rights under the contract by the usual legal proceedings in the ordinary tribunals, or which limits the time within which he may thus enforce his rights, is void.

§ 235. Duty of Party Attempting Rescission

Rescission, when not effected by consent, can be accomplished only by the use, on the part of the party rescinding, of reasonable diligence to comply with the following rules:

1. He must rescind promptly, upon discovering the facts which entitle him to rescind, if he is free from duress, menace, undue influence, or disability, and is aware of his right to rescind; and,

2. He must restore to the other party everything of value which he has received from him under the contract; or must offer to restore the same, upon condition that such party shall do likewise, unless the latter is unable, or positively refuses to do so.

WISCONSIN STATUTES ANNOTATED

§ 103.465   Restrictive Covenants in Employment Contracts[4]

A covenant by an assistant, servant or agent not to compete with his employer or principal during the term of the employment or agency, or thereafter, within a specified territory and during a specified time is lawful and enforceable only if the restrictions imposed are reasonably necessary for the protection of the employer or principal. Any such restrictive covenant imposing an unreasonable restraint is illegal, void and unenforceable even as to so much of the covenant or performance as would be a reasonable restraint.

DEALERSHIP PRACTICES

135.01   Short Title

This chapter may be cited as the "Wisconsin Fair Dealership Law".

135.02   Definitions

In this chapter:

(1) "Person" means a natural person, partnership, joint venture, corporation or other entity.

(2) "Dealership" means a contract or agreement, either expressed or implied, whether oral or written, between 2 or more persons, by which a person is granted the right to sell or distribute goods or services, or use a trade name, trademark, service mark, logotype, advertising or other commercial symbol, in which there is a community of interest in the business of offering, selling or distributing goods or services at wholesale, retail, by lease, agreement or otherwise.

(3) "Grantor" means a person who grants a dealership.

(4) "Community of interest" means a continuing financial interest between the grantor and grantee in either the operation of the dealership business or the marketing of such goods or services.

(5) "Dealer" means a person who is a grantee of a dealership.

(6) "Good cause" means:

(a) Failure by a dealer to comply substantially with essential and reasonable requirements imposed upon him by the grantor, or sought to be imposed by the grantor, which requirements are not discriminatory as compared with requirements imposed on other similarly situated dealers either by their terms or in the manner of their enforcement; or

(b) Bad faith by the dealer in carrying out the terms of the dealership.

4.   Enacted 1957.

135.03   Cancellation and Alteration of Dealerships

No grantor, directly or through any officer, agent or employee may terminate, cancel, fail to renew or substantially change the competitive circumstances of a dealership agreement entered into after April 5, 1974 without good cause. The burden of proving good cause shall be on the grantor.

135.04   Notice of Termination or Change in Dealership

Except as provided in this section, a grantor shall provide a dealer at least 90 days' prior written notice of termination, cancellation, nonrenewal or substantial change in competitive circumstances. The notice shall state all the reasons for termination, cancellation, nonrenewal or substantial change in competitive circumstances and shall provide that the dealer has 60 days in which to rectify any claimed deficiency. If the deficiency is rectified within 60 days the notice shall be void. The notice provisions of this section shall not apply if the reason for termination, cancellation or nonrenewal is insolvency, the occurrence of an assignment for the benefit of creditors or bankruptcy. If the reason for termination, cancellation, nonrenewal or substantial change in competitive circumstances is nonpayment of sums due under the dealership, the dealer shall be entitled to written notice of such default, and shall have 10 days in which to remedy such default from the date of delivery or posting of such notice.

135.05   Application to Arbitration Agreements

This chapter shall not apply to provisions for the binding arbitration of disputes contained in a dealership agreement concerning the items covered in § 135.03, if the criteria for determining whether good cause existed for a termination, cancellation, nonrenewal or substantial change of competitive circumstances, and the relief provided is no less than that provided for in this chapter.

135.06   Action for Damages and Injunctive Relief

If any grantor violates this chapter, a dealer may bring an action against such grantor in any court of competent jurisdiction for damages sustained by him as a consequence of the grantor's violation, together with the actual costs of the action, including reasonable actual attorney fees, and the dealer also may be granted injunctive relief against unlawful termination, cancellation, nonrenewal or substantial change of competitive circumstances.

135.07   Nonapplicability

This chapter does not apply:

(1) To a dealership to which a motor vehicle dealer or motor vehicle distributor or wholesaler as defined in § 218.01(1) is a party in such capacity.

(2) To the insurance business.

(3) Where goods or services are marketed by a dealership on a door to door basis.

PART IV: FOREIGN

ENGLAND

LAW REFORM (FRUSTRATED CONTRACTS) ACT, 1943

6 & 7 Geo. VI, c. 40

1. Adjustment of Rights and Liabilities of Parties to Frustrated Contracts

(1) Where a contract governed by English law has become impossible of performance or been otherwise frustrated, and the parties thereto have for that reason been discharged from the further performance of the contract, the following provisions of this section shall, subject to the provisions of section two of this Act, have effect in relation thereto.

(2) All sums paid or payable to any party in pursuance of the contract before the time when the parties were so discharged (in this Act referred to as "the time of discharge") shall, in the case of sums so paid, be recoverable from him as money received by him for the use of the party by whom the sums were paid, and, in the case of sums so payable, cease to be so payable:

Provided that, if the party to whom the sums were so paid or payable incurred expenses before the time of discharge in, or for the purpose of, the performance of the contract, the court may, if it considers it just to do so having regard to all the circumstances of the case, allow him to retain or, as the case may be, recover the whole or any part of the sums so paid or payable, not being an amount in excess of the expenses so incurred.

(3) Where any party to the contract has, by reason of anything done by any other party thereto in, or for the purpose of, the performance of the contract, obtained a valuable benefit (other than a payment of money to which the last foregoing subsection applies) before the time of discharge, there shall be recoverable from him by the said other party such sum (if any), not exceeding the value of the said benefit to the party obtaining it, as the court considers just, having regard to all the circumstances of the case and, in particular,—

(a) the amount of any expenses incurred before the time of discharge by the benefitted party in, or for the purpose of, the performance of the contract, including any sums paid or payable by him to any other party in pursuance of the contract and retained or recoverable by that party under the last foregoing subsection, and

(b) the effect, in relation to the said benefit, of the circumstances giving rise to the frustration of the contract.

(4) In estimating, for the purposes of the foregoing provisions of this section, the amount of any expenses incurred by any party to the contract,

173

the court may, without prejudice to the generality of the said provisions, include such sum as appears to be reasonable, in respect of overhead expenses and in respect of any work or services performed personally by the said party.

(5) In considering whether any sum ought to be recovered or retained under the foregoing provisions of this section by any party to the contract, the court shall not take into account any sums which have, by reason of the circumstances giving rise to the frustration of the contract, become payable to that party under any contract of insurance unless there was an obligation to insure imposed by an express term of the frustrated contract or by or under any enactment.

(6) Where any person has assumed obligations under the contract in consideration of the conferring of a benefit by any other party to the contract upon any other person, whether a party to the contract or not, the court may, if in all the circumstances of the case it considers it just to do so, treat for the purposes of subsection (3) of this section any benefit so conferred as a benefit obtained by the person who has assumed the obligations as aforesaid.

2. Provision as to Application of this Act. * * *

(2) This Act shall apply to contracts to which the Crown is a party in like manner as to contracts between subjects.

(3) Where any contract to which this Act applies contains any provision which, upon the true construction of the contract, is intended to have effect in the event of circumstances arising which operate, or would but for the said provision operate, to frustrate the contract, or is intended to have effect whether such circumstances arise or not, the court shall give effect to the said provision and shall only give effect to the foregoing section of this Act to such extent, if any, as appears to the court to be consistent with the said provision.

(4) Where it appears to the court that a part of any contract to which this Act applies can properly be severed from the remainder of the contract, being a part wholly performed before the time of discharge, or so performed except for the payment in respect of that part of the contract of sums which are or can be ascertained under the contract, the court shall treat that part of the contract as if it were a separate contract and had not been frustrated and shall treat the foregoing section of this Act as only applicable to the remainder of that contract.

(5) This Act shall not apply—

(a) to any charterparty, except a time charterparty or a charterparty by way of demise, or to any contract (other than a charterparty) for the carriage of goods by sea; or

(b) to any contract of insurance, save as is provided by subsection (5) of the foregoing section; or

(c) to any contract to which section seven of the Sale of Goods Act, 1893 (which avoids contracts for the sale of specific goods which perish before the risk has passed to the buyer) applies, or to any other contract for the sale, or for the sale and delivery, of specific goods, where the contract is frustrated by reason of the fact that the goods have perished.

3.   Short Title and Interpretation

(1) This Act may be cited as the Law Reform (Frustrated Contracts) Act, 1943.

(2) In this Act the expression "court" means, in relation to any matter, the court or arbitrator by or before whom the matter falls to be determined.

STATUTE OF FRAUDS

29 Car. II, c. 3, 1677.

AN ACT FOR THE PREVENTION OF FRAUDS AND PERJURIES

§ 4.   And be it further enacted by the authority aforesaid, That from and after the said four and twentieth day of June no action shall be brought (1) whereby to charge any executor or administrator upon any special promise, to answer damages out of his own estate; (2) or whereby to charge the defendant upon any special promise to answer for the debt, default or miscarriages of another person; (3) or to charge any person upon any agreement made upon consideration of marriage; (4) or upon any contract or sale of lands, tenements, or hereditaments, or any interest in or concerning them; (5) or upon any agreement that is not to be performed within the space of one year from the making thereof; (6) unless the agreement upon which such action shall be brought, or some memorandum or note thereof, shall be in writing, and signed by the party to be charged therewith, or some other person thereunto by him lawfully authorized.

7.   And be it further enacted, that all declarations or creations of trusts or confidences of any lands, tenements or hereditaments, shall be manifested and proved by some writing signed by the party who is by law enabled to declare such trust, or by his last will in writing, or else they shall be utterly void and of none effect.

§ 17.   And be it further enacted by the authority aforesaid, that from and after the said four and twentieth day of June no contract for the sale of any goods, wares and merchandizes, for the price of ten pounds sterling or upwards, shall be allowed to be good, except the buyer shall accept part of the goods so sold, and actually receive the same, or give something in earnest to bind the bargain, or in part payment, or that some note or memorandum in writing of the said bargain be made and signed by the parties to be charged by such contract, or their agents thereunto lawfully authorized.

†